Individual and Family Stress and Crises

Janice Gauthier Weber

Los Angeles | London | New Delhi
Singapore | Washington DC

For information:

SAGE Publications, Inc.
2455 Teller Road
Thousand Oaks, California 91320
E-mail: order@sagepub.com

SAGE Publications India Pvt. Ltd.
B 1/I 1 Mohan Cooperative Industrial Area
Mathura Road, New Delhi 110 044
India

SAGE Publications Ltd.
1 Oliver's Yard
55 City Road
London EC1Y 1SP
United Kingdom

SAGE Publications Asia-Pacific Pte. Ltd.
33 Pekin Street #02-01
Far East Square
Singapore 048763

Printed in the United States of America

Library of Congress Cataloging-in-Publication Data

Weber, Janice Gauthier
Individual and family stress and crises / Janice Gauthier Weber.
    p. cm.
Includes bibliographical references and index.
ISBN 978-1-4129-3691-0 (pbk.)
   1. Stress (Psychology) 2. Stress management. 3. Family assessment. 4. Adaptability (Psychology)
I. Title.

BF575.S75W434 2011
155.9'042—dc22   2010035401

This book is printed on acid-free paper.

10 11 12 13 14 10 9 8 7 6 5 4 3 2 1

Acquisitions Editor:	Kassie Graves
Editorial Assistant:	Veronica K. Novak
Production Editor:	Libby Larson
Permissions Editor:	Adele Hutchinson
Copy Editor:	Melinda Masson
Typesetter:	C&M Digitals (P) Ltd.
Proofreader:	Caryne Brown
Indexer:	Judy Hunt
Cover Designer:	Candice Harman
Marketing Manager:	Stephanie Adams

Contents

Individual and Family Stress and Crises

Preface

Motivation to write this book came from the inability to locate an appropriate text for a class of juniors, seniors, and graduate students that I had taught for over 15 years using excerpts from different texts and journal articles. I had asked numerous publishing company representatives over those years for an appropriate text but had met with no success. Students did not seem to like the practice of assigning readings from multiple sources and "skipping around" in a text. For many years, I had been "stressing" over the lack of an appropriate text.

The purpose of this book is to fill a void in the field of family science. This book is directed primarily at upper-level undergraduate students and graduate students enrolled in courses in family science programs (family life education, family studies, etc.) at 4-year colleges and universities. The contents will help to meet the course requirements for certification in family life education. After reading this book, individuals will know stress and crisis terminology and models, have an understanding of how crises develop, know how to perform primary and secondary prevention, and know how to manage a crisis through assessment, planning, intervention, and follow-up.

Students in disciplines other than family science, such as nursing, criminal justice, sociology, and education, will also benefit from the text because any professional could encounter someone who is in crisis. For example, educators, school principals, managers, postal workers, human resource personnel, and other frontline workers, such as emergency medical technicians, police, and emergency room personnel, are in contact with people under stress on a daily basis.

Crisis management requires not just years of training or a degree but knowledge of what to do as well as what not to do and the skills that go along with that knowledge (Hoff, 1989, 1995, 2001). In light of the times in which we live (terrorism, war, tsunamis, more frequent and intense hurricanes, economic uncertainty, rapid technological change, etc.), anyone, including lay individuals, can benefit from the information presented in the text, particularly the information on crisis management. Louisianans experienced four major hurricanes as I was writing this book. With thousands of people experiencing major stressors, there are not enough professional crisis interventionists to work with the individuals and families affected by the storms. Paraprofessionals in these situations could prevent unnecessary crises by intervening immediately after the stressor. The protocol in the shelter visited by this author appeared to be "Wait until someone 'freaks out' and then attend to him or her." No crisis prevention measures were taken; individuals received just the provision of survival needs. Emotional health was an afterthought.

Boss (2002) raised the question "Do we focus on the individual or the family?" I say that we must be prepared to do both. We do not always have access to the family, as when students are living away from home to attend a university. Families may not even know that their members are experiencing a crisis, so we must be prepared to assist individuals alone as well as within the context of the family. In addition, even when we are performing crisis management with a family, each individual may have a different definition of the situation, as well as different manifestations, resources, and coping strategies. Hill (1958) recognized this when he stated that "each responsible member experiences a roller-coaster pattern" (p. 147). Also when working with families, we generally can chart only one individual's perspective at a time. Managing family crises requires a combination of family and individual processes (Boss, 1987; Burr, Klein, & Associates, 1994). With that in mind, this book addresses both individual and family models and sociological and psychological concepts in order to understand individuals and families under stress and in crisis.

The text uses the term *stress theory* rather than *crisis theory*. Individual models tend to be called crisis models while family models tend to be called stress models in the literature. The term *stress theory* accounts for the fact that individuals and families do not always experience a crisis when they experience stress; thus the label *crisis theory* seems more deterministic than *stress theory*.

The book is organized into three parts. Part I, the introduction, includes two chapters, one on the history of stress theory and another on definitions of terms. Part II presents the stress and crisis models while Part III presents how to apply the models to crisis management.

References

Boss, P. (1987). Family stress. In M. Sussman & S. Steinmetz (Eds.), *Handbook of marriage and the family* (pp. 695–723). New York: Plenum Press.

Boss, P. (2002). *Family stress management: A contextual approach.* Thousand Oaks, CA: Sage.

Burr, W. R., Klein, S. R., & Associates. (1994). *Reexamining family stress: New theory and research*. Thousand Oaks, CA: Sage.

Hill, R. (1958). Generic features of families under stress. *Social Casework, 49*, 139–150.

Hoff, L. A. (1989). *People in crisis: Understanding and helping* (3rd ed.). Menlo Park, CA: Addison Wesley.

Hoff, L. A. (1995). *People in crisis: Understanding and helping* (4th ed.). San Francisco: Jossey-Bass.

Hoff, L. A. (2001). *People in crisis: Clinical and public health perspectives* (5th ed.). San Francisco: Jossey-Bass.

Acknowledgments

SAGE would like to thank the following reviewers:

Sadguna Anasuri, University of Wisconsin–Stout

Suzanne Bartle-Haring, The Ohio State University

Julia A. Malia, The University of Tennessee–Knoxville

Julie A. Maschhoff, Illinois State University

Michael J. Merten, Oklahoma State University

Megan J. Murphy, Iowa State University

Carolyn Slotten, Miami University, Oxford, Ohio

Mixon Ware, Eastern Kentucky University

Mari S. Wilhelm, University of Arizona

HISTORY AND DEFINITION OF STRESS THEORY

Part I of this book consists of two chapters. The first chapter gives a brief overview of the history of stress theory. The second chapter attempts to clarify definitions of concepts.

CHAPTER 1

The History
of Stress Theory

This chapter presents the history of stress theory, a relatively new theory that is still evolving. Although limited to dealing with one major aspect of clients' lives, stress theory's "applicability is far-reaching" (Ingoldsby, Smith, & Miller, 2004, p. 147). The terms *stress theory* and *crisis theory* have been used interchangeably. This text uses the term *stress theory* as the title acknowledges that, although sometimes stress is of crisis proportions, stress is not always of that severity.

A theory is an explanation of observations (Babbie, 2004) that can show us how to intervene (Burr, 1995), predict behavior, and guide research. There are different types of theories. Stress theory is a social theory that explains observations about stress, an aspect of social life. Theories use concepts that represent classes of phenomena to explain observations. A variable, a special type of concept that varies, is composed of a set of attributes (Babbie, 2004). The attributes *male* and *female* compose the variable *gender* as gender varies from male to female. When we put together concepts showing their relationships, we form conceptual frameworks or models. Chapters in Part II of this book include conceptual frameworks/models of stress theory. Although stress theory is a relatively new development, most likely people have dealt with stress since the beginning of the human race.

Boss (1987) points out that "in the Talmud and the Bible, we read that families have been concerned with events of change, trouble, disaster, and ambiguity since the beginning of recorded time" (p. 696). Early stress researchers in England wrote "considerably on problem families, labeling them as deviant, antisocial, and lower class" (Hill, 1958, p. 144). Early American researchers, in contrast to English researchers, concentrated on the processes of family maladjustment rather than on stereotyping families (Hill, 1958). The late 1970s through the late 1980s saw a shift in research from family weaknesses to family strengths and coping strategies (Burr, 1989). Research on stress not only varied in focus from weaknesses to strengths; it also varied in the unit of analysis from individuals, to families, to communities.

In this chapter, a brief history of the development of individual stress theory appears first, followed by the history of the development of family stress theory. Although this text is primarily aimed at people interested in families, individual stress theory has made valuable contributions to understanding family stress (Boss, 2002), and both individual and family stress theories are important in family stress management.

Individual Stress Theory

Contributions to individual stress theory came largely from psychobiology, sociology, psychiatry, and anthropology. The earlier researchers were psychobiologists, followed by sociologists, psychiatrists, and anthropologists. The models briefly discussed in this section are presented in detail in Part II of this text. See Figure 1.1 for a timeline of individual stress theory development. We begin with the contributions of psychobiology.

Figure 1.1   Timeline of Development of Individual Stress Theory

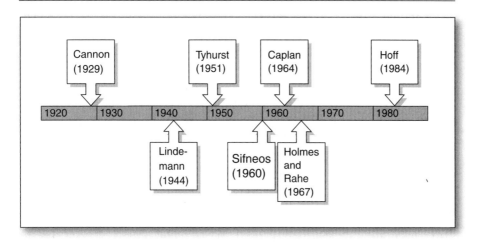

Psychobiology

Early psychobiologists found a connection between emotional stress and physiology. Cannon (1929) did early experimental work showing that stimuli associated with emotional arousal led to changes in physiological processes. Later, the relationship between ordinary life events and illness was demonstrated. More recently technological advances facilitated research showing specific physiological responses to stress. Shortly after the work of early psychobiologists, sociologists began contributing to the stress research.

Sociology

Lindemann (1944), a sociologist, described individual bereavement experiences of surviving relatives of those who died in the Melody Lounge Cocoanut Grove fire. In studying surviving relatives of the people who perished in the fire, he found that those who had positive outcomes had gone through a process. The grieving process that he observed is discussed later in Part III: Crisis Management. Following the work in sociology, psychiatrists contributed to the stress literature.

Psychiatry

Early psychiatrists contributing to stress theory included Tyhurst (1951, 1957a, 1957b), Caplan (1964, 1974), Holmes and Rahe (1967), and Sifneos (1960). While Tyhurst (1951, 1957a, 1957b) developed a model describing the natural history of individual reactions to disaster, which are discussed in Part II of this book, Holmes and Rahe (1967) conceived of life events as stressors, which require change in the individual's ongoing life pattern. Their Social Readjustment Rating Scale (SRRS) (Holmes & Rahe, 1967) appears in Chapter 2. To this day, the scale is used to assess vulnerability of individuals and cited in the literature (e.g., Lewis, Lewis, Daniels, & D'Andrea, 2003). Caplan's (1974) focus on prevention of mental health disturbances was different from that of Tyhurst (1951, 1957a, 1957b) and Holmes and Rahe (1967). He developed a stage theory of crisis development (Caplan, 1964), which is presented in Part II of this book. Also in Part II of this book, Sifneos' model, useful in guiding crisis assessment, appears. Although psychiatric models dominated the 1950s and 1960s, the 1980s saw a contribution to stress theory from anthropology.

Anthropology

Hoff (1989, 1995, 2001), a nurse anthropologist, developed the Crisis Paradigm to explain what happens when individuals experience crises and to help manage individual crises. The Crisis Paradigm is presented in Part II of this book. Family stress theory developed parallel to the development of individual stress theory.

Family Stress Theory

Independent of the individual stress research summarized above, a considerable body of stress theory and research evolved within the family field (McCubbin, Patterson, & Wilson, 1981). Burr (1989) divided the development of family stress theory into three stages or eras. In this book, I add the fourth era, the postmodern era. The models briefly discussed in the eras are presented in detail in Part II of this text. See Figure 1.2 for a timeline of family stress theory development.

The First Era (1920s to Late 1940s)

The first era in the development of family stress theory began with research in the 1920s and ended with efforts toward theory development in the mid-1940s (Burr, 1989). Graduate students did much of the early research in the 1920s while Angell, a sociologist from the University of Michigan, wrote one of the first published studies on family stress in 1936. The research of Cavan and Ranck (1938) from the University of Chicago followed. Both studies examined the effects of the Great Depression of the 1930s on families. Both also studied families on the sociopsychological/family level using the case study approach and inductive (specific to general) method to examine the effects of the stressor of the sudden loss or reduction of income on families as well as individuals (Boss, 1987).

Angell (1936) found that family integration and adaptability had an impact on how families reacted to the sudden loss of income. He defined integration as the family's "bonds of coherence and unity" consisting of "common interests, affection, and a sense of economic interdependence" (p. 15) and adaptability as flexibility (vs. rigidity) in a family's structure. Adaptability consisted of philosophy of life (materialistic vs. nonmaterialistic), family mores (traditional vs. nontraditional), and responsibility (irresponsibility vs. responsibility). He called the more adaptable families "plastic" families, which were the nonmaterialistic, nontraditional, responsible families. Angell distinguished three degrees of integration and adaptability producing nine types of families (highly integrated, highly adaptable; highly integrated, moderately adaptable; highly integrated, inadaptable; moderately integrated, highly adaptable; moderately integrated, moderately adaptable;

Figure 1.2 Timeline of Development of Family Stress Theory

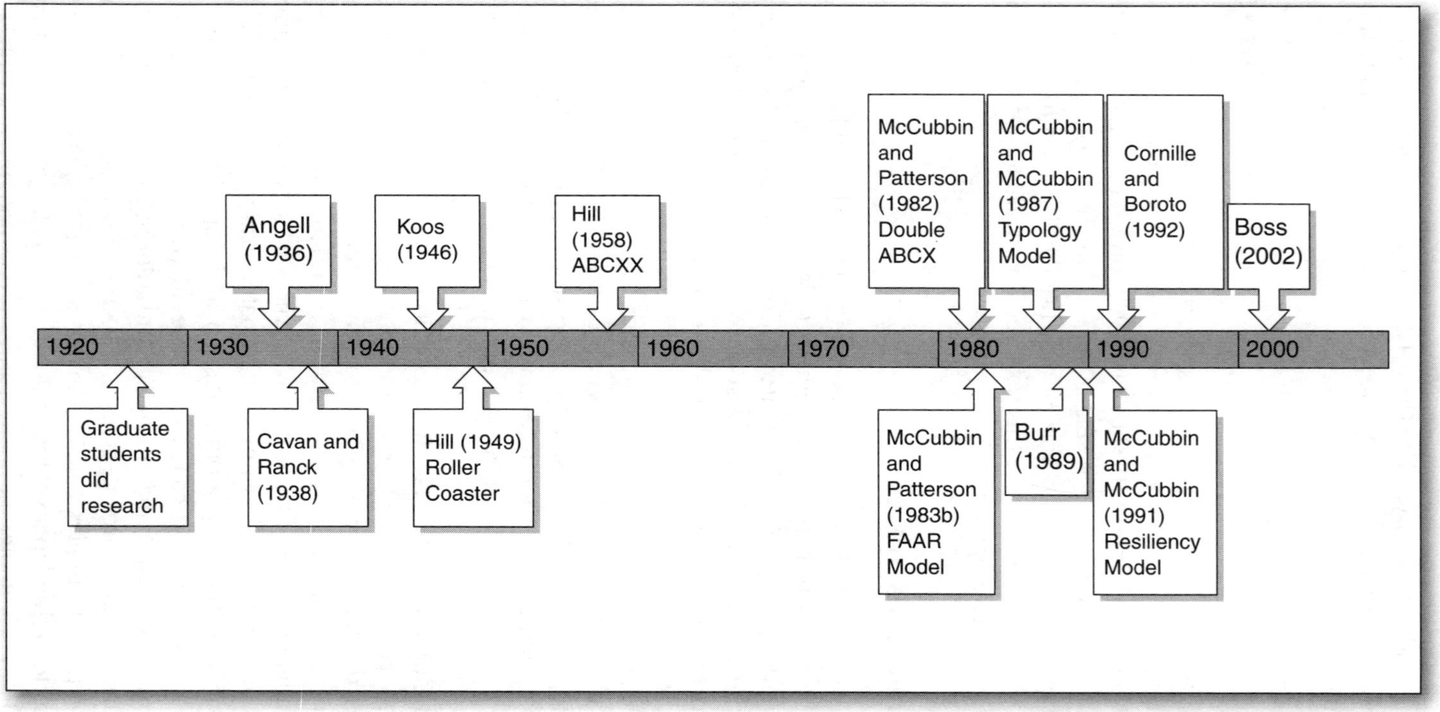

moderately integrated, inadaptable; integrated, highly adaptable; unintegrated, moderately adaptable; and unintegrated, unadaptable). No unintegrated, highly adaptable families were found in the study. Angell found that
the families accommodated more easily when there was a maximum of integration and adaptability and that "even a moderate degree of adaptability
will pull families with any integration at all through all but the worst crises"
(p. 181). Two years following the publication of Angell, Cavan and Ranck
(1938) published their findings.

Cavan and Ranck (1938), a sociologist and a psychiatric social worker,
respectively, presented "a theoretical statement of the process of organization,
crisis, disorganization, and reorganization, as related to the family" (p. 2). They
applied group theories to the family in stating that three criteria characterized a
well-organized (vs. disorganized) family: (a) "a high degree of unity," (b) "reciprocal functioning," and (c) "a definite function in the larger community of which it
is a part" (p. 2). Evidence of the first characteristic, unity, included the degree of

- acceptance and contribution to family objectives, such as caring for
  children, planning for children's education, establishing a permanent
  home, and providing affectional relations;
- subordination of personal ambitions to family objectives;
- conduct controlled by accepted family traditions and ideals, not
  through external compulsion; and
- satisfaction for interests (amusement, intellectual stimulation, finances)
  found within the family.

Cavan and Ranck (1938) defined the second characteristic of organized
families, reciprocal functioning, as when family "members have been assigned
and have accepted definite roles which are complementary to each other"
(pp. 3–4). Evidence of having a function in the community included
three characteristics: (a) being self-supporting, (b) abiding by the law,
and (c) maintaining friendly relationships with neighbors.

Cavan and Ranck (1938) believed that it was important to study family
members (individuals) as well as the family as a whole and that it was important for individual members to be well organized. They defined the well-
organized family member as one who accepted family and community roles.
The person then organized his or her life around those roles. The well-
organized person also found socially acceptable and personally satisfactory
ways to achieve the goals implied by the roles.

Early family stress researchers (Angell, 1936; Cavan & Ranck, 1938) used
the term *crisis* for what we now label *stressor* in stress theory, leading to
some confusion among those studying the theory. Despite this drawback,

this first body of research led to the first efforts of development of family stress theory (Burr, 1989) by sociologist Earl Koos (1946). Koos made the first effort at creating a stress theory with "the profile of trouble" (p. 107). Koos's research and profile, which appear in Part II of this book, led to the second era of family stress theory development.

The Second Era (Late 1940s to Late 1970s)

The second era, from the late 1940s to the late 1970s, consisted of major theoretical development (Burr, 1989). Hill (1949), another sociologist, called Koos's (1946) profile of families in trouble the Truncated Roller Coaster Profile of Adjustment. Named the father of family stress theory (Boss, 2002), Hill (1949, 1958) made the next attempt at developing family stress theory when he developed the ABCX "Formula"/Model, which became the center of family stress theory, in this era. According to Boss (1987), Hill (1958) made a substantial contribution to scientific inquiry into family stress with his ABCX Formula, whose variables remain a foundation of current family stress theory. Much of the remainder of this era consisted of testing the ABCX Formula (Burr, 1989). A shift in the focus of research led to the third era of family stress theory development.

The Third Era (Late 1970s to Mid-1980s)

From the late 1970s through the late 1980s, the third era saw a change in focus of research from family weaknesses to family strengths, coping strategies, and family system concepts (Burr, 1989). McCubbin and Patterson (1982, 1983a, 1983b), two family social scientists, expanded on the ABCX Formula to develop the Double ABCX Model, which included coping as well as other variables. Family stress researchers in this era based their studies on the Double ABCX Model (Burr, 1989). A shift in focus to processes signaled the beginning of the fourth era in the development of family stress theory.

The Fourth Era (Mid-1980s to Present)

The fourth era in the development of family stress theory saw a shift to a more postmodern approach by changing focus to processes, shared family meanings, culture, and contexts as well as family strengths.

Based on the premise that there are multiple realities and multiple truths, postmodern therapies reject the idea that reality is external and can be grasped. People create meaning in their lives through conversations with others. The postmodern approaches avoid pathologizing clients, take a dim view of diagnosis, avoid searching for underlying causes of problems, and place a high value on discovering clients' strengths and resources. Rather than endless talking about problems, the focus of therapy is on creating solutions in the present and the future. (Corey, 2005, p. 471)

The fourth, postmodern, era of stress theory development began with a focus on shared family meanings created through family member interactions appearing in the Family Adjustment and Adaptation Response (FAAR) Model (McCubbin & Patterson, 1983b; Patterson, 1988, 1989, 1993, 2002; Patterson & Garwick, 1994). In 1987, the husband and wife team of Marilyn McCubbin, a nurse, and Hamilton McCubbin, family social scientist, expanded on the Double ABCX Model to develop the Typology Double ABCX Model, later called the Typology Model of Family Adjustment and Adaptation.

The change from concentrating on the causes of stress and family weaknesses to concentrating on family strengths appeared in this era of stress theory development. With this change in concentration, the concept of resilience was added to the stress literature beginning in the late 1980s (Rutter, 1987; Stinnett & DeFrain, 1985). Expanding on the Typology Model of Family Adjustment and Adaptation that they had published in 1987, M. A. McCubbin and H. I. McCubbin (1991, 1993) developed the Resiliency Model of Family Stress, Adjustment, and Adaptation. While adding to the literature, by considering culture and a more postmodern view, the Resiliency Model was still based on the ABCX Formula/Model (Hill, 1949, 1958).

Another shift in stress theory development of this era came as focus on processes occurred. Robert Burr (1989), a family scientist, proposed using the general ecosystemic theory to explain family stress. He modified the Profile of Trouble (Koos, 1946) to illustrate the processes that families experience. The Family Distress Model (Cornille & Boroto, 1992; Cornille, Boroto, Barnes, & Hall, 1996; Cornille, Mullis, & Mullis, 2006) also focused on processes and considered culture.

Wesley Burr and Associates (1994) called on scholars to "set aside positivist views in favor of a family systems paradigm. . . . They suggested that scholars liberate themselves from the ABCX Model" (Boss, 2002, pp. 33–34). Despite that suggestion, during this era, Boss expanded on the ABCX Formula to develop the Contextual Model of Family Stress, which considered culture. Boss suggested that the postmodern era of family stress theory development began with her model. Regardless of what this era is called or when exactly it began, it saw the development of models focusing on family meanings, family processes, family strengths, and family contexts and models that considered culture, making them more postmodern in approach.

Summary of the History of Stress Theory

Individual stress theory and family stress theory had parallel developments beginning in the early 1920s. Individual stress theorists came mainly from the fields of psychobiology, sociology, psychiatry, and anthropology. Family stress theorists came mainly from sociology, psychiatric social work, nursing, and family science. The development of family stress theory occurred in four eras. Part II of this book presents stress theory models. In the models there are inconsistencies in definitions of concepts. For example, early family stress researchers used the term *crisis* for what we now label *stressor* in stress theory, leading to some confusion among those studying the theory. Because of this and other varying definitions of concepts, definitions are presented in Chapter 2.

References and Suggestions for Further Reading

Angell, R. C. (1936). *The family encounters the depression.* Gloucester, MA: Peter Smith. (Reprinted in 1965)

Babbie, E. (2004). *The practice of social research* (10th ed.). Belmont, CA: Wadsworth/Thomson.

Boss, P. (1987). Family stress. In M. B. Sussman & S. K. Steinmetz (Eds.), *Handbook of marriage and the family* (pp. 695–723). New York: Plenum Press.

Boss, P. (2002). *Family stress management: A contextual approach* (2nd ed.). Thousand Oaks, CA: Sage.

Burr, R. G. (1989). *Reframing family stress theory: From the ABC-X Model to a Family Ecosystemic Model.* Unpublished master's thesis, Brigham Young University, Provo, UT.

Burr, W. R. (1995). Using theories in family science. In R. D. Day, K. R. Gilbert, B. H. Settles, & W. R. Burr (Eds.), *Research and theory in family science* (pp. 73–88). Pacific Grove, CA: Brooks/Cole.

Burr, W. R., Klein, S. R., & Associates. (1994). *Reexamining family stress: New theory and research.* Thousand Oaks, CA: Sage.

Cannon, W. B. (1929). *Bodily changes in pain, hunger, fear and rage.* New York: D. Appleton & Co.

Caplan, G. (1964). *Principles of preventive psychiatry.* New York: Basic Books.

Caplan, G. (1974). *Support systems and community mental health.* New York: Behavioral Publications.

Cavan, R. S., & Ranck, K. H. (1938). *The family and the depression: A study of one hundred Chicago families.* Chicago: The University of Chicago Press.

Corey, G. (2005). *Theory and practice of counseling & psychotherapy* (7th ed.). Belmont, CA: Thomson Brooks/Cole.

Cornille, T. A., & Boroto, D. R. (1992). The Family Distress Model: A conceptual and clinical application of Reiss' strong bonds finding. *Contemporary Family Therapy, 14*(3), 181–198.

Cornille, T. A., Boroto, D. R., Barnes, M. F., & Hall, P. K. (1996). Dealing with family distress in schools. *Families in Society: The Journal of Contemporary Human Services, 77*(7), 435–445.

Cornille, T. A., Mullis, A. K., & Mullis, R. L. (2006, November). *How to use Internet coverage about disasters to teach about family resilience.* PowerPoint presented at the meeting of the National Council on Family Relations, Minneapolis, MN.

Hill, R. (1949). *Families under stress.* New York: Harper & Brothers.

Hill, R. (1958). Generic features of families under stress. *Social Casework, 49,* 139–150.

Hoff, L. A. (1984). *People in crisis: Understanding and helping* (2nd ed.). Menlo Park, CA: Addison Wesley.

Hoff, L. A. (1989). *People in crisis: Understanding and helping* (3rd ed.). Menlo Park, CA: Addison Wesley.

Hoff, L. A. (1995). *People in crisis: Understanding and helping* (4th ed.). Menlo Park, CA: Addison Wesley.

Hoff, L. A. (2001). *People in crisis: Clinical and public health perspectives* (5th ed.). San Francisco: Jossey-Bass.

Holmes, T. H., & Rahe, R. H. (1967). The Social Readjustment Rating Scale. *Journal of Psychosomatic Research, 11,* 213–218.

Ingoldsby, B. B., Smith, S. R., & Miller, J. E. (2004). *Exploring family theories.* Los Angeles: Roxbury.

Koos, E. L. (1946). *Families in trouble.* Morningside Heights, NY: King's Crown.

Lewis, J. A., Lewis, M. D., Daniels, J. A., & D'Andrea, M. J. (2003). *Community counseling: Empowerment strategies for a diverse society* (3rd ed.). Pacific Grove, CA: Thomson Brooks/Cole.

Lindemann, E. (1944). Symptomatology and management of acute grief. *American Journal of Psychiatry, 101,* 141–148.

McCubbin, H. I., & Patterson, J. M. (1982). Family adaptation to crises. In H. I. McCubbin, A. Cauble, & J. Patterson (Eds.), *Family stress, coping, and social support* (pp. 26–47). Springfield, IL: Charles C. Thomas.

McCubbin, H. I., & Patterson, J. M. (1983a). Family stress and adaptation to crises: A Double ABCX Model of family behavior. In D. H. Olson & R. C. Miller (Eds.), *Family studies review yearbook: Vol. 1* (pp. 87–106). Beverly Hills, CA: Sage.

McCubbin, H. I., & Patterson, J. M. (1983b). The family stress process: The Double ABCX Model of family adjustment and adaptation. In H. I. McCubbin, M. Sussman, & J. M. Patterson (Eds.), *Social stress and the family: Advances and developments in family stress theory and research* (pp. 7–37). New York: Haworth.

McCubbin, H. I. Patterson, J. M., & Wilson, L. R. (1981). *FILE: Family Inventory of Life Events and Changes: Research instrument.* St. Paul: Family Social Science, University of Minnesota.

McCubbin, M. A., & McCubbin, H. I. (1987). Family stress theory and assessment: The T-double ABCX Model of family adjustment and adaptation. In H. I. McCubbin & A. Thompson (Eds.), *Family assessment inventories for research and practice* (pp. 3–32). Madison: University of Wisconsin.

McCubbin, M. A., & McCubbin, H. I. (1991). Family stress theory and assessment: The Resiliency Model of Family Stress Adjustment and Adaptation. In H. I. McCubbin & A. Thompson (Eds.), *Family assessment inventories for research and practice* (pp. 3–31). Madison: University of Wisconsin.

McCubbin, M. A., & McCubbin, H. I. (1993). Families coping with illness: The Resiliency Model of Family Stress Adjustment and Adaptation. In C. Danielson, B. Hamel-Bissell, & P. Winstead-Fry (Eds.), *Families, health & illness: Perspectives on coping and intervention* (pp. 21–64). St. Louis, MO: Mosby.

Patterson, J. M. (1988). Families experiencing stress: I. The Family Adjustment and Response Model, II. Applying the FAAR Model to health-related issues for intervention and research. *Family Systems Medicine, 6*(2), 202–237.

Patterson, J. M. (1989). A family stress model: The Family Adjustment and Adaptation Response. In C. Ramsey (Ed.), *The science of family medicine* (pp. 95–117). New York: Guilford Press.

Patterson, J. M. (1993). The role of family meanings in adaptation to chronic illness and disability. In J. M. Patterson, A. P. Turnbull, S. K. Behr, D. L. Murphy, & J. G. Marquis (Eds.), *Cognitive coping, families, and disability* (pp. 221–238). Baltimore: Brookes.

Patterson, J. M. (2002). Integrating family resilience and family stress theory. *Journal of Marriage and Family, 64,* 349–360.

Patterson, J. M., & Garwick, A. W. (1994). Levels of meaning in family stress theory. *Family Process, 33,* 287–304.

Rutter, M. (1987). Psychosocial resilience and protective mechanisms. *American Journal of Orthopsychiatry, 57*(3), 316–331.

Sifneos, P. E. (1960). A concept of "emotional crisis." *Mental Hygiene, 44,* 169–179.

Stinnett, N., & DeFrain, J. (1985). *Secrets of strong families.* Boston: Little, Brown.

Tyhurst, J. S. (1951). Individual reactions to community disaster: The natural history of psychiatric phenomena. *American Journal of Psychiatry, 107,* 764–769.

Tyhurst, J. S. (1957a). Psychological and social aspects of civilian disaster. *Canadian Medical Association Journal, 76,* 385–393.

Tyhurst, J. S. (1957b). The role of transition states—including disaster—in mental illness. In *Symposium on preventive and social psychiatry* (pp. 149–169). Washington, DC: Walter Reed Army Institute of Research and the National Research Council.

CHAPTER 2

Definitions

The problem with defining concepts of stress theory is that there are inconsistencies in definitions used by professionals (Boss, 2002). In addition, some conceptual frameworks/models use different concepts to mean the same thing as other concepts used in other conceptual frameworks. Because theoretical definitions directly affect practice (crisis intervention strategies) and research, it is essential to clarify definitions (Boss, 1987). Following are concepts used interchangeably and their most consistent definitions. It is important to be familiar with these concepts that are used interchangeably. As you read the rest of the book, you may want to refer back to this chapter.

Stressor

A stressor is anything that potentially leads to change (Boss, 2002) because change is stressful for an organism. Stressors are neutral and lead to a state of stress when they require change (Boss, 2002). Since the dimensions of stressors are variant and multiple, we need to classify, type, or categorize them and define those divisions (Boss, 1987). Table 2.1 shows some of the many ways that stressors can be classified, typed, or categorized. Classifications are based on origin, clarity, choice, duration, and whether a stressor occurs alone or with other stressors. Some classifications of stressors are more difficult to cope with than other types; therefore the classification of the stressor influences the degree of stress (Boss, 2002). Identifying the classification of a stressor will assist someone helping with crisis management to choose appropriate interventions as appropriate interventions relate to the classification of stressors (Hoff, 1989, 1995, 2001). It is also essential that researchers describe the classification of the stressors they investigate (Boss, 1987).

Table 2.1 Classifications of Stressors

Individual	Family	Community
Internal	External	
Situational	Transitional	Social/cultural
Nonambiguous	Ambiguous	
Volitional	Nonvolitional	
Hazardous event/situation	Precipitating factor/incident	
Chronic	Acute	
Isolated	Cumulative	

Source: Adapted from Boss (2002).

Individual, Family, or Community Stressors

Patterson (1988) classified stressors based on whether they emerge or originate from an individual, a family, or a community. Examples of individual stressors include acute illness, loss of job, and starting school. Examples of family stressors include divorce, sexual abuse, moving, and having a child. Examples of community stressors include tornadoes, wars, taxes, and bank failures. Individual, family, or community stressors could be further classified based on other factors.

Internal or External Stressors

The classification of stressors as either internal or external is based on their source or origin (Hill, 1949). The location of blame or perceived responsibility, which is subjective, determines how to classify stressors as internal or external. According to Cloward and Piven (cited in Hoff, 1989, 1995, 2001), individuals have greater difficulty coping with external (originating outside the individual) stressors than internal (originating inside the individual) stressors since external individual stressors are usually out of the individual's control.

For families, however, it is more difficult to cope with stressors that originate within the family (internal/intrafamily) than to cope with those that originate outside the family (external/extrafamily) (Hill, 1958). Internal/intrafamily stressors tend to push family members apart while external/extrafamily stressors tend to pull family members closer together. Families view external family stressors as beyond their control while they view internal stressors as within control of family members, leading to such negative reactions as blame, thus being more stressful. On the other hand, external family stressors such as hurricanes tend to pull the family together. See Table 2.2 for lists of some family stressors typically classified as internal and external.

Some stressors are difficult to classify as internal or external because they could fall in either category, depending on the circumstances. For instance, if someone is arrested for committing a crime, the arrest would be classified as an internal family stressor (originating within the family), while if someone is arrested but he or she did not commit the crime, the arrest could be classified as an external family stressor (originating outside the family). Besides Hill (1949) and Patterson (1988), Hoff (1989, 1995, 2001) classified stressors based on their origin using three classifications rather than two.

Table 2.2 Examples of Internal and External Family Stressors

Internal	*External*
Abuse	Discrimination
Chronic gambling	Economic depression
Contracting AIDS	Lawsuits
Desertion	Natural disasters
Inability to bear children	Political revolution
Increased tasks and time commitments	Rape
Infidelity	Robbery
Mental illness	Terrorism
Nonsupport	War
Premature or unwanted pregnancy	
Role conflict	
Running away	
Running for election	
School problems	
Strained relationships	
Suicide	

Situational, Transitional, or Social/Cultural Stressors

Hoff (1989, 1995, 2001) actually called stressors crisis origins and classified them as situational, transitional, and/or social/cultural. She posited that some stressors could have multiple origins. Although she was referring to individual stressors, we could classify some family and community stressors using her concepts.

Situational stressors. Hoff (1989, 1995, 2001) further classified situational crisis origins into material, personal/physical, and/or interpersonal losses. She said that situational origins are usually unanticipated and sometimes relate to personal life choices. A heart attack, a stressor of personal/physical origin, often relates to the life choices of diet and exercise. Other examples of personal/physical origins include diagnoses of fatal illnesses, loss of limbs, or other bodily disfigurements. Examples of material origins include fires and natural disasters. Interpersonal/social origin examples include deaths of loved ones and divorces. While situational stressors are usually unexpected, transitional stressors usually are expected.

Transitional stressors. Transitional stressors are life passages from one status to another as from infancy to childhood. Transitions involve stress because they require change in such things as roles and responsibilities. Transitional origins consist of two types: universal/normative/evolutional and non-universal/non-normative.

Universal/normative/evolutional transitions are developmental/life cycle transitions. Since universal/normative/evolutional transitions are expected or anticipated, we can prepare for them. Universal/normative/evolutional transitions can be further classified as either individual or family.

Individual universal/normative/evolutional transitions, which are based on the age of the individual, are experienced by everyone until death. The only exception to experiencing all of the individual universal transitions is when one dies prematurely. Individual universal/normative/evolutional transitions identified by Erikson (1963) include the following:

Prenatal to infancy

Infancy to childhood

Childhood to puberty/adolescence

Adolescence to adulthood/maturity

Maturity to middle age

Middle age to old age

Old age to death

Family universal/normative/evolutional transitions occur based on the age of the oldest child (Duvall, 1946, 1971, 1977). There are three general categories of family development, with five major stages, that can be broken down into eight substages embedded in those categories. See Table 2.3. Each time there is a change from one substage to another, such as from single married couple to child-rearing family, there is a transition. Unlike with individual transitions, every family does not necessarily experience all family transitions since some people never marry, marry and never have children, divorce, or divorce and remarry. Because of divorce and remarriage, families may recycle some of the stages and transitions. While universal/normative/evolutional transitions are experienced by almost everyone, non-universal/non-normative transitions are not usually experienced by everyone.

Non-universal/non-normative transitions signal a shift in status not experienced by every individual or family. Besides being classified as individual or family, non-universal/non-normative, transitions can be classified as either anticipated or unanticipated. Individuals anticipate some non-universal transitions such as choosing to change status from homemaker to

Table 2.3 Family Life Cycle Stages

Categories	Major Stages	Substages	
Founding Family	Beginning Stage	Stage 1:	Single married couple (no children)
Expanding Family	Expanding Stages	Stage 2:	Child-rearing families (children 0–30 months)
		Stage 3:	Families with preschoolers (children 2.5–6 years)
	Developing Stages	Stage 4:	Families with school-agers (children 6–13 years)
		Stage 5:	Families with teenagers (children 13–20 years)
Contracting Family	Launching Stage	Stage 6:	Families launching
	Aging Stages	Stage 7:	Empty nest (middle-aged parents, time when all children leave home until retirement)
		Stage 8:	Retirement (retirement to death of both spouses)

Source: Adapted from Duvall (1971).

worker, while some non-universal transitions are unanticipated, such as when someone is laid off unexpectedly, and changes from worker to home-maker. A family non-universal/non-normative transition example includes a shift from having a home to being homeless. Crises originating from transi-tional states or situational origins are easier to manage than those from social/cultural origins.

Social/cultural stressors. Social/cultural stressors may be further clas-sified as those stemming from values, socialization, deviance, or conflict. Stressors originating from values about race, age, gender, or sexual prefer-ence include those stemming from stressors related to discrimination. An example of a stressor originating from socialization includes wife abuse, as her spouse may have been socialized in his family of origin to control his wife by whatever means possible, and she may have been socialized in her family to be passive. Stressors originating from deviant behaviors could be from deviant behaviors of self or of others. A person could experience the stressor of being a victim of a robbery or a perpetrator of a robbery. A clash between people for and against abortion is an example of a stressor with a conflict origin as well as the origin of values, socialization, and deviance, demonstrating how stressors can have multiple origins making them more difficult to manage. Also affecting difficulty of management is degree of clarity of the stressor.

Nonambiguous or Ambiguous Stressors

Boss (1988) classified stressors based on their clarity as nonambiguous or ambiguous. Her classifications were based on research of families of military personnel who were missing in action during the Vietnam War. Nonambiguous stressors were usually easier to manage.

Nonambiguous stressors. Nonambiguous stressors are those where the facts are clear (Boss, 1988). Families know when, how, how long, and to whom the stressor occurs. An example of a nonambiguous stressor would be the death of an elderly person when a doctor has informed the family of the severity of the person's condition.

Ambiguous stressors. Ambiguous stressors are those where the facts about what is happening, such as when, how, how long, and/or to whom, are unclear (Boss, 1988). Ambiguous stressors are more difficult to deal with than nonambiguous stressors since it is not clear when trouble will come. A parent having Alzheimer's disease is an example of an ambiguous stressor. In that situation, it is not clear who has the parenting role. Sometimes the parent may be able to act as a parent, and other times the child must parent his or her parent.

Many people had losses that were ambiguous after the terrorist attacks of September 11, 2001. It was not clear how long it would be before their loved ones would be found dead or alive or found at all, which made it difficult for them to do grief work. The ambiguous situation is more stressful than unambiguous situations when family members know that a person died and can have rituals surrounding the transition.

Volitional or Nonvolitional Stressors

The element of choice determines whether a stressor is volitional or nonvolitional. The stress from volitional stressors is usually easier to manage than that from nonvolitional stressors.

Volitional stressors. Volitional stressors are those that are wanted and sought out. Examples include such things as freely choosing job change, a college entrance, or a wanted pregnancy (Boss, 1988). Volitional stressors are chosen, whereas nonvolitional stressors are not chosen.

Nonvolitional stressors. Nonvolitional stressors are those "that are not sought out but just happen, such as being laid off or the sudden loss of someone loved" (Boss, 1988, p. 40). Generally, nonvolitional stressors will lead to more stress than volitional stressors. For example, being fired from a job (nonvolitional) will usually lead to more stress than quitting a job (volitional).

Hazardous Event/Situation or Precipitating Factor/Incident

When a crisis occurs, there may be two stressors—a hazardous event or situation (Stressor 1) and a precipitating factor or incident (Stressor 2) (Golan, 1969; Sifneos, 1960). Whether a stressor is a hazardous event/situation or a precipitating factor/incident is based on order of occurrence, with the hazardous event/situation occurring prior to the precipitating factor/incident.

Hazardous event/situation. While a hazardous event or situation is stressful, the individual may become vulnerable or at risk for a crisis only after it occurs and may not experience crisis at all or until another stressor happens (precipitating factor or incident). If a stressor is severe and a crisis is experienced immediately following the stressor, the hazardous event and the precipitating factor are the same stressor. Sometimes the death of a child is both hazardous event and precipitating factor. The stressor of losing a child to death is so severe that a person usually goes into crisis immediately.

Precipitating factor/incident. The precipitating factor or incident (second stressor) is often minor (Hoff, 1989, 1995, 2001). It has been called the straw that broke the camel's back (Golan, 1969; Sifneos, 1960). When someone seeks assistance with crisis management, it is important to identify both the hazardous event and the precipitating factor. If someone saw a program about depression on television and it spurred him or her to seek assistance, the program is the precipitating factor. The hazardous event was the experience that led to the depression, and crisis workers base crisis management on the hazardous event, not the precipitating factor, the television program. Boss (1988) tells of a family that went into crisis after seeing the funeral of President John F. Kennedy on television (precipitating factor). The family had experienced a child's death 10 years earlier (hazardous event) and had never fully grieved, leaving its members vulnerable to a crisis; thus successful crisis management must be based on the loss of the child and not the president's death.

Chronic or Acute Stressors

Stressors can also be classified according to their duration as either chronic or acute. The duration of the stressor determines whether it is chronic or acute.

Chronic stressors. Chronic stressors are those that last a long time, "such as diabetes, chemical addiction, or racial discrimination" (Boss, 1988, p. 40). Chronic stressors, also called *strains,* usually do not lead to crisis in and of themselves (Patterson, 1988). They do make people more vulnerable to crisis, however, as they are generally using resources to cope with the distress associated with the chronic stressors. The more strain that an individual or family has, the more resources required to cope, and the more vulnerable (at risk) he or she is to crisis (Patterson, 1988). There always will be *some* strain in a family (Patterson, 1988). Strains are more likely to be hazardous situations than precipitating factors such as when someone has diabetes (hazardous situation) and begins to lose eyesight because of the diabetes (precipitating factor). Strains also are more likely to be ambiguous than acute stressors.

Patterson (1988) and Boss (1988) further classified strains. Patterson said that strains emerge from three main sources: (1) unresolved distress from prior stressors (e.g., divorce); (2) stress because role performance does not meet someone's expectations (e.g., when a parent cannot spend as much time as he or she would like with a child); and (3) when outcomes of coping are negative (e.g., alcoholism). Kanner, Coyne, Schaefer, and Lazarus (1981) referred to the second group, strains, associated with performance of roles of daily living, as *hassles.* Boss (1988) classified strains as an *illness* (e.g., Alzheimer's disease); an *economic condition* (e.g., poverty or wealth); a *social condition* (e.g., discrimination for age, gender, or race); or *living near a constant danger* (e.g., a volcano), *near a noise producer* (e.g., train tracks), or *in a constantly noisy atmosphere* (e.g., a home with many children). Any of these strains (chronic stressors) can make family members more vulnerable to a crisis, particularly when an acute stressor occurs.

Acute stressors. Acute stressors are those that happen suddenly and last only a short time but are severe (Boss, 1988), such as hurricanes, tornadoes, or accidents. They happen suddenly, and then they are over. Boss (1988) says that people know more what they have to deal with for acute stressors than for chronic stressors. Although they are less ambiguous than chronic stressors, the severity of acute stressors often makes them more difficult to manage. Also determining difficulty of management is whether a stressor occurs alone or at the same time as other stressors.

Isolated or Cumulative Stressors

Stressor classifications based on whether a stressor occurs alone or at the same time as other stressors are isolated stressors or cumulative stressors. Scales have been developed to measure cumulative stressors both for individuals of different ages and for families.

Isolated stressors. An isolated stressor is a stressor that occurs alone without any other stressors occurring at the same time (Boss, 1988). If a hurricane occurs while the individual or family is experiencing no other stressors, the hurricane is an isolated stressor. Generally, isolated stressors are easier to manage than cumulative stressors.

Cumulative stressors. Cumulative stressors are stressors that occur at the same time or "one right after the other so that there is no resolution before the next one occurs" (Boss, 1988, p. 40), such as when someone is going through a transition, has a chronic disease, and flunks a test. Cumulative stressors are more likely to occur than isolated stressors as individuals and families are often in transition. *Pileup* is a term used to describe the occurrence of cumulative stressors.

Individual cumulative stressors or individual pileup. *Individual cumulative stressors or individual pileup* can be measured using the Coddington Life Events Scales (CLES) (Coddington, 1972), the College Schedule of Recent Experience (CSRE) (Anderson, 1972), and the Social Readjustment Rating Scale (SRRS) (Holmes & Rahe, 1967). The SSRS is sometimes called the Social Readjustment Rating Questionnaire (SSRQ) since the original article on the scale's development uses both names (Holmes & Rahe, 1967). Coddington (1972) developed the four scales of the CLES to measure cumulative stressors for preschool, elementary, junior high, and senior high age groups. The scales are copyrighted and published by Multi-Health

Systems, Inc. The CSRE (Anderson, 1972), developed specifically to measure cumulative stressors in college students, consists of 47 items with weighted scores for each item. See Table 2.4. The sum of the scores represents the "total magnitude change value" for a 12-month period (Anderson, 1972).

The SRRS (Holmes & Rahe, 1967), designed for use with adults, consists of 43 items with weighted scores for each item (Table 2.5). To assess pileup, individuals circle those items that occurred within the last year and add the values of each item. A score of 0–150 is considered within normal

Table 2.4 College Schedule of Recent Experience (CSRE)

	Events	Values
1.	Entering college	50
2.	Marriage	77
3.	Troubles with the boss	38
4.	Working while attending school	43
5.	Death of spouse	87
6.	Major change in sleeping habits	34
7.	Death of a close family member	77
8.	Major change in eating habits	30
9.	Change in or choice of a major field of study	41
10.	Revision of personal habits	45
11.	Death of a close friend	68
12.	Minor violations of the law	22
13.	Outstanding personal achievement	40
14.	Pregnancy	68
15.	Major change in the health or behavior of a family member	56
16.	Sexual difficulties	58
17.	In-law troubles	42
18.	Major change in number of family get-togethers	26
19.	Major change in financial state	53
20.	Gaining a new family member	50

	Events	Values
21.	Change in residence or living conditions	42
22.	Conflict or change in values	50
23.	Marital separation from mate	74
24.	Major change in church activities	36
25.	Marital reconciliation with mate	58
26.	Being fired from work	62
27.	Divorce	76
28.	Changing to a different line of work	50
29.	Major change in the number of arguments with spouse	50
30.	Major change in responsibilities at work	47
31.	Wife beginning or ceasing work outside the home	41
32.	Major change in working hours	42
33.	Major change in usual type and/or amount of recreation	37
34.	Major change in the use of drugs	52
35.	Taking on a mortgage or loan less than $10,000	52
36.	Major personal injury or illness	65
37.	Major change in the use of alcohol	46
38.	Major change in social activities	43
39.	Major change in the amount of participation in cocurricular activities	38
40.	Major change in the amount of independence and responsibility	49
41.	Vacation or travel	33
42.	Engaged to be married	54
43.	Changing to a new school	50
44.	Change in dating habits	41
45.	Trouble with school administration	44
46.	Broken marital engagement	60
47.	Major change in self-concept or self-awareness	57

Source: Reprinted by permission from College Schedule of Recent Experience by Gail E. Anderson. Copyright 1972 by Gail E. Anderson. By permission of Gail E. Anderson.

Table 2.5   Social Readjustment Rating Scale (SRRS)

Rank	Life Event	Mean Value
1	Death of spouse	100
2	Divorce	73
3	Marital separation	65
4	Jail term	63
5	Death of close family member	63
6	Personal injury or illness	53
7	Marriage	50
8	Fired at work	47
9	Marital reconciliation	45
10	Retirement	45
11	Change in health of a family member	44
12	Pregnancy	40
13	Sex difficulties	39
14	Gain of new family member	39
15	Business readjustment	39
16	Change in financial state	38
17	Death of a close friend	37
18	Change to different line of work	36
19	Change in number of arguments with spouse	35
20	Mortgage over $10,000	31
21	Foreclosure of mortgage or loan	30
22	Change in responsibilities at work	29
23	Son or daughter leaving home	29
24	Trouble with in-laws	29
25	Outstanding personal achievement	28
26	Wife begins or stops work	26
27	Begin or end of school	26

Rank	Life Event	Mean Value
28	Change in living conditions	25
29	Revision of personal habits	24
30	Trouble with boss	23
31	Change in work hours or conditions	20
32	Change in residence	20
33	Change in schools	20
34	Change in recreation	19
35	Change in church activities	19
36	Change in social activities	18
37	Mortgage or loan less than $10,000	17
38	Change in sleeping habits	16
39	Change in number of family get-togethers	15
40	Change in eating habits	15
41	Vacation	13
42	Christmas	12
43	Minor violations of the law	11

Source: Holmes & Rahe (1967).

limits; 151–199, mild stress; 200–299, moderate stress; and 300 and above, major stress (major pileup). Major pileup relates to serious negative health changes 2 years following the pileup. Types of stressors appearing on the SRRS include personal, family, financial, and occupational. Although the scale is intended for use with individuals, out of the 43 items, 11 of the 14 most stressful are related to family. Other scales were developed specifically to measure family cumulative stressors or pileup.

Family cumulative stressors or family pileup. *Family cumulative stressors or family pileup* can be measured by the Family Inventory of Life Events (FILE) (McCubbin, Patterson, & Wilson, 1982), the Young Adult–Family Inventory of Life Events and Strains (YA-FILES) (Grochowski & McCubbin, 1991), and the Adolescent–Family Inventory of Life Events (A-FILE) (McCubbin & Patterson, 1991a). The FILE consists of 17 items (Table 2.6). A low, moderate,

Table 2.6 Family Inventory of Life Events (FILE)

I. Intrafamily Strains	1. Increase of husband/father's time away from family.
	2. Increase of wife/mother's time away from family.
	3. A member appears to have emotional problems.
	4. A member appears to depend on alcohol or drugs.
	5. Increase in conflict between husband and wife.
	6. Increase in arguments between parent(s) and child(ren).
	7. Increase in conflict among children in the family.
	8. Increased difficulty in managing teenage child(ren).
	9. Increased difficulty in managing school-age child(ren) (6–12 years).
	10. Increased difficulty in managing preschool-age child(ren) (2.5–6 years).
	11. Increased difficulty in managing toddler(s) (1–2.5 to 6 years).
	12. Increased difficulty in managing infant(s) (0–1 year).
	13. Increase in the number of "outside activities" that the child(ren) are involved in.
	14. Increased disagreement about a member's friends or activities.
	15. Increase in the number of problems or issues, which don't get resolved.
	16. Increase in the number of tasks or chores, which don't get done.
	17. Increased conflict with in-laws or relatives.
II. Marital Status	18. Spouse/parent was separated or divorced.
	19. Spouse/parent has an "affair."
	20. Increased difficulty in resolving issues with a "former" or separated spouse.
	21. Increased difficulty with sexual relationship between husband and wife.
III. Pregnancy and Childbearing Strains	22. Family member experiencing menopause.
	23. Spouse had unwanted or difficult pregnancy.
	24. An unmarried member became pregnant.
	25. A member had an abortion.
	26. A member gave birth to or adopted a child.
IV. Finance and Business Strains	27. Took out a loan or refinanced a loan to cover increased expenses.
	28. Went on welfare.
	29. Change in conditions (economic, political, weather), which hurts family investments and/or income.

	30. Change in agriculture market, stock market, or land values, which hurts family investments and/or income.
	31. A member started a new business.
	32. Purchased or built a home.
	33. A member purchased a car or another major item.
	34. Increasing the financial debts due to overuse of credit cards.
	35. Increased strain on family "money" for medical/dental expenses.
	36. Increased strain on family "money" for food, clothing, energy, and home care.
	37. Increased strain on family "money" for child(ren)'s education.
	38. Delay in receiving child support or alimony payments.
V. Work–Family Transitions and Strains	39. A member changed to a new job/career.
	40. A member lost or quit a job.
	41. A member retired from work.
	42. A member started or returned to work.
	43. A member stopped working for extended period (e.g., laid off, leave of absence, strike).
	44. Decrease in satisfaction with job/career.
	45. A member had increased difficulty with people at work.
	46. A member was promoted at work or given more responsibilities.
	47. Family moved to a new home/apartment.
	48. A child/adolescent member changed to a new school.
VI. Illness and Family "Care" Strains	49. Parent/spouse became seriously ill or injured.
	50. Child became seriously ill or injured.
	51. Close relative or friend of the family became seriously ill.
	52. A member became physically disabled or chronically ill.
	53. Increased difficulty in managing a chronically ill or disabled member.
	54. Member of close relative was committed to an institution or nursing home.
	55. Increased responsibility to provide direct care or financial help to husband's and/or wife's parent(s).
	56. Experienced difficulty in arranging for satisfactory child care.
VII. Losses	57. A parent/spouse died.
	58. A child member died.
	59. Death of husband's or wife's parent or close relative.
	60. Close friend of the family died.
	61. Married son or daughter was separated or divorced.
	62. A member "broke up" a relationship with a close friend.

(Continued)

Table 2.6 (Continued)

VIII. Transitions "In and Out"	63. A member was married. 64. A young adult member left home. 65. A young adult member began college (or post–high school training). 66. A member moved back home or a new person moved into the household. 67. A parent/spouse started school (or training program) after being away from school for a long time.
IX. Family Legal Violations	68. A member went to jail or juvenile detention. 69. A member was picked up by police or arrested. 70. Physical or sexual abuse or violence in the home. 71. A member ran away from home. 72. A member dropped out of school or was suspended from school.

Source: Reprinted by permission from *Family Assessment: Resiliency, coping, and adaptation (inventories for research and practice)* by Hamilton I. McCubbin, Joan M. Patterson, and Lance R. Wilson. Copyright 1982 by Hamilton I. McCubbin. By permission of Hamilton I. McCubbin.

or high score on the FILE depends on the life cycle stage of the family (McCubbin & Patterson, 1991b). The FILE measures pileup or family vulnerability to crisis from the adult family members' perspectives.

Based on the FILE (McCubbin et al., 1982), the A-FILE (McCubbin & Patterson, 1991a), designed to record an adolescent's (or 12- to 18-year-old's) perceptions of his or her family's pileup of stressors experienced in the last year or his of her vulnerability to crisis, consists of 50 items. A subset of the 50 items (27 items) assesses stressors prior to the last year (those that take longer to adapt to or are chronic). It includes all events experienced by any family member since what happens to one member affects the others according to a family systems perspective.

The YA-FILES (Grochowski & McCubbin, 1991), a modification of the A-FILE, measures both individual and family cumulative stress or pileup and vulnerability to crisis of college freshmen (young adults). The 77-item instrument consists of two parts. Part I results in a young adult–family stress index (family pileup) while Part II results in a young adult–college stress index (individual pileup). Whether the stressor is isolated or cumulative, how the stressor is defined will impact the response.

Definition of the Stressor

The definition of a stressor is the meaning of the stressor. Other terms used in lieu of *definition* are *appraisal, assessment, interpretation,* and *perception.* The definition of a stressor may be categorized as negative/unpleasant or positive/pleasant. Each category will elicit different responses (emotions, behaviors, thoughts, and physical reactions).

For an individual, possible definitions of an unplanned pregnancy include a challenge (positive/pleasant) and the end of life as one knows it (negative/unpleasant). A family may define an unplanned pregnancy as a blessed event (positive/pleasant) or as the end of the family as its members know it (negative/unpleasant). Different individuals within a family may have different definitions. When individual family members' definitions are the same, they are congruent, and there is a collective perception (Boss, 1988). Based on family systems theory, the whole is greater than the sum of its parts; therefore, the family's definition may supersede an individual member's definition even when the family definition is a distortion of reality (Boss, 2002). In addition, family systems theory purports that when a family member changes his or her definition, the family will also begin to change. The definition of a stressor may affect the hardships experienced, or the hardships may affect the definition of the stressor.

Hardships

Hardships are demands on coping resources made by a stressor (Hill, 1949). Coping resources will be discussed in detail later in this chapter. Individual family members, the family system, and/or the community may make these demands (McCubbin & Patterson, 1983a). Examples of family hardships include demands on the family resources of energy, time, and space when a new baby comes into the family. If the hardships are unmanaged, stress occurs (McCubbin & Patterson, 1983a).

Stress

Stress is a *state* of individuals, families, and/or communities in response to the stimulus of a stressor and resulting hardships (Boss, 1987). Stress is normal and neutral (neither positive nor negative) (Boss, 1988; Selye, 1956). It is a continuous outcome variable in that there are degrees of stress (Boss, 1988) as well as a categorical variable. See Table 2.7. Types of individual stress based

Table 2.7 Classifications of Stress

Deprived	Optimal	Excessive
Level I	Level II	Level III
Individual	Family	Community
Desirable	Undesirable	
Eustress	Distress	

on degrees of stress include deprived, optimal, and excessive (Selye, 1956). A *deprived* degree of stress may result in a lack of motivation while *optimal* stress tends to lead to motivation. *Excessive* stress may lead to crisis.

Types of family stress based on degree include Level I, Level II, and Level III (Burr, 1989). Robert Burr (1989) classified family stress into the three levels based on the level of change required to manage the stress successfully (result in positive outcome). Wesley Burr and Associates (1994) found support for these levels based on types of coping strategies used for acute stress but not for chronic stress. For a Level I stress, first-order changes (e.g., changes in rules, coping strategies) could manage the stress successfully; for Level II stress, second-order changes (e.g., changes in metarules or rules about rules) are needed; and for Level III stress, third-order changes (e.g., changes in values, philosophy of life, sacred vs. secular orientation, beliefs, assumptions) are needed (Burr, Klein, & Associates, 1994). Examples of different levels of coping strategies appear later in this chapter. Other categorizations of stress, which are not based on degree of stress, include individual, family, or community; desirable or undesirable; and eustress or distress.

Individual, Family, or Community Stress

Selye (1978) defined individual stress as the state of pressure/tension when the individual reacts to a stressor. Boss (1988) defined family stress as a state of pressure/tension in the family system in response to a stressor. In addition, if the community experiences stress, we can define community stress as the state of pressure/tension when the community reacts to a stressor. The individual, family, or community may experience stress as desirable or undesirable.

Desirable or Undesirable Stress

Whether stress is desirable or undesirable depends on the definition/perception/assessment/appraisal given to a stressor and the degree of stress. An optimal degree of stress is desirable for motivation. The stress of the deadline of an assignment can motivate a student to begin work on a term paper. Stress from the stressor of a physical illness of a family member can motivate a family to spend more time together. In these cases, stress is desirable. When the degree of stress is excessive, stress is likely to be defined as undesirable. The stress of having several final exams in one day can lead a student to feel too overwhelmed to concentrate and study. In this case, stress is undesirable. In addition to classification based on desirability, stress can also be categorized based on how it is experienced.

Eustress or Distress

Sometimes the state of stress is experienced as a positive or pleasant state called eustress (Selye, 1956). When the definition of a stressor is positive, we are more likely to experience eustress. Sometimes stress is experienced as a negative or unpleasant state called distress (McCubbin & Patterson, 1983a). When the definition of a stressor is negative, we are more likely to experience distress. Even though a stressor is defined in a positive way (desirable), distress may still be experienced, as in the birth of a baby. Distress in a family results when a stressor leads to disruption in family processes (roles, routines, rituals) and the stressor requires the family to use new processes (make changes). The process of coping is used to manage distress.

Coping

Coping is the transformation process of managing distress by each individual and by the family (Patterson, 1988). According to Boss (1987), if even *one* member manifests distress symptoms, the family is not coping successfully. Coping resources are used to cope with distress.

Coping Resources

Coping resources refer to assets (characteristics, traits, or competencies) used to manage distress from stressors. Classifications for resources vary from author to author but not to a great degree and are based on when they are used and on origin. Classifications of coping resources based on when they are used include resistance/adjustment and adaptive. The terms *resistance resources* (McCubbin & McCubbin, 1987; McCubbin, Thompson,

Pirner, & McCubbin, 1988) and *adjustment resources* (McCubbin & McCubbin, 1987) refer to resources used after a stressor but prior to a crisis to try to prevent a crisis from occurring. *Adaptive resources* (Patterson, 1988) refer to resources used to recover from a crisis. Both resistance/ adjustment and adaptive resources can be further classified based on origin. Classifications of resources based on origin include personal/individual/ psychological, family/intrafamilial/microenvironmental, and community/ social (McCubbin & Patterson, 1983a; Patterson, 1988). It would be impossible to list all possible resources; however, Patterson (1988) discussed the most important resources from the stress literature. Table 2.8 lists those and other common resources.

Personal/Individual/Psychological Coping Resources

Personal, individual, or psychological coping resources are those assets possessed by an individual. Of those listed in Table 2.8, self-esteem (positive self-worth) and self-mastery have been found to be critical for coping with distress, yet they are the most threatened by crises (Patterson, 1988). While individual family members possess certain resources, the collective family possesses resources as well.

Family/Intrafamily/Microenvironmental Coping Resources

Family, intrafamily, or microenvironmental coping resources are those assets possessed by the collective members of the family. Olson, Russell, and Sprenkle (1979) integrated the most prominent family resources, the family's adaptability and cohesion, into the Circumplex Model of Marital and Family Systems. Based on the Circumplex Model, we can determine a family's type and whether the family is balanced, midrange, or unbalanced. Researchers (Olson et al., 1989) found balanced families cope better with stress than unbalanced families. While the collective family possesses certain resources, the community collective possesses resources as well.

Community Coping Resources

Community coping resources are assets possessed by the community. Major classifications of community resources include persons, groups, and institutions. Further classifications of institutional community resources include mesoenvironmental and macroenvironmental. *Mesoenvironmental* means the middle-level environment (services of institutions such as schools,

Table 2.8 Types of Coping Resources

I. Personal/Individual/Psychological	
Primary	*Subsets*
Health	physical
	emotional
Intelligence	
Knowledge	
Personality traits	extroversion
	optimism
	self-esteem
	sense of humor
	sense of mastery
	social ties to community
Skills	to earn money
	to manage home
Time	
II. Family/Intrafamily	
Microenvironmental	
Appreciation	
Clear boundaries	generational
Communication skills	messages clear and direct
Instrumental	verbal–nonverbal congruency
Affective	
Egalitarian marital roles	
Organization	
Regular and varied interaction	
Respect for individuality	
Support	
Trust	
Type is balanced	adaptability
	cohesion

(Continued)

Table 2.8 (Continued)

III. Community/Social	
Primary	*Subsets*
Persons	
Groups	coworkers
	friends
	health care providers
	neighbors
	physicians
	relatives
	self-help groups
Institutions	
Mesoenvironmental	schools, churches, employers
Macroenvironmental	government policies

churches, and employers), while *macroenvironmental* means the larger-level environment (government policies) (McCubbin & McCubbin, 1987). In order for coping resources to relieve distress, they must be used. The act of using a coping resource is called a coping strategy.

Coping Strategies

Coping strategies are behaviors/activities for getting and/or using coping resources to restore balance between demands on resources (hardships) and resources, thus reducing distress (McCubbin et al., 1988). Major classifications of coping strategies include negative/dysfunctional/unhealthy/disabling or positive/functional/healthy/enabling (based on outcome); individual, family, or community (based on who uses a coping strategy); Level I, II, or III (based on level of abstraction); and adjustment/resistance or adaptation (based on when a coping strategy is used).

Negative/Dysfunctional/Unhealthy/Disabling and Positive/Functional/Healthy/Enabling Coping Strategies

Negative/dysfunctional/unhealthy/disabling coping strategies. Negative/dysfunctional/unhealthy/disabling coping strategies are coping strategies that, although they may relieve distress in the short run, lead to harmful side effects/consequences/outcomes in the long run. They become stress producers (stressors) rather than stress reducers (Hoff, 1989). Negative coping strategies increase vulnerability because of the harmful side effects/consequences/outcomes (Boss, 1987). Examples of such coping strategies are abuse of alcohol, food, illegal drugs, medications, sex, shopping, and/or work and family violence. Although the intent of such coping strategies may be positive, the results of such strategies are negative/dysfunctional/unhealthy/disabling, such as when someone drinks alcoholic beverages (coping strategy), temporarily relieving distress but resulting in alcoholism (negative/dysfunctional/unhealthy/disabling outcome).

Positive/functional/healthy/enabling coping strategies. Positive/functional/healthy/enabling coping strategies have positive/functional/healthy/enabling consequences or outcomes most of the time (Burr et al., 1994). It is clear that overdrinking alcoholic beverages will lead to negative outcomes; however, Burr et al. (1994) point out that even what appear to be the most helpful strategies can have negative consequences or outcomes in some situations, an area that needs further research. For example, use of social support, a positive coping strategy, can lead to undermining self-efficacy, self-esteem, and/or autonomy (negative consequences or outcomes). Both positive and negative coping strategies may be used by individuals, families, or communities.

Individual, Family, or Community Coping Strategies

Individual coping strategies. Lazarus (1966) classified individual coping strategies into three general categories:

1. Direct actions

2. Defensive reappraisals

3. Anxiety-reaction patterns

Direct actions include behaviors or activities aimed at strengthening the individual's resources (e.g., learning skills), attack patterns (e.g., violence), and avoidance patterns (e.g., physical or intellectual flight). Defensive reappraisals include externalization of blame, scapegoating, and displacement. According to Lazarus (1966), anxiety-reaction patterns (e.g., seeking counseling, keeping a diary, drinking alcohol) occur when the stressor is ambiguous. Some of the coping strategies identified by Lazarus can be classified as positive/healthy/functional/enabling while others can be classified as negative/unhealthy/

dysfunctional. While individuals use their own coping strategies, families use coping strategies as a system.

Family coping strategies. Family coping strategies are behaviors/ activities performed by the family and by each individual family member (Boss, 1987). Coping strategies aim at maintaining family integration and morale and member self-esteem. Family coping strategies have been classified based on level of abstraction (Burr, 1989) and on when they occur (McCubbin & McCubbin, 1987). In addition, McCubbin and McCubbin (1987) grouped specific family coping strategies into five general patterns:

1. Reducing the number and/or intensity of demands on resources

2. Acquiring additional resources

3. Maintaining existing resources

4. Managing tension

5. Changing the meaning of a situation

These patterns of family coping strategies can be classified based on level of abstraction and on when they occur.

Level I, II, and III coping strategies. *Level I, II, and III coping strategy* classifications suggested a developmental pattern in the use of family coping strategies, with less abstract strategies used first followed by more abstract strategies (R. G. Burr, 1989). Levels I, II, and III refer to the levels of abstraction, with Level III being the most abstract (W. R. Burr, Day, & Bahr, 1993). Wesley Burr and Associates (1994) proposed that the developmental pattern occurred, with Level I strategies used more extensively early in the process and Level II and/or III strategies later when lower-level strategies failed to reduce distress, but that this was not necessarily true for all stress. With severe stress, a family may go directly to Level III coping strategies without using Level I or Level II coping strategies first.

Level I coping strategies used to cope with Level I stress refer to those that require only first-order changes, such as attempts to change behavior patterns, role expectations, or rules. Level I coping strategies can be categorized as cognitive, emotional, relationship, communication, community, spiritual, and individual development activities (Burr et al., 1994). See Table 2.9. Burr et al. (1994) developed the conceptual framework of Level I coping strategies by examining published research and listing specific coping strategies found in that research. They then grouped the strategies leading to the conceptual framework. Six of the seven general areas of coping strategies involve family aspects: cognition, emotion, relationships, communication,

Table 2.9 Level I Family Coping Strategies

Cognitive Activities	
Accept the situation and others.	1. Quickly accept and confront the situation.
	2. Accept the differences in family members' responses to the situation.
	3. Accept limitations; do not try to do or be everything.
Gain useful knowledge.	1. Find information and facts about the situation.
	2. Understand the essential nature of the situation.
Change how the situation is viewed or defined.	1. Separate the stress into manageable parts.
	2. Do not have false hopes, but have faith in own ability to handle the situation.
	3. Have an optimistic attitude of life, self, and others.
	4. Do not blame others or become preoccupied with blaming; instead be solution-oriented.
	5. View it as a family-centered concern and not as an individual's problem.
	6. Reframe the situation by defining the problem in a more positive way.
Emotional Activities	
Express feelings and affection.	1. Express positive and negative feelings and emotions openly.
	2. Be honest, clear, and direct in expressing affection.
	3. Be clear and direct in expressing commitment to each other.
Avoid or resolve disabling expressions of emotion.	1. Reduce anxiety by taking time to get away or relax when needed.
	2. Avoid or reduce disturbing emotional feelings by self-punishment, consuming alcohol, smoking, crying, and withdrawing.
	3. Be passive about the situation.
Be aware of and sensitive to each other's emotional needs.	1. Be sensitive to each other's needs.
	2. Share feelings of the experience with each other to be more aware of each other's specific situation.

(Continued)

Table 2.9 (Continued)

Relationship Activities	
Develop family cohesion and togetherness.	1. Do things together to develop and increase family integration.
	2. Do things with children and maintain stability.
Maintain family adaptability and flexibility.	1. Be flexible and willing to change family roles, behaviors, and attitudes.
Cooperate as a family.	1. Be unified and committed to cooperation as a family.
	2. Offer family members mutual support and access to the family's collective coping experience.
Build and improve trusting relationships with others.	1. Develop trusting relationships with others.
	2. Increase tolerance of one another.
	3. Have more tolerance of family members.
Communication Activities	
Be open and honest.	1. Be open in your communication with other family members.
	2. Be honest in your communications with others.
	3. Exchange information with one another.
	4. Talk to someone about the situation.
Listen to each other.	1. Listen to other family members.
	2. Be effective in the quantity and quality of your communication.
Be more sensitive to nonverbal communication.	1. Be sensitive to and aware of nonverbal communication.
Community Activities	
Seek help and support from others.	1. Seek and accept help from relatives when needed.
	2. Seek and accept help from community services when needed.

Fulfill expectations in organizations.	1. Accept and live up to expectations of organizations to which the family belongs.
	2. Remain part of your organizations or community.
Spiritual Activities	
Be more involved in religious activities.	1. Be more involved in your religious activities.
Increase or seek help from God.	1. Believe in God.
Individual Development Activities	
Develop autonomy, independence, and self-sufficiency.	1. Be involved in self-development; it allows for more independence and self-sufficiency.
Keep active hobbies.	1. Spend time on hobbies and activities with friends.

Source: Adapted from Burr, Klein, & Associates (1994).

community, and spiritual life. The seventh refers to the individualistic process of enhancing individual family member development.

According to Patterson (1988), first-order (Level I) change is used during times of relative stability to cope with minor stressors and *avoid* crisis. Burr (1989), on the other hand, proposed that Level I coping strategies were used to cope with Level I crises rather than to prevent crises. Most likely, both Patterson and Burr were correct in that Level I coping strategies are probably used both to manage everyday stress and to try to manage the acute distress of a crisis. According to Burr, if the Level I coping strategies were not effective at managing crises, stress might have increased to Level II or Level III stress, and families would have needed to use Level II or III coping strategies.

Level II coping strategies used to cope with Level II stress are more complex and abstract than Level I coping strategies and deal with such things as metarules and other fundamental aspects of the family's basic organization, such as processes. Metarules are rules about rules of transformation. Level II coping strategies include such behaviors/activities as reviewing and/or changing the way of governing the family, hierarchies of power (Burr, Day, & Bahr, 1993), decision-making methods, and the way of making rules (Burr et al., 1994). Level II strategies may also involve the structure of "processes such as trying to communicate in different ways, being more or less loving, being more or less supportive, and changing the amount of cooperation versus competition" (Burr et al., 1994, p. 179). When a mother begins making the family rules after the death of the father, a metarule (the rule about who makes the rules) changes. When Level II coping strategies do not relieve the family stress, the stress may increase to Level III stress, and the family may employ Level III coping strategies.

Level III coping strategies used to cope with Level III stress refer to those concerning the abstract beliefs and assumptions that make up a family's philosophy of life (family paradigm) (Burr et al., 1993). A Level III coping strategy is a questioning of and sometimes a change of paradigm/ schema. Questioning spiritual beliefs occurs at this level. Families may employ Level III coping strategies without first using Level I or Level II if the level of stress is severe, as in the case of the September 11, 2001, attacks. Some family members and friends of those lost in the towers thought that they could no longer pray to a God that allowed the event to happen.

Adjustment/resistance or adaptation coping strategies. *Adjustment/ resistance or adaptation coping strategies* are classifications of family coping strategies based on when the coping strategies are used (McCubbin & McCubbin, 1987, 1991). Adjustment/resistance coping strategies are those the family uses to cope with distress after a stressor but before a crisis. The basic adjustment/resistance coping strategies include avoidance, elimination, and assimilation (McCubbin & McCubbin, 1987, 1991). Avoidance and elimination help to keep the family from having to change the family structure much.

Avoidance is "defined as family efforts to deny or ignore the stressor and other demands in the belief and hope that they will go away or resolve themselves" (McCubbin & McCubbin, 1991, p. 13). We often say that a family is "in denial" when this happens. It appears that families are doing nothing when they use avoidance as a coping strategy. Elimination is changing or removing the stressor or altering the definition of the stressor (McCubbin & McCubbin, 1991). A family may change its definition of a stressor from "the end of the world" to "a manageable challenge." Assimilation is the family's absorption of demands by making only minor changes within the family (McCubbin & McCubbin, 1991). Sharing roles that were previously segregated is an example of assimilation.

Adaptation coping strategies are those the family uses when the family is in crisis. Adaptation strategies identified by McCubbin and McCubbin (1991) include synergizing, interfacing, compromising, and maintaining the family system. "Synergizing refers to family efforts to coordinate and pull together as a unit to accomplish a shared lifestyle and orientation which cannot be achieved by any member alone but only through mutuality and interdependence" (p. 24). Sharing spiritual beliefs falls in the category of synergizing. Interfacing refers to working "with the community to achieve a new and better 'fit'" (p. 24). Participating in community activities illustrates this concept. Compromising is defined as accepting and lending support to a less-than-perfect resolution. A family learning to live with a family member's chronic illness and make the best of the time that they do have together illustrates this concept. Maintaining the family system refers to attending to the needs of family members and of the family unit. While these family coping strategies are used when a family is in distress, there are also coping strategies to use when a community is in distress.

Community coping strategies. Community coping strategies are behaviors/activities performed by the community to reduce distress. Community coping is outside the realm of this book. A good resource on community coping strategies is the book *Disaster and Mass Trauma: Global Perspectives on Post-Disaster Mental Health Management* (Kalayjian, 1995). When coping strategies used after a stressor to reduce distress do not work, a crisis may occur.

Crisis

A crisis is an acute (lasting a few hours to a few weeks), moderate to severe, distressed state of being. It is a categorical variable since an individual, a family, or a community is either in or out of crisis, (Boss, 1988). It is also a continuous variable as one could have a Level I, II, or III crisis, with Level III being the most severe (Burr, 1989).

Although crisis is a state of dysfunction, when someone or a family is in crisis, we do not label that person or family as dysfunctional. The label *dysfunctional* describes a chronic condition, whereas a crisis is an acute (temporary) condition that happens to both healthy/functional and unhealthy/dysfunctional individuals and families.

The terms *stress* and *crisis* do *not* mean the same thing. Nor do *stressor* and *crisis*. Confusion of the terms resulted from some early theorists and researchers using the terms interchangeably. We know that an individual, a family, or a community is in a state of crisis by the manifestations/symptoms/indicators/signals that it exhibits.

Individual Manifestations/
Symptoms/Indicators/Signals of Crisis

There are manifestations, symptoms, indicators, or signals of distress that we can use to identify when an individual is in crisis (Hoff, 1989, 1995,

2001). Individuals may experience some of these after a stressor and not go into crisis. In that case, they are in a vulnerable state but not in a state of crisis. They are still able to function and meet goals even though they are in distress. An individual in crisis will experience a greater number of manifestations/symptoms/indicators/signals with greater severity than a vulnerable individual.

Individual manifestations/symptoms/indicators/signals of distress can be classified into four general groups—behavioral, cognitive, emotional, and physical or biophysical (see Table 2.10). Some also use two other categories of manifestations, spiritual and interpersonal. Upon examining the manifestations of the classifications *spiritual* and *interpersonal*, it becomes apparent that each is a subset of one of the main classifications. For example, anger at God is an emotional manifestation (anger) directed at God, making it spiritual in nature. Thinking that no one cares is a cognitive manifestation (thinking) about interpersonal relationships. Lashing out at someone is a behavioral manifestation in an interpersonal relationship.

Different individuals will experience different manifestations/symptoms/indicators/signals when they are in crisis. Some may experience more of

Table 2.10 Some Individual Manifestations/Symptoms/Indicators/Signals of Distress

Behavioral	Cognitive	Emotional	Physical/Biophysical
Arguing	Apathy	Anger	Abdominal pain
Excessive activity	Blame	Anxiety	Chills
Fewer social contacts	Boredom	Fear	Colds
Increased startle response	Confusion	Depressions	Decreased appetite
Isolation	Cynicism	Emotional shock	Dizziness
Lack of intimacy	Difficulty understanding communication	Envy	Energy loss
Lashing out	Distressing dreams	Guilt	Exhaustion
Nagging	Distrust	Insecurity	Fainting

Behavioral	Cognitive	Emotional	Physical/Biophysical
Pacing	Disturbed thinking	•Irritability	Frequent urination
Somatic complaints	Frustration	Little joy	Headaches
Substance abuse	Hallucinating	Numbness (no feeling)	Increased blood pressure
Violent behavior	Hypo- or hyperalertness	Rage	Increased heart rate
	Inability to solve problems	Shame	Menstrual irregularities
	Intrusive thoughts		Muscle aches
	Low productivity		Numbness
	Negative attitude		Perspiring
	Negative self-talk		Rash
	No new ideas		Respiratory problems
	Not oriented to time or place		Sleep disturbances (insomnia or excessive sleep)
	• Overwhelmed		Stomach problems (nausea, diarrhea, cramps)
	Preoccupation with thoughts of stressor		Teeth grinding
	Racing thoughts		Tight chest
	• Resentment		Visual difficulties
	Slowed thinking		Vomiting
	• Spacing out		Weakness
	Suicidal thoughts		Weight change
			Worsening of chronic illness

one type of manifestation/symptom/indicator/signal than another. Although people of all ages share many crisis manifestations/symptoms/indicators/ signals (Greenstone & Leviton, 2002), children often find it difficult to name their feelings, so they act them out in their behaviors. Table 2.11 lists typical crisis manifestations/symptoms/indicators/signals in children of different ages.

Family Manifestations/Symptoms/Indicators/Signals of Crisis

When a family is in a state of crisis (temporarily dysfunctional), family boundaries, roles, rules, and tasks are affected (Boss, 1988, 2002), and old ways of reaching goals no longer work. Some family crisis manifestations include inability to perform usual roles and tasks, inability to make decisions, inability to solve problems, inability to care for each other in the usual way, and focus on individual survival. Kanel (1998) calls family crises *runaways*. To relieve the manifestations of crisis, individuals and families use crisis management.

Crisis Management

Crisis management is an attempt to relieve the crisis manifestations of the crisis state and return to the same or higher level of functioning compared to before the stressor that led to the crisis occurred. Individuals and families use the same type of coping strategies to manage crises as they use to try to prevent crises. Sometimes they use a community resource, such as crisis counselors, to assist them. When crisis counselors are used, it is called formal crisis management. A detailed discussion of formal crisis management appears in Part III of this book.

Recovery/Reorganization

Recovery/reorganization has been referred to both as a period of time and as a state of being. The beginning of recovery/reorganization is a turning point. The recovery/reorganization state begins when there is a change in the (a) stressor, (b) resources used for coping, (c) coping strategies used, or (d) definition of the stressor (Boss, 1988). Changing any combination or even just one of the above can begin recovery. Sometimes it is possible to change only one or two. Recovery/ reorganization lasts from when crisis manifestations begin to decrease until achievement of a somewhat steady level of organization. Recovery can take only hours or years (Boss, 1988). When recovery ends, we can identify the crisis outcome.

Table 2.11 Typical Manifestations/Symptoms/Indicators/Signals of Crisis in Children

	Preschool Ages 1–5	*Early Childhood Ages 5–11*	*Preadolescent Ages 11–14*	*Adolescent Ages 14–18*
Behavioral	Clinging to parents Thumb sucking	Aggressiveness Avoiding school Clinging Competition for attention Irritability Whining	Attention-seeking behavior Fighting Rebellion Refusal to do chores Withdrawal	Decline in struggles over parental control Delinquent and/or irresponsible behavior
Cognitive	Loss of interest in preschool Night terrors Speech difficulties	Confusion Loss of interest in school Nightmares Night terrors Poor concentration	Denial Loss of interest in school, peers, and social activities	Apathy Blame Decline in interest in opposite sex and school Poor concentration
Emotional	Fear of animals, being left alone, the dark	Anxiety Fear of abandonment, dark, personal harm	Anger Anxiety Fear of impending loss of family members, friends, or home or of personal harm	Anger at the perceived unfairness of a crisis occurring in their lives Fear of loss Guilt
Physical	Bed wetting Constipation Immobility Loss of bladder and/or bowel control	Sleep disturbances	Aches Appetitive, and/or sleep disturbances Bowel problems Psychosomatic complaints Skin eruption	Appetite and sleep disturbances Asthma Bowel problems Decreased energy Headaches Menstrual problems Rashes Tension

Source: Adapted from Greenstone & Leviton (2002).

Crisis Outcomes/Resolutions

Crisis outcomes/resolutions can be classified as negative, neutral, or positive. A negative outcome/resolution is not returning to the same level of organization or functioning as that prior to the crisis but rather ending up at a lower level of organization or functioning. Originally, when the individual or family returned to the same level or higher level of functioning that it had prior to the stressor, it was called a positive outcome. Boss (1988) points out that returning to the same level of functioning as prior to the stressor might not actually be a positive outcome, as in the case of an abusive relationship. If a wife returns from the hospital to receive treatment for injuries from spousal abuse and a family returns to the same abusive patterns, Boss asserts, this is not a positive outcome, even though the family has recovered to the prior level of functioning. Whether returning to the prior level of functioning is positive or neutral, then, depends on the level of functioning prior to the crisis. In the case cited above, it was a neutral outcome. A positive outcome in that case would have been ending up at a higher level of functioning, in which case there would no longer be abuse in the relationship. In the case of a positive outcome, the crisis would have served a useful purpose.

Purpose of Crises

The purpose of a crisis is to present an opportunity to reach a higher level of functioning. When an individual or a family experiences a crisis, it can take the opportunity to grow and develop from the experience and have a positive outcome/resolution or choose not to take the opportunity and have a neutral or negative outcome/resolution. The distress from a crisis can act as a motivator to change unhealthy family patterns, as in the case of spouse abuse. When individuals and families resist crisis or have positive outcomes, they are sometimes called resilient.

Resilience, Resiliency, and Resilient

The concepts of resilience, resiliency, and resilient are treated in a separate section, as they are relatively new concepts in stress theory. The concepts go with the trend to focus research on individual and family strengths (Stinnett & DeFrain, 1985); however, the definitions of resilience, resiliency, and resilient are inconsistent in the literature (Patterson, 2002). The concepts need both that are clear conceptual and operational definitions (Patterson, 2002). I propose that the concepts of resilience, resiliency, and resilient, which were borrowed from the research of psychologists (Garmezy, 1987; Garmezy & Masten, 1986; Rutter, 1987), are just new terms for concepts that already exist in stress theory. Since the concepts of resilience, resiliency, and resilient appear in the literature of researchers and practitioners, it is important to agree on definitions.

Although practitioners and researchers do not agree on definitions of the concepts, they do tend to agree that they are descriptive of both individuals and families (Hetherington & Blechman, 1996; Patterson, 2002). The terms have been referred to as protective factors/characteristics (Boss, 2006) or strengths (Stinnett & DeFrain, 1985), protective/adaptive processes (Hetherington & Blechman, 1996; Walsh, 1998), and positive outcomes (Patterson, 2002). Walsh (1998) defines resilience as a capacity (a resource) and as a process. Protective factors/characteristics or strengths are called resources in stress theory. Protective/adaptive processes are called coping strategies, and positive outcomes are called high levels of recovery/reorganization. Is adding resiliency, resilience, and resilient to our repertoire of concepts just introducing another set of terms? What, if any, impact will the terms have on how crisis managers perform crisis management? Regardless of the answer to the questions, a consistency of definitions is important to both researchers and practitioners. Meanwhile, for strategies for increasing family resilience, see *Strengthening Family Resilience* by Froma Walsh (1998).

Summary of Definitions

This chapter presented the major concepts used in stress theory, their most salient definitions, their classifications, and their relationships to each other. People often confuse the concepts of stressors, stress, and crises. Remember a stressor is something that happens (an event) or is going on (a situation) while both stress and a crisis are states of being, with a crisis being a moderate to severe state of distress. A terrorist attack is a stressor. Stress is the state of the individual, family, or community after experiencing a stressor. If temporary dysfunction results, the dysfunctional state is called a state of crisis. The crisis can be managed with coping strategies that use coping resources during recovery/reorganization in which the crisis manifestations/symptoms/indicators/signals diminish. The outcome of recovery/organization may be negative, neutral, or positive.

EXERCISE

2.1 Identify a personal crisis that occurred at least 2 years ago. Write a narrative about the crisis. Following is a narrative example that will be used to illustrate each of the models presented in Part II of the text:

When I was 32 years old, less than a month before my thirty-third birthday, my husband died due to melanoma, a deadly skin cancer. The cancer had moved to his lungs and basically smothered him, and I helplessly watched him die. We had a 15-month-old son. After staying in the hospital with my husband for his last 2 weeks of life, I watched him take his last breath on July 24, 1984. I sat with him for a while before I called the nurse as I knew there was nothing that could be done to save him. The nurse in turn advised my sister-in-law, who had been in the waiting room. Until that time, I did not know that family members had been taking turns staying in the waiting room so that I would not be alone after my husband died. I did not cry. Even though I knew he was going to die and I anticipated his death, I was in shock when it actually happened, and I was relieved. I wouldn't have to watch him suffer anymore. I stayed at the hospital until the funeral home staff arrived to pick up the body. I asked that they cross his legs at his ankles as he was comfortable like that. They said that they would try. As I walked out of the hospital door into the sunny day, I remember thinking that it seems like everything should stop, but everything just keeps on going like nothing happened. The people walking in the door and driving their cars did not know that my husband had just died at the age of 37. Someone slept at my house that night so I wouldn't be alone. I don't remember who it was. I didn't sleep much that night, but my husband came to me in a dream. Fortunately, my husband's brother and his wife made all of the funeral arrangements. All I did was pick the shirt he would wear. It was a Western-style shirt that I had sewn for him. I had embroidered some red flowers on the front. When I first saw him in the casket, I put a picture of our son in his pocket. He was so cold and hard. Getting to the funeral home was interesting. I think my father brought me. Whoever it was, I needed to give him directions, and I couldn't remember where to turn. Whoever was driving couldn't understand why I couldn't remember where to turn. My brain just wasn't working very well. I don't remember crying very much. I had cried so much before when my husband was sick and going through treatments, and I was exhausted from taking care of him and our baby. Fortunately, my parents were always there to take care of the baby when I needed to take my husband to the hospital for a treatment or a surgery. My three girlfriends from out of state came for the funeral and stayed a couple of days. We went out to a club one night, and people were staring and making comments that we were gay. I guess it was because we were dancing together and holding hands. Another friend came about a week later and helped clean the house. In the weeks that followed, my parents fixed dinner for my son and me each weekday so I did not have to be concerned with meal preparation after work. My mother also babysat for my son when I had to work late or go out of town for business meetings. I tried to find books about widowhood to read, but at the time I only found one in my library. I applied for Social Security benefits for my son and a plaque from the Veterans Administration for my husband's grave. A month after my husband died, I was back at work. I was almost back to functioning normally, but I did forget about an appointment, which was unlike me.

2.2 Use the appropriate instrument to identify your level of pileup for the year prior to the crisis in Exercise 2.1 and add to the narrative reasons for choosing a particular instrument as well as an interpretation of results from the instrument.

References and Suggestions for Further Reading

Anderson, G. E. (1972). *College schedule of recent experience.* Unpublished master's thesis, North Dakota State University, Fargo.

Boss, P. (1977). A clarification of the concept of psychological father presence to families experiencing ambiguity of boundary. *Journal of Marriage and Family, 39*(1), 141–151.

Boss, P. (1987). Family stress: Perception and context. In M. Sussman & S. Steinmetz (Eds.), *Handbook on marriage and the family* (pp. 695–723). New York: Plenum.

Boss, P. (1988). *Family stress management.* Newbury Park, CA: Sage.

Boss, P. (2002). *Family stress: A contextual approach.* Thousand Oaks, CA: Sage.

Boss, P. (2006). *Loss, trauma, and resilience: Therapeutic work with ambiguous loss.* New York: Norton.

Burr, R. G. (1989). *Reframing family stress theory: From the ABC-X Model to a Family Ecosystemic Model.* Unpublished master's thesis, Brigham Young University, Proro, UT.

Burr, W. R. (1973). *Theory construction and the sociology of the family.* New York: John Wiley & Sons.

Burr, W. R., Day, R. D., & Bahr, K. S. (1993). *Family science.* Pacific Grove, CA: Brooks/Cole.

Burr, W. R., Klein, S. R., & Associates. (1994). *Reexamining family stress: New theory and research.* Thousand Oaks, CA: Sage.

Caplan, G. (1964). *Principles of preventive psychiatry.* New York: Basic Books.

Carter, B., & McGoldrick, M. (1999). Overview: The expanded family life cycle—Individual, family, and social perspectives. In B. Carter & M. McGoldrick (Eds.), *The expanded family life cycle: Individual, family, and social perspectives* (3rd ed., pp. 1–26). Boston: Allyn and Bacon.

Coddington, R. D. (1972). The significance of life events as etiologic factors in the diseases of children II: A study of the normal population. *Journal of Psychosomatic Research, 16,* 205–213.

Coohey, C., & Marsh, J. (1995). Promotion, prevention, and treatment: What are the differences? *Research on Social Work Practice, 5,* 524–538.

Corsini, R. J., & Wedding, D. (1989). *Current psychotherapies.* Itasca, IL: F. E. Peacock.

Duvall, E. (1946). Conceptions of parenthood. *American Journal of Sociology, 52*(3), 193–203.

Duvall, E. (1971). *Marriage and family development* (5th ed.). Philadelphia: J. B. Lippincott.

Duvall, E. (1977). *Marriage and family development* (6th ed.). Philadelphia: J. B. Lippincott.

Erikson, E. (1963). *Childhood and society* (2nd ed.). New York: Norton.

Golan, N. (1969). When is a client in crisis? *Social Casework, 50,* 389–394.

Garmezy, N. (1987). Stress, competence, and development: Continuities in the study of schizophrenic adults, children vulnerable to psychopathology, and the search for stress-resistant children. *American Journal of Orthopsychiatry, 57*(2), 159–174.

Garmezy, N., & Masten, A. S. (1986). Stress, competence, and resilience: Common frontiers for therapist and psychopathologist. *Behavior Therapy, 17,* 500–521.

Greenstone, J. L., & Leviton, S. C. (2002). *Elements of crisis intervention: Crises and how to respond to them.* Pacific Grove, CA: Brooks/Cole.

Grochowski, J. R., & McCubbin, H. I. (1991). YA-FILES: Young Adult Family Inventory of Life Events and Changes. In H. I. McCubbin & A. I. Thompson (Eds.), *Family assessment inventories for research and practice* (pp. 111–123). Madison: University of Wisconsin.

Hetherington, E. M., & Blechman, E. A. (1996). *Stress, coping, and resiliency in children and families.* Mahwah, NJ: Erlbaum.

Hill, R. (1949). *Families under stress.* New York: Harper & Brothers.

Hill, R. (1958). Generic features of families under stress. *Social Casework, 49,* 139–150.

Hoff, L. A. (1989). *People in crisis: Understanding and helping* (3rd ed.). Menlo Park, CA: Addison Wesley.

Hoff, L. A. (1995). *People in crisis: Understanding and helping* (4th ed.). Menlo Park, CA: Addison Wesley.

Hoff, L. A. (2001). *People in crisis: Clinical and public health perspectives* (5th ed.). San Francisco: Jossey-Bass.

Holmes, T. H., & Rahe, R. H. (1967). The Social Readjustment Rating Scale. *Journal of Psychosomatic Research, 11,* 213–218.

Ivey, A. E., Gluckstern, N. B., & Ivey, M. B. (1997). *Basic attending skills* (3rd ed.). North Amherst, MA: Microtraining Associates.

Kalayjian, A. S. (1995). *Disaster and mass trauma: Global perspectives on post-disaster mental health management.* Long Branch, NJ: Vista.

Kanel, K. (1998). *A guide to crisis intervention.* Pacific Grove, CA: Brooks/Cole.

Kanner, A. D., Coyne, J. C., Schaefer, C., & Lazarus, R. S. (1981). Comparison of two modes of stress measurement: Daily hassles and uplifts versus major life events. *Journal of Behavioral Medicine, 4,* 1–39.

Koos, E. L. (1946). *Families in trouble.* Morningside Heights, NY: King's Crown.

Lazarus, R. (1966). *Psychological stress and the coping process.* New York: McGraw-Hill.

Lindemann, E. (1944). Symptomology and management in acute grief. *American Journal of Psychiatry, 101,* 141–148.

McCubbin, H. I., & McCubbin, M. A. (1991). Family stress theory and assessment: The Resiliency Model of Family Stress, Adjustment, and Adaptation. In H. I. McCubbin & A. I. Thompson (Eds.), *Family assessment inventories for research and practice* (pp. 2–32). Madison: University of Wisconsin. (Originally published in 1987)

McCubbin, H. I., & Patterson, J. M. (1983a). Family stress and adaptation to crises: A Double ABCX Model of family behavior. In D. H. Olson & B. Miller (Eds.), *Family studies review yearbook* (pp. 87–106). Beverly Hills, CA: Sage.

McCubbin, H. I., & Patterson, J. M. (1983b). The family stress process: The Double ABCX Model of family adjustment and adaptation. In H. I. McCubbin, M. Sussman, & J. M. Patterson (Eds.), *Social stress and the family: Advances and developments in family stress theory and research* (pp. 7–37). New York: Haworth.

McCubbin, H. I., & Patterson, J. M. (1991a). A-FILE: Adolescent Family Inventory of Life Events and Changes. In H. I. McCubbin & A. I. Thompson (Eds.), *Family assessment inventories for research and practice* (pp. 99–110). Madison: University of Wisconsin.

McCubbin, H. I., & Patterson, J. M. (1991b). FILE: Family Inventory of Life Events and Changes. In H. I. McCubbin & A. I. Thompson (Eds.), *Family assessment inventories for research and practice* (pp. 79–98). Madison: University of Wisconsin.

McCubbin, H. I., Patterson, J. M., & Wilson, L. R. (1982). *FILE.* St. Paul: University of Minnesota.

McCubbin, H. I., Thompson, A. I., Pirner, P. A., & McCubbin, M. A. (1988). *Family types and strengths.* Edina, MN: Burgess International Group.

McCubbin, M. A., & McCubbin, H. I. (1987). Family stress theory and assessment: The T-Double ABCX Model of Family Adjustment and Adaptation. In H. I. McCubbin & A. I. Thompson (Eds.), *Family assessment inventories for research and practice* (pp. 3–32). Madison: University of Wisconsin.

Olson, D., Russell, C., & Sprenkle, D. H. (1979). Circumplex model of marital and family systems II: Clinical research and intervention. In J. Vincent (Ed.), *Advances in family intervention, assessment and theory.* Greenwich, CT: JAI Press.

Olson, D. H., McCubbin, H. I., Barnes, H., Larsen, A., Muxen, M., & Wilson, M. (1989). *Families: What makes them work* (2nd ed.). Los Angeles: Sage.

Patterson, J. M. (1988). Families experiencing stress: I. The Family Adjustment and Adaptation Response Model. *Family Systems Medicine, 6*(2), 202–237.

Patterson, J. M. (2002). Integrating family resilience and family stress theory. *Journal of Marriage and Family, 64,* 349–360.

Peake, T. H., Borduin, C. M., & Archer, R. P. (1988). *Brief psychotherapies: Changing frames of mind.* Newbury Park, CA: Sage.

Rutter, M. (1987). Psychosocial resilience and protective mechanisms. *American Journal of Orthopsychiatry, 57*(3), 316–331.

Selye, H. (1956). *The stress of life.* New York: McGraw-Hill.

Selye, H. (1978). *The stress of life* (Rev. ed.). New York: McGraw-Hill.

Sifneos, P. E. (1960). A concept of "emotional crisis." *Mental Hygiene, 44,* 169–179.

Slaikeu, K. A. (1990). *Crisis intervention: A handbook for practice and research* (2nd ed.). Boston: Allyn & Bacon.

Stinnett, N., & DeFrain, J. (1985). *Secrets of strong families.* Boston: Little, Brown.

Tyhurst, J. S. (1957). The role of transition states—including disasters—in mental illness. In *Symposium on preventive and social psychiatry* (pp. 149–169). Washington, DC: Walter Reed Army Institute of Research and the National Research Council.

Walsh, F. (1998). *Strengthening family resilience.* New York: Guilford Press.

Watzlawick, P., Weakland, J., & Fisch, R. (1974). *Change: Principles of problem formation and problem resolution.* New York: Norton.

Wikler, L. (1981). Chronic stresses of families of mentally retarded children. *Family Relations, 30*(2), 281–288.

INDIVIDUAL AND FAMILY STRESS MODELS

Part II of this book considers both individual and family stress models because both individual and family indicators are important to understanding and predicting the outcome of the family stress process (Boss, 2002). An understanding of the models will help guide research and intervention. Some models will work better to guide intervention with specific clients based on various factors such as the type of stressor experienced.

The Profile of Trouble, the Truncated Roller Coaster Profile of Adjustment, and the Family Ecosystemic Model of Stress

Chapter 3 presents three models with similar figures, the Profile of Trouble, the Truncated Roller Coaster Profile of Adjustment, and the Family Ecosystemic Model of Stress. The models are presented in the chronological order of their development. The Profile of Trouble was developed first; thus it is presented first.

The Profile of Trouble

From his 3-year longitudinal study of mainly immigrants living in "old, poorly lighted, poorly heated, and unventilated" (Koos, 1946, p. 4) housing in New York City, Earl Lomon Koos, while employed by the Columbia University Department of Sociology, developed the first conceptual framework of family stress, the "Profile of Trouble" (p. 107). Figure 3.1 illustrates Koos's (1946) profile to indicate the "structure" of family troubles observed in the study.

He identified the families' normal interaction, the point the initiating cause took effect, the point at which the families' interaction dropped, the point of recovery, and the angle of recovery.

a – a'—normal interaction/organization. In Figure 3.1, *a – a'* indicates the family's normal interaction or organization. Koos (1946) began his research using the term family *organization* and then changed to family *interaction* when discussing his graphic device, and he determined the level of family organization/interaction using four criteria:

1. The amount of consciousness and acceptance by each family member of his or her and others' roles in the family

2. The extent to which family members worked toward the good of the family and of each individual

3. How much the family members found satisfaction with the family unit

4. Whether the family had a sense of direction and was moving in that direction

Comparing the families to each other, Koos (1946) ranked and divided the families into three categories of family organization/interaction: better than average, average, and below average.

b—the point at which the initiating cause takes effect. The lowercase *b* represents the point at which the initiating cause takes effect. Koos (1946) also referred to initiating causes as troubles or, in today's terminology, stressors. The lowercase *b* represents the point at which the stressor takes effect, not the point at which the stressor occurs, as other authors indicate when referring to Koos's model. Koos's model in fact indicates that the effects of the stressor may not be immediate.

c—the point at which family interaction drops. In the illustration, *c* indicates the point at which family interaction drops or, in today's terminology, the lowest point of the crisis. Following this turning point, the family begins a period of recovery. The next variable identified by Koos (1946) in his framework was the point of recovery.

d—the point of recovery. In Koos's (1946) model, *d* represents the point of recovery. Based on recovery, Koos grouped the profiles into four general types of variations found in the families he studied. In the first variation (Figure 3.1a), the families recovered to their pretrouble levels of interaction or organization. Figure 3.1b illustrates the second variation in which the families recovered to higher levels. In this second type, family interaction rose to a higher-than-pretrouble level. This happened in only one family in the sample of the families

Figure 3.1 Four General Types of the Profile of Trouble

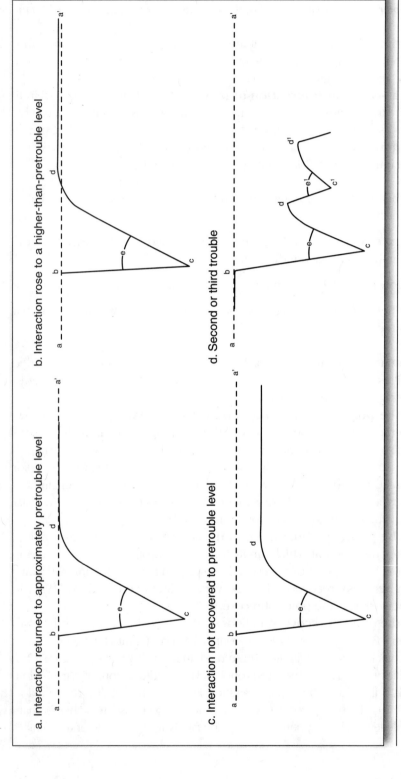

a. Interaction returned to approximately pretrouble level

b. Interaction rose to a higher-than-pretrouble level

c. Interaction not recovered to pretrouble level

d. Second or third trouble

Source: Koos (1946).

studied. In the third variation, the families did not recover to their previous levels of interaction. In this third type (Figure 3.1c), family interaction did not recover fully. These families remained below the pretrouble level. In the fourth variation (Figure 3.1d), before the families had completely recovered from the initial "trouble," a second and sometimes third trouble occurred. In this fourth type, only incomplete recovery from one trouble took place before a second or even a third trouble brought further erosion of the family's interaction. In addition to the point of recovery, Koos's model includes identifying the angle of recovery.

e—the angle of recovery. In the Profile of Trouble, *e* represents the angle of recovery. The size of the angle depends on the length of time that it takes to recover—the smaller the angle, the shorter the recovery period while the larger the angle, the longer the recovery period. Koos (1946) found an inverse relationship between adequacy of interaction/organization and length of time troubles affected the family. The majority of the pretrouble families with average interaction/organization resolved their troubles within 4 weeks, while the pretrouble below-average families' troubles tended to last more than 8 weeks.

Critique of the Profile of Trouble

A criticism of Koos's presentation of the Profile of Trouble is the fact that he changed terminology during the course of his discussion of the device, as Koos (1946) began his discussion using the term family *organization* and then changed to family *interaction*. Also, Koos used the term *trouble* to refer to both the stressor and the state of crisis. In addition, he used the term *cause*, which we no longer use because it sounds deterministic. Although Koos's model is the first to refer to families, each individual in the family may be at a different phase of the model at the same time (Burr, Klein, & Associates, 1994). On the positive side, besides being the first conceptual framework in family stress theory, Koos's model takes us from before the stressor to after recovery from the crisis.

Summary of the Profile of Trouble

Koos's (1946) Profile of Trouble suggests that families operate at three general levels of family interaction/organization, better than average, average, and below average. The initiating cause/trouble/stressor leads to decreased family interaction/organization that varies for each family, for each family member, and for each initiating cause/trouble/stressor. Families recover at different rates, producing varying angles of recovery. Koos identified four basic variations of recovery, including recovering to the pretrouble level of organization, recovering to higher-than-pretrouble organization, recovering to lower-than-pretrouble organization, and experiencing a second trouble before complete recovery. Although Koos used the terms family *organization* and family *interaction* interchangeably, overall the model is very useful in illustrating the course of a family or an individual crisis. In addition, it became the basis of the work of Hill (1949) in his development of the Truncated Roller Coater Profile of Adjustment.

Truncated Roller Coaster Profile of Adjustment

From his study of families experiencing the stressors of departure/separation from and reunion with the husband because of war, Reuben Hill, grandfather of the study of family (Hill, 2009), drew upon Koos's (1946) Profile of Trouble to describe "the course of family adjustment in the face of crisis" (Hill, 1949, p. 13). Hill (1949, 1958) is considered the father of family stress theory for his ABCX Formula, discussed in a later chapter. Hill (1949, 1958) was actually testing Koos's model in his research. He described Koos's Profile of Trouble as the truncated form of a roller coaster. Hill labeled the parts of Koos's model differently from Koos, using the terminology of *organization*, *crisis*, *disorganization*, and *reorganization*, terms previously presented by Cavan and Ranck (1938). Hill (1949) stated that "each responsible member" of the family "experiences a roller-coaster pattern of personal shock, disorganization, recovery, readjustment" (pp. 14–15), implying that the model can be used to track personal crises as well as family crises.

Conceptual Framework of the
Truncated Roller Coaster Profile of Adjustment

The following conceptual framework is based on Hill's (1949) fourth chapter, where he presents some of the findings of his research. Hill broke down adjustment patterns into periods (see Figure 3.2). In Hill's model,

1 represents the precrisis family level of organization;

2 represents anticipatory reactions and preparation for the first stressor;

3 represents reaction to the first stressor/the first disorganization;

4 represents the adjustment process;

5 represents the level of organization after reorganization/adjustment is complete;

6 represents anticipatory reactions and preparation for the second impending stressor;

7 represents reactions to the second stressor/the second disorganization;

8 represents the reorganization/readjustment process; and

9 represents the level of reorganization.

Like Koos (1946), Hill found more than one pattern of adjustment: good adjustment to separation and good adjustment to reunion (Figure 3.2a), good adjustment to separation and poor adjustment to reunion (Figure 3.2b), fair adjustment to separation and good adjustment to reunion (Figure 3.2c), fair adjustment to separation and poor adjustment to reunion (Figure 3.2d), and poor adjustment to separation and good adjustment to reunion (Figure 3.2e).

1. Precrisis Family Level of Organization

The first period in Hill's (1949) model is the precrisis family organization. Hill operationalized family organization as family adaptability and integration and marital adjustment. Hill found that family adaptability, family integration, and marital adjustment constituted "the most important statistically identifiable factors making for successful adjustment to crisis" (p. 128). Adaptability and integration were determined with qualitative data while marital adjustment was quantitatively determined.

Adaptability. Adaptability included previous success in meeting family crises; predominance of nonmaterialistic goals; flexibility and willingness to shift traditional roles of husband and wife or of father and mother, if necessary; acceptance of responsibility by all family members in performing family duties; and presence of equalitarian patterns of family control and decision making. Hill (1949) found adaptability "to be of more importance than integration in adjustment to crisis" (p. 232). Hill rated adaptability as high, medium, or low. He also rated integration as high, medium, or low.

Integration. Family integration means the "bonds of coherence and unity running through family life, of which common interest, affection, and a sense of economic interdependence are perhaps the most prominent" (Angell, 1936, p. 15). Integration as discussed by Hill (1949) included willingness to sacrifice personal interest to attain family objectives, pride in the family tree and in the ancestral traditions, presence of strong patterns of emotional interdependence and unity, and high participation as a family in joint activities. He found that families with any combination of medium integration to high integration and medium adaptation to high adaptation tended to make a good adjustment to a crisis. The third variable used to determine family organization was marital adjustment.

Figure 3.2 Five General Types of Truncated Roller Coaster Profiles of Adjustment

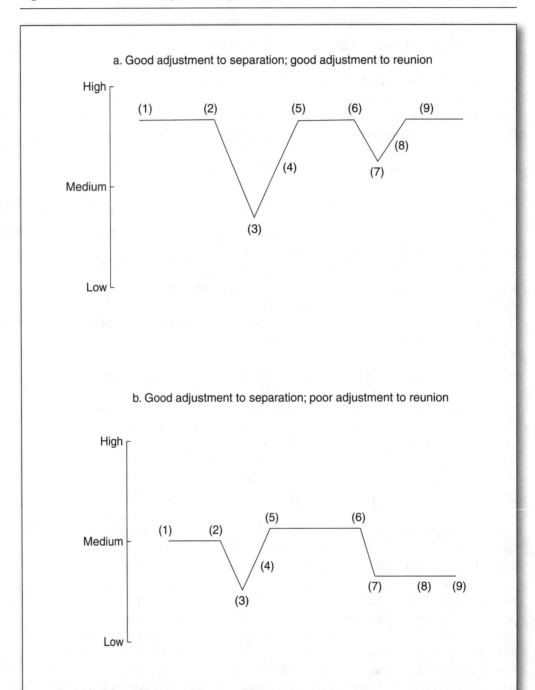

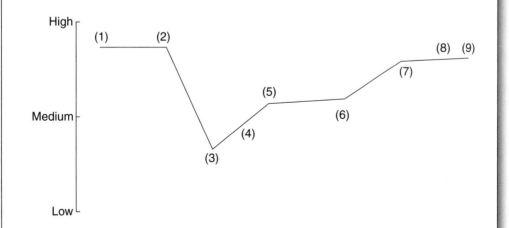

c. Fair adjustment to separation; good adjustment to reunion.

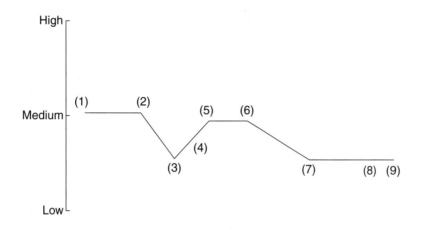

d. Fair adjustment to separation; poor adjustment to reunion.

Figure 3.2 (Continued)

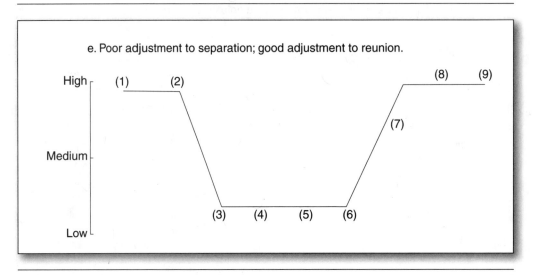

e. Poor adjustment to separation; good adjustment to reunion.

Source: Hill (1949).

Marital Adjustment. Locke (1968) defined marital adjustment as "the process of adaptation of the husband and wife in such a way as to avoid or resolve conflicts" (p. 45). Hill used the Burgess-Cottrell Marital Adjustment Scale (Burgess & Cottrell, 1939, cited in Hill, 1949) to measure marital adjustment. Hill rated marital adjustment based on scores on the Marital Adjustment Scale as good (70 and over), fair (40–69), or poor (0–39). Burgess, Locke, and Thomas (1963) described a marriage with good adjustment as "a union in which the husband and wife are in agreement on the chief issues of marriage" (p. 295).

2. Anticipatory Reactions and Preparation for the First Stressor

The second period in Hill's (1949) model, anticipatory reactions and preparation, is how the family members reacted to knowing that the husband would be leaving and how they did or did not prepare. Hill presented a figure in his first chapter that labeled what his fourth chapter called anticipatory reactions and preparation as the crisis. To this day, his first-chapter figure is reproduced in the literature (Ingoldsby, Smith, & Miller, 2004; Lamanna & Riedmann, 2000), although it is mislabeled, causing some individuals to label stressors (events or situations) as crises (states of being). The figure is purposefully not reproduced in this chapter in an attempt to stop its unwitting reproduction. According to Hill's figures in his results chapter, the point labeled *3* is the crisis. In the inaccurate figure, the point labeled *2* in the accurate figure was labeled the crisis.

The anticipatory reactions described by Hill varied and included such manifestations as emotional shock, worry, and calm. Some definitions of the impending separation describe it as an "opportunity to think out marital problems and decide whether the marriage was worth continuing" (Hill, 1949, p. 55) or as a job to be done. Anticipatory preparation included such behaviors as wives starting a job, husbands changing jobs, moving in with in-laws, moving to apartments from larger homes, building or buying homes, and crying.

Hill (1949) researched predictable stressors (separation and reunion). Of course, all stressors are not predictable, so not all families will experience this second period of Hill's model, anticipatory disturbance and preparation. All families experiencing a crisis will experience Hill's third period, reaction to the first stressor/the first disorganization.

3. Reaction to the First Stressor/ the First Disorganization

Hill (1949) described the third period as the immediate reaction to the stressor, the husband's/father's absence, including emotional upset and type of activity. He also called this period *disorganization*. The point labeled *3* in Figure 3.2 is actually the period of the worst disorganization. In today's terminology, we call this the crisis period.

Hill found that emotional reactions leading to good adjustment ranged from "excitement, through feelings of unreality, to calm" (p. 249). When families felt indifferent about separation, they adjusted well. When families reacted emotionally with extreme loneliness, emotional upset, and numbness, they adjusted poorly to separation. Hill found crying to be a common activity in this period. After this period of disorganization, Hill found that families began a fourth period that he named the adjustment process.

4. The Adjustment Process

Hill (1949) also called the fourth period, adjustment process, "recovery." He found efforts to manage new responsibilities in this period through reorganization of roles, reallocation of duties, and/or reallocation of responsibilities (coping strategies). The fourth period led to the period called the level of organization after adjustment.

5. The Level of Organization After Adjustment/Recovery Is Complete

Good adjustment was defined as the attainment of a working dynamic equilibrium in which reorganization of roles into complementary patterns has been satisfactorily completed, duties and responsibilities have been reallocated, and the emotional strains and stresses of readjustment will not be leaving serious scars on family relations. The length of time from the introduction of the stressor to adjustment was months in Hill's (1949) sample. Length of time to adjustment to the crisis was not predictive of degree of adjustment.

6. Anticipatory Reactions and Preparation for the Second Impending Stressor

Hill's (1949) research included reactions to the reunion of families separated by war, a second stressor for the families. Since the reunion was predictable, Hill studied the families' reactions to the impending reunion. Sometimes the anticipatory reactions were of joy, sometimes there was no reaction, and sometimes couples planned divorces. When the reunion actually took place, the families moved to what Hill called the seventh period, reactions to the second stressor or the second disorganization.

7. Reactions to the Second Stressor/ the Second Disorganization

Some families in Hill's (1949) study experienced a second disorganization or crisis after the second stressor of reunion while others did not experience disorganization after the reunion. Families did not adjust well when they were indifferent about reunion. Sometimes the immediate reaction to reunion actually was a rise followed by a drop in organization. The drop happened when the "honeymoon" ended and the family had to meet daily needs, but the drop was usually not steep, and usually recovery was much quicker than recovery from the stressor of separation.

8. The Reorganization/Readjustment Process

In Hill's (1949) model, *8* represents the gradual readjustment to family living. This reorganization process was found to lead to a new level of reorganization.

9. The Level of Reorganization

In Hill's (1949) model, *9* represents the reorganization after the second stressor of reunion. Based on Hill's findings, we can conclude that a family can recover to an organization level that is higher than, lower than, or equal to the level of organization at the time the stressor occurred. Later clinical observations inductively support this finding, but this point still needs further support (Boss, 1987).

Critique of Truncated Roller Coaster Profile of Adjustment

Hill (1949) combined quantitative and qualitative research to test Koos's Profile of Trouble (1946) and found support for it. Hill's Truncated Roller Coaster Profile of Adjustment is a relabeling of Koos's work. Like Koos's Profile of Trouble, Hill's profile takes us from before the stressor (precrisis) until crisis resolution and beyond. Hill goes further to illustrate the effects of a second stressor. There are some flaws in Hill's work, however, in that Hill used the terms *stressor* and *crisis* as synonyms (Boss & Mulligan, 2003).

Summary of Truncated Roller Coaster Profile of Adjustment

Hill (1949) tested Koos's (1946) Profile of Trouble and renamed it the Truncated Roller Coaster Profile of Adjustment. Hill found support for Koos's work. Although there are criticisms of Hill's work, the main one being calling a stressor a crisis, he did a monumental job of studying a large sample both quantitatively and qualitatively. Like Hill, Robert Burr (1989) based his model on the work of Koos.

Family Ecosystemic Model of Stress

Robert Burr (1989), a family scientist, modified the Koos (1946) Profile of Trouble to develop the Family Ecosystemic Model of Stress, based on family ecosystemic theory. Family ecosystemic theory concerns itself with discovering processes (behavior or interactions) and looking at interactions, feelings, meanings, purposes, and patterns nonpositivistically (without causation).

Burr (1989) combined the concept of levels of abstraction (Constantine, 1986; Reiss, 1981; Sluzki, 1983; Watzlawick, Weakland, & Fisch, 1974) and the idea that stress is a process (Reiss, 1981) with the concept of coping (Boss, McCubbin, & Lester, 1979; McCubbin, 1979; McCubbin, Dahl, Lester, Benson, & Robertson, 1976) in the Family Ecosystemic Model of Stress. A "new insight" of the model is that, as families cope with stress, there tends to be a developmental sequence involving three levels of abstraction. See Figure 3.3.

Normally families transform inputs (elements from outside the family put inside) into outputs (elements from inside the family put outside) easily (Kantor & Lehr, 1975). Burr (1989) says that the process of stress begins when feedback (information about outputs) indicates that the family does not have the requisite variety of rules (adequate rules) to use transformation processes (actions to change inputs into outputs) that meet the family's standards.

Conceptual Framework of Family Ecosystemic Model of Stress

Burr (1989) discusses four processes in describing the Family Ecosystemic Model of Stress. See Figure 3.3.

First Process: Old "Normal" Level

The horizontal line at the left in the model shows the "normal" (pre-stressor) level of family processes. It represents the processes families experience before experiencing a stressor.

Figure 3.3   The Family Ecosystemic Model of Stress

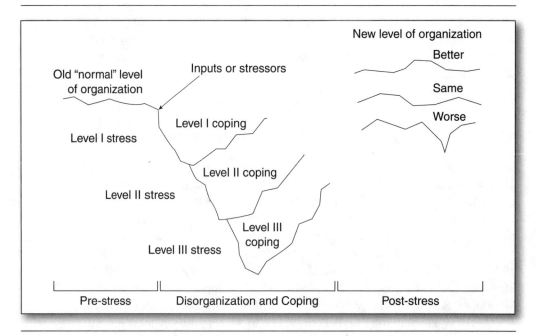

Source: Adapted from Burr (1989).

Second Process: Inputs or Stressors

The arrow points to the time when a stressor or stressors occur. Stressors are inputs into the family system for which there is a lack of requisite variety of rules of transformation to transform inputs into desired outputs (Burr, 1989).

Third Process: Stress and Coping

The Family Ecosystemic Model (Burr, 1989) views coping as transformation processes that families go through to adjust to inputs that they do not know how to handle with their usual transformation processes or when their usual transformation processes are disrupted. In Figure 3.3, the descending lines in the Family Ecosystemic Model of Stress represent the stress and corresponding coping processes.

In addition, Burr (1989) says that a family may stay at one level of stress and coping for years before moving to a different level or never move on, and that not all families go through the developmental sequence of coping. Some families may go directly to Level II or Level III stress and coping.

Level I Stress and Coping. At this point, families tend to use processes that try to create Level I (first-order) changes in the family. If the Level I processes are successful, the family moves out of Level I crisis and into a period of recovery, and it is not necessary to try Level II (second-order) coping strategies. See Chapter 2 for a discussion of levels of coping strategies.

Level II Stress and Coping. If the Level I processes (coping strategies) are not successful in coping with the distress, the family experiences Level II stress, which is a crisis, and tries to create Level II change using Level II coping strategies. See the line that continues downward from "Level I stress & coping" in Figure 3.3.

Level III Stress and Coping. If Level II coping strategies are not successful at relieving distress, the family experiences a Level III stress, which is a crisis. At this point, Level III coping processes are employed. See Chapter 2 for examples of different levels of stress and coping strategies.

Fourth Processes: New "Normal" Levels

When coping processes start to help families handle stress, families begin to return to or develop new "normal" processes, indicated by the ascending lines in the diagram. Once the coping processes are successful, families operate either at their previous levels of processing or at new "normal" levels, indicated by the horizontal lines at the far right of the figure.

Critique of the Family Ecosystemic Model of Stress

Burr (1989) contributed to stress theory by incorporating the levels of abstraction for stress and coping. The Family Ecosystemic Model is non-positivistic (not concerned with finding causes of crises) (Burr, 1989). On the other hand, Burr's illustration might be improved by indicating stress on the downward stroke in the figure and coping with the upward stroke.

Summary of the Family Ecosystemic Model of Stress

Burr (1989) modified Koos's (1946) Profile of Trouble by adding levels of abstraction for stress and coping, and called his model the Family Ecosystemic Model of Stress. Burr contended that as inputs come into a family, it uses transformation processes to manipulate the inputs to obtain desired outputs to meet goals. The family members monitor the outputs through feedback (information about outputs), which enables the members to determine whether they are meeting goals. If there is not a requisite variety of rules (adequate rules) to handle the inputs, the family experiences stress, which it adapts to through transformation processes called coping strategies.

According to the Family Ecosystemic Model of Stress, prior to the input of a particular stressor, the family operates with "normal" transformation processes. After the input of a stressor, the family copes using Level I, II, and/or III coping processes, depending on the severity of the stress/crisis. These processes may go on for years. The family then recovers to a new "normal" level of transformation processes.

Summary

This chapter presented three family stress models, the Profile of Trouble, the Truncated Roller Coaster Profile of Adjustment, and the Family Ecosystemic Model of Stress. Both the Profile of Trouble and the Family Ecosystemic Model are based on the first conceptual framework of family stress, the Profile of Trouble. The figures for each of the models are the same, but they are labeled differently. The Truncated Roller Coaster Profile of Adjustment goes beyond the Profile of Trouble to illustrate a second stressor. The Family Ecosystemic Model of Stress adds levels of abstraction for both stress and coping as well as the idea that stress is a process. Although each model is a family model, the authors of the Profile of Trouble and the Truncated Roller Coaster Profile of Adjustment—Koos and Hill, respectively—recognized that each family member may experience a different pattern. Sketching the stress and crisis experiences can assist helpers by allowing them to visualize what the client may have a difficult time verbalizing. The sketches can also help clients visualize the stress/crisis process.

EXERCISES

3.1.   Draw and label a Profile of Trouble to illustrate the crisis from Exercise 2.1. Label the level of interaction/organization both before "the point at which the initiating cause takes effect" and after "the point of recovery."

3.2.   Outline the crisis from Exercise 2.1 using Koos's (1946) terminology. Explain your choices. Below is an example of such an outline based on the case presented at the end of Chapter 2.

   I. a – a'—normal interaction/organization (better than average, average, below average): average

      A. Amount of consciousness and acceptance by each family member of his or her and others' family roles (better than average, average, below average): average; after 11 years of marriage we had worked out satisfactory family roles

      B. Extent to which family members worked toward family and individual good (better than average, average, below average): better than average; since having a baby, family goals were particularly important

      C. How much family members found satisfaction with family unit (better than average, average, below average): average; there was satisfaction with the baby, but couple activities were limited because of husband's illness

      D. Whether the family had a sense of direction and was moving in that direction (better than average, average, below average): average, because of husband's illness family could only have short-term goals

   II. b—the point at which the initiating cause takes effect: The initiating cause was husband's death

   III. c—the point at which the family interaction drops (better than average, average, below average): below average

      A. Amount of consciousness and acceptance by each family member of his or her and others' family roles (better than average, average, below average): below average; my parents took care of my son for a period of time—a few days, I think—so I was not performing my role as parent

B. Extent to which family members worked toward family and individual good (better than average, average, below average): below average; I was not taking care of my son, and self-care was based on what others told me to do

C. How much family members found satisfaction with family unit (better than average, average, below average): below average; the family unit had been redefined, and ways to find satisfaction would need to be redefined as well

D. Whether the family had a sense of direction and was moving in that direction (better than average, average, below average): below average; family goals would need to be redefined by me as a single parent

IV. d—the point of recovery (better than average, average, below average): average to better than average

A. Amount of consciousness and acceptance by each family member of his or her and others' family roles (better than average, average, below average): average; I accepted my role as head of household and my son as a growing child, although I did use him to meet some of my emotional needs as I let him sleep in my bed when he woke in the night

B. Extent to which family members worked toward family and individual good (better than average, average, below average): better than average; affects of decisions on the family as well as on individuals were considered since I took time to attend support groups, which was good for me as an individual

C. How much family members found satisfaction with family unit (better than average, average, below average): average; the family unit was lacking a male companion and father figure

D. Whether the family had a sense of direction and was moving in that direction (better than average, average, below average): better than average; less than a month after my husband died, a bid was put on a home that we had considered buying before his death

V. e—the angle of recovery: small

Now complete your outline being sure to address all of the following concepts.

I. a – a'—normal interaction/organization (better than average, average, below average)

A. Amount of consciousness and acceptance by each family member of his or her and others' family roles (better than average, average, below average)

B. Extent to which family members worked toward family and individual good (better than average, average, below average)

C. How much family members found satisfaction with family unit (better than average, average, below average)

D. Whether the family had a sense of direction and was moving in that direction (better than average, average, below average)

II. b—the point at which the initiating cause takes effect

III. c—the point at which the family interaction drops (better than average, average, below average)

    A. Amount of consciousness and acceptance by each family member of his or her and others' family roles (better than average, average, below average)

    B. Extent to which family members worked toward family and individual good (better than average, average, below average)

    C. How much family members found satisfaction with family unit (better than average, average, below average)

    D. Whether the family had a sense of direction and was moving in that direction (better than average, average, below average)

IV. d—the point of recovery (better than average, average, below average)

    A. Amount of consciousness and acceptance by each family member of his or her and others' family roles (better than average, average, below average)

    B. Extent to which family members worked toward family and individual good (better than average, average, below average)

    C. How much family members found satisfaction with family unit (better than average, average, below average)

    D. Whether the family had a sense of direction and was moving in that direction (better than average, average, below average)

V. e—the size of the angle of recovery

3.3. Draw and label a Truncated Roller Coaster Profile of Adjustment to illustrate the crisis from Exercise 2.1.

3.4. Outline the crisis from Exercise 2.1 using Hill's (1949, 1958) terminology. Following is an example of this assignment based on the case study presented in Chapter 2.

I. Precrisis Level of Family Organization (high, medium, low): medium

    A. Integration (high, medium, low): medium

        1. Willingness to sacrifice personal interest to attain family objectives (high, medium, low): high; I sacrificed my personal interests to care for my husband and child

        2. Pride in the family tree and in the ancestral traditions (high, medium, low): medium; there was pride in the family tree from one side of the family but not the other

        3. Presence of strong patterns of emotional interdependence and unity (high, medium, low): low; we did not share our emotions very readily

4. High participation as a family in joint activities (high, medium, low): low; other than going to doctors' visits, we did not share many activities

5. Strong affectional ties between father and mother, father and children, mother and children, and children and children (high, medium, low): medium

   a. Father and mother (high, medium, low): medium; focused on illness and child
   b. Father and children (high, medium, low): low; father was not able to pick up and hold child because of illness; he seemed to disengage
   c. Mother and children (high, medium, low): medium; child was source of emotional satisfaction
   d. Children and children (high, medium, low): only one child

B. Adaptability (high, medium, low): medium

   1. Previous success in meeting family crises (high, medium, low): medium; had recovered from other crises, as when the husband was diagnosed with cancer, but not to prior level of functioning

   2. Predominance of nonmaterialistic goals (high, medium, low): high; goals were within financial means—for example, we lived in a mobile home at the time

   3. Flexibility and willingness to shift traditional roles of husband and wife or of father and mother, if necessary (high, medium, low): low; husband could barely perform his roles, much less shift roles

   4. Acceptance of responsibility by all family members in performing family duties (high, medium, low): low; primary responsibility for all household duties and child care was mine due to husband's illness

   5. Presence of equalitarian patterns of family control and decision making (high, medium, low): high; decisions were made as a couple

C. Marital Adjustment (poor, fair, good): fair to good

   1. Wife (poor, fair, good): good; there were no disagreements

   2. Husband (poor, fair, good): fair; husband could not really participate as a marital partner in many ways

II. Anticipatory Stress Reactions: I don't know what my husband's stress reactions were, as he did not share his feelings and thoughts with me, but I was calm.

III. Reaction to the First Stressor/the First Disorganization

A. Amount of consciousness and acceptance by each family member of his or her and others' family roles (better than average, average, below average): below average; my parents took care of my son for a period of time—a few days, I think—so I was not performing my role as parent

B. Extent to which family members worked toward family and individual good (better than average, average, below average): below-average; I was not taking care of my son, and self-care was based on what others told me to do

C. How much family members found satisfaction with family unit (better than average, average, below average): below average; the family unit had been redefined, and ways to find satisfaction would need to be redefined as well

D. Whether the family had a sense of direction and was moving in that direction (better than average, average, below average): below-average; family goals would need to be redefined by me as a single parent

IV. Adjustment Process/Recovery

A. Reorganization of roles since I took on the role of business owner

B. Reallocation of duties since I took on the duties of taking care of business matters

C. Reallocation of responsibilities since I became the only responsible adult in the family

V. Level of Organization After Adjustment/Recovery Is Complete (high, medium, low): high

A. Integration (high, medium, low): high

1. Willingness to sacrifice personal interest to attain family objectives (high, medium, low): high; I was willing to stay in a position in order to keep my family from moving

2. Pride in the family tree and in the ancestral traditions (high, medium, low): medium; there was pride in the family tree from one side of the family but not the other

3. Presence of strong patterns of emotional interdependence and unity (high, medium, low): high; my son and I said that we loved each other often

4. High participation as a family in joint activities (high, medium, low): high; my son went with me wherever I went when it was appropriate

5. Strong affectional ties between father and mother, father and children, mother and children, and children and children (high, medium, low): high

   a. Father and mother (high, medium, low): father was dead
   b. Father and children (high, medium, low): father was dead
   c. Mother and children (high, medium, low): high; my son and I showed affection by hugging and kissing often
   d. Children and children (high, medium, low): only one child

B. Adaptability (high, medium, low): high

1. Previous success in meeting family crises (high, medium, low): medium; had recovered from other crises as when the husband was diagnosed with cancer but not to prior level of functioning

2. Predominance of nonmaterialistic goals (high, medium, low): high; goals were within financial means—for example, we lived in a mobile home at the time

3. Flexibility and willingness to shift traditional roles of husband and wife or of father and mother, if necessary (high, medium, low): this no longer applied since husband was dead

4. Acceptance of responsibility by all family members in performing family duties (high, medium, low): high; I accepted that I was a single parent with all that goes with it

5. Presence of equalitarian patterns of family control and decision making (high, medium, low): this no longer applied since husband was dead

C. Marital Adjustment (poor, fair, good): husband was dead

1. Wife (poor, fair, good): husband was dead

2. Husband (poor, fair, good): husband was dead

VI. Anticipatory Reactions and Preparation for the Second Impending Stressor: There was no major second stressor within the next 2 years

VII. Reactions to the Second Stressor/the Second Disorganization

VIII. Reorganization/Readjustment Process

IX. Level of Reorganization (high, medium, low)

A. Integration (high, medium, low)

1. Willingness to sacrifice personal interest to attain family objectives (high, medium, low)

2. Pride in the family tree and in the ancestral traditions (high, medium, low)

3. Presence of strong patterns of emotional interdependence and unity (high, medium, low)

4. High participation as a family in joint activities (high, medium, low)

5. Strong affectional ties between father and mother, father and children, mother and children, and children and children (high, medium, low)

   a. Father and mother (high, medium, low)
   b. Father and children (high, medium, low)
   c. Mother and children (high, medium, low)
   d. Children and children (high, medium, low)

B. Adaptability (high, medium, low)

1. Previous success in meeting family crises (high, medium, low)

2. Predominance of nonmaterialistic goals (high, medium, low)

3. Flexibility and willingness to shift traditional roles of husband and wife or of father and mother, if necessary (high, medium, low)

4. Acceptance of responsibility by all family members in performing family duties (high, medium, low)

5. Presence of equalitarian patterns of family control and decision making (high, medium, low)

C. Marital Adjustment (poor, fair, good)

1. Wife (poor, fair, good)
2. Husband (poor, fair, good)

Now complete the outline below for your crisis.

I. Precrisis Level of Family Organization (high, medium, low)

A. Integration (high, medium, low)

1. Willingness to sacrifice personal interest to attain family objectives (high, medium, low)

2. Pride in the family tree and in the ancestral traditions (high, medium, low)

3. Presence of strong patterns of emotional interdependence and unity (high, medium, low)

4. High participation as a family in joint activities (high, medium, low)

5. Strong affectional ties between father and mother, father and children, mother and children, and children and children (high, medium, low)

B. Adaptability (high, medium, low)

1. Previous success in meeting family crises (high, medium, low)

2. Predominance of nonmaterialistic goals (high, medium, low)

3. Flexibility and willingness to shift traditional roles of husband and wife or of father and mother, if necessary (high, medium, low)

4. Acceptance of responsibility by all family members in performing family duties (high, medium, low)

5. Presence of equalitarian patterns of family control and decision making (high, medium, low)

C. Marital Adjustment (poor, fair, good)

1. Wife (poor, fair, good)
2. Husband (poor, fair, good)

II. Anticipatory Stress Reactions

III. Reaction to the First Stressor/the First Disorganization

IV. Adjustment Process/Recovery

V. Level of Organization After Adjustment/Recovery Is Complete (high, medium, low)

   A. Integration (high, medium, low)

      1. Willingness to sacrifice personal interest to attain family objectives (high, medium, low)

      2. Pride in the family tree and in the ancestral traditions (high, medium, low)

      3. Presence of strong patterns of emotional interdependence and unity (high, medium, low)

      4. High participation as a family in joint activities (high, medium, low)

      5. Strong affectional ties between father and mother, father and children, mother and children, and children and children (high, medium, low)
         a. Father and mother (high, medium, low)
         b. Father and children (high, medium, low)
         c. Mother and children (high, medium, low)
         d. Children and children (high, medium, low)

   B. Adaptability (high, medium, low)

      1. Previous success in meeting family crises (high, medium, low)

      2. Predominance of nonmaterialistic goals (high, medium, low)

      3. Flexibility and willingness to shift traditional roles of husband and wife or of father and mother, if necessary (high, medium, low)

      4. Acceptance of responsibility by all family members in performing family duties (high, medium, low)

      5. Presence of equalitarian patterns of family control and decision making (high, medium, low)

   C. Marital Adjustment (poor, fair, good)

      1. Wife (poor, fair, good)
      2. Husband (poor, fair, good)

VI. Anticipatory Reactions and Preparation for the Second Impending Stressor

VII. Reactions to the Second Stressor/the Second Disorganization

VIII. Reorganization/Readjustment Process

IX. Level of Reorganization (high, medium, low)

   A. Integration (high, medium, low)

1. Willingness to sacrifice personal interest to attain family objectives (high, medium, low)

2. Pride in the family tree and in the ancestral traditions (high, medium, low)

3. Presence of strong patterns of emotional interdependence and unity (high, medium, low)

4. High participation as a family in joint activities (high, medium, low)

5. Strong affectional ties between father and mother, father and children, mother and children, and children and children (high, medium, low)

   a. Father and mother (high, medium, low)

   b. Father and children (high, medium, low)

   c. Mother and children (high, medium, low)

   d. Children and children (high, medium, low)

B. Adaptability (high, medium, low)

1. Previous success in meeting family crises (high, medium, low)

2. Predominance of nonmaterialistic goals (high, medium, low)

3. Flexibility and willingness to shift traditional roles of husband and wife or of father and mother, if necessary (high, medium, low)

4. Acceptance of responsibility by all family members in performing family duties (high, medium, low)

5. Presence of equalitarian patterns of family control and decision making (high, medium, low)

C. Marital Adjustment (poor, fair, good)

1. Wife (poor, fair, good)

2. Husband (poor, fair, good)

3.5. Draw and label a Family Ecosystemic Model of Stress to illustrate the family crisis from Exercise 2.1.

3.6 Outline the crisis from Exercise 2.1 using the concepts from the Family Ecosystemic Model of Stress. Following is an example based on the case study presented in Chapter 2.

I. First Process: Old "Normal" Level: Level I processes were used to cope prior to the stressor

   A. Getting new information about melanoma and treatments
   B. Seeking help from relatives to care for son
   C. Turning to community agencies such as hospitals for assistance

II. Second Process: Input(s) or Stressor(s): husband's death

III. Third Process: Stress & Coping

   A. Level I: had Level II stress

      1. Stress

      2. Coping

         a. Cognitive

            1) Accepted the situation and others

               a) Quickly accepted and confronted the situation

               b) Accepted limitations; did not try to do or be everything

            2) Gained useful knowledge

               a) Found information and facts about the situation

               b) Understood the essential nature of the situation

            3) Changed how the situation was viewed or defined

               a) Separated the stress into manageable parts

               b) Did not have false hopes, but had faith in own ability to handle the situation

               c) Did not blame others or become preoccupied with blaming; instead was solution-oriented

         b. Emotional Activities

            1) Expressed feelings and affection

               a) Was honest, clear, and direct in expressing affection

         c. Relationship Activities

            1) Developed family cohesion and togetherness

               a) Did things with child and maintained stability

            2) Maintained family adaptability and flexibility

               a) Was flexible and willing to change family roles, behaviors, and attitudes

         d. Communication Activities

            1) Was open and honest

               a) Was open and honest in communications with others

         e. Community Activities

            1) Sought help and support from others

               a) Sought and accepted help from relatives when needed

               b) Sought and accepted help from community services when needed

     f. Spiritual Activities

       1) Was more involved in religious activities

       2) Increased or sought help from God

         a) Believed in God

  B. Level II

    1. Stress

      a. Amount of consciousness and acceptance by each family member of his or her and others' family roles (better than average, average, below average): below average; my parents took care of my son for a period of time—a few days, I think—so I was not performing my role as parent

      b. Extent to which family members worked toward family and individual good (better than average, average, below average): below average; I was not taking care of my son, and self-care was based on what others told me to do

      c. How much family members found satisfaction with family unit (better than average, average, below average): below average; the family unit had been redefined, and ways to find satisfaction would need to be redefined as well

      d. Whether the family had a sense of direction and was moving in that direction (better than average, average, below average): below average; family goals would need to be redefined by me as a single parent

    2. Coping

      a. Used crisis counseling in the form of psychologist visits

      b. Changed who made rules from husband and me to only me

  C. Level III: had Level II stress

    1. Stress

    2. Coping

IV. Fourth Processes: New "Normal" Levels: went back to using Level I coping strategies to cope with stresses

  A. Getting new information about melanoma and widowhood

  B. Seeking help from relatives to care for son

Now complete the following outline for your crisis.

  I. First Process: Old "Normal" Level

  II. Second Process: Input(s) or Stressor(s)

References and Suggestions for Further Reading

Angell, R. C. (1936). *The family encounters the depression.* Gloucester, MA: Peter Smith. (Reprinted in 1965)

Boss, P. (1987). Family stress. In M. B. Sussman & S. K. Steinmetz (Eds.), *Handbook of marriage and the family* (pp. 695–723). New York: Plenum Press.

Boss, P. (2002). *Family stress management: A contextual approach.* Thousand Oaks, CA: Sage.

Boss, P., McCubbin, H. I., & Lester, G. (1979). The corporate executive wife's coping patterns in response to routine husband-father absence. *Family Process, 18,* 79–86.

Boss, P., & Mulligan, C. (2003). *Family stress: Classic and contemporary readings.* Thousand Oaks, CA: Sage.

Burgess, E. W., Locke, H. J., & Thomas, M. M. (1963). *The family: From institution to companionship.* New York: American Book.

Burr, R. G. (1989). *Reframing family stress theory: From the ABC-X Model to a Family Ecosystemic Model.* Unpublished master's thesis, Brigham Young University, Provo, UT.

Burr, W. R., Klein, S. R., & Associates. (1994). *Reexamining family stress: New theory and research.* Thousand Oaks, CA: Sage.

Cavan, R. S., & Ranck, K. H. (1938). *The family and the depression: A study of one hundred Chicago families.* Chicago: The University of Chicago Press.

Constantine, L. L. (1986). *Family paradigms.* New York: Guilford Press.

Hill, E. J. (2009). Memories of my "rich uncle," Reuben Hill. *National Council on Family Relations Report, 45*(1), F8, F10.

Hill, R. (1949). *Families under stress.* New York: Harper & Brothers.

Hill, R. (1958). Generic features of families under stress. *Social Casework, 49*, 139–150.

Ingoldsby, B. B., Smith, S. R., & Miller, J. E. (2004). *Exploring family theories.* Los Angeles: Roxbury.

Kantor, D., & Lehr, W. (1975). *Inside the family.* New York: Harper & Row.

Koos, E. L. (1946). *Families in trouble.* Morningside Heights, NY: King's Crown.

Lamanna, M. A., & Riedmann, A. (2000). *Marriages and families: Making choices in a diverse society* (7th ed.). Belmont, CA: Wadsworth.

Locke, H. J. (1968). *Predicting adjustment in marriage: A comparison of a divorced and a happily married group.* New York: Greenwood Press.

McCubbin, H. I. (1979). Integrating coping behavior in family stress theory. *Journal of Marriage and Family, 4,* 237–244.

McCubbin, H. I., Dahl, B., Lester, G., Benson, D., & Robertson, M. (1976). Coping repertoires of families adapting to prolonged war-induced separations. *Journal of Marriage and Family, 38,* 471–478.

McCubbin, H. I., & Patterson, J. M. (1983). The family stress process: The Double ABCX Model of family adjustment and adaptation. In H. I. McCubbin, M. Sussman, & J. M. Patterson (Eds.), *Social stress and the family: Advances and developments in family stress theory and research* (pp. 7–37). New York: Haworth.

Patterson, J. M. (1988). Families experiencing stress: I. The Family Adjustment and Response Model II. Applying the FAAR Model to health-related issues for intervention and research. *Family Systems Medicine, 6*(2), 202–237.

Patterson, J. M. (2002). Integrating family resilience and family stress theory. *Journal of Marriage and Family, 64,* 349–360.

Reiss, D. (1981). *The family's construction of reality.* Cambridge, MA: Harvard University Press.

Sluzki, C. E. (1983). Process, structure and world views: Toward an integrated view of systemic models in family therapy. *Family Process, 22,* 469–476.

Watzlawick, P., Weakland, J. H., & Fisch, R. (1974). *Change: Principles of problem formation and problem resolution.* New York: Norton.

CHAPTER 4

The ABCX Formula and the Double ABCX Model

The ABCX Formula

Besides the Truncated Roller Coaster Profile of Adjustment, Reuben Hill (1949, 1958), based on prior research conducted by himself and others (Angell, 1936; Cavan & Ranck, 1938), developed the ABCX Formula, better known as the ABCX Model, to explain "the crisis-proneness and freedom from crisis among families" (Hill, 1958, p. 143). Although Hill referred to the components of the ABCX Formula in his 1949 work, he did not label the components as A, B, C, and X until 1958. The ABCX Formula is the basis of most family stress models, leading Hill to be called the father of family stress theory (Boss, 2002). The ABCX Formula focuses primarily on precrisis variables of families: A (the crisis-precipitating event/stressor) interacting with B (the family's crisis-meeting resources) interacting with C (the definition the family makes of the event) produces X (the crisis).

Conceptual Framework of the ABCX Formula

$$A \qquad\qquad B \qquad\qquad C ———X$$

A. *The Crisis-Precipitating Event/Stressor*

Hill (1958) used the terms *crisis-precipitating event* and *stressor* to mean "a situation for which the family has had little or no prior preparation and must therefore be viewed as problematic" (p. 139). He contended that crisis-precipitating events affect families differently based on the hardships that accompany them. Hill (1958) defined hardships as complications of a stressor that demand competencies (resources) from the family. Whether or not a stressor led to hardships (and how many) determined whether a family defined a stressor positively or negatively. Examples of hardships of families that experienced the stressor of the husband/father conscription into the armed forces found by Hill (1949) included sharp changes in income, housing inadequacies, enforced living with in-laws or other relatives, illness of wife or children, wife's having to work and to take on both parenting roles, and child-discipline problems stemming from the father's absence. According to Hill, the crisis-precipitating event or stressor interacted with the family's crisis-meeting resources.

B. *The Family's Crisis-Meeting Resources*

Since the family resources Hill (1958) described appeared after the stressor and prior to the crisis, a more appropriate term for *B* might be *the family's stressor-meeting resources*. That being said, Hill defined family crisis-meeting resources as factors in family organization that, by their presence, kept the family from crisis or, by their absence, urged a family into crisis. In other words, resources determined the adequacy (crisis-proofness) or inadequacy (crisis-proneness) of the family. Hill summarized the family's crisis-meeting resources previously studied, such as family integration and family adaptability, from Angell (1936). According to Hill, the crisis-precipitating event and the family's resources interacted with the family's definition of the event.

C. *The Definition the Family Makes of the Event*

Hill (1958) said that the subjective definition the family made of the event equaled the meaning or interpretation of the event and its accompanying hardships for the family. According to Hill, the tendency to define the stressor events and the accompanying hardships of the stressor as crisis-producing/-provoking versus challenging made the family more crisis-prone. According to Hill, the crisis-precipitating event, the family's resources, and the family's definition of the event interacted to lead to crisis.

X. *The Crisis*

A family in crisis, according to Hill (1958), would have role patterns in flux and shifting expectations, resulting in "slowed up affectional and emotion-satisfying performances" (p. 146). Families in crisis might experience sharp changes in the sexual area, such as in the frequency and pattern of sexual relations. This crisis manifestation is frequently experienced when the stressor is the loss of a child.

Critique of the ABCX Formula

The ABCX Formula describes only precrisis variables and the crisis. Calling the resources crisis-meeting is misleading. Stressor-meeting is a more appropriate description, considering where the resources appear in the formula, after the stressor and prior to the crisis. It is a linear, deterministic model. Despite its limitations, the ABCX Formula is the basis of most family stress models and led to Hill's being called the father of family stress theory (Boss, 2002).

Summary of the ABCX Formula

According to the ABCX Formula, A (the crisis-precipitating event/ stressor) interacting with B (the family's crisis-meeting resources) interacting with C (the definition the family makes of the event) produces X (the crisis). Hill (1958) contended that hardships were attributes of the stressor event and that whether a family defined a stressor positively or negatively was affected by whether the stressor led to hardships in the family. Hill defined the B factor/family resources as the adequacy (crisis-proofness) or inadequacy (crisis-proneness) of family organization.

The C factor in the formula is the definition, meaning, or interpretation of the A factor/stressor. According to Hill (1958), the tendency to define the stressor events and the accompanying hardships of the stressor as crisis-producing makes a family more crisis-prone. A family in a crisis state, according to Hill, will have role patterns in flux and expectations shifting, resulting in "slowed up affectional and emotion-satisfying performances" (p. 146). The ABCX Formula has some problems, such as being linear and deterministic, but it withstood the test of time as the basis of most family stress models (Boss, 2002), such as the Double ABCX Model.

The Double ABCX Model

Family scientists Hamilton McCubbin and Joan Patterson (1982, 1983a, 1983b), based on their longitudinal "study of families who had a husband/ father held captive or unaccounted for" in the Vietnam War, expanded upon

Hill's (1958) ABCX Formula by adding postcrisis variables to explain and predict how families recover from crisis and why some are better able to adapt than others (Patterson, 1988). Using Hill's ABCX Formula as a foundation, McCubbin and Patterson (1982, 1983b) added (1) additional life stressors and strains; (2) psychological, intrafamilial, and social resources; (3) changes in the family's definition; (4) family coping strategies; and (5) a range of outcomes, with family coping strategies being the Double ABCX Model's major contribution to stress theory. See Figure 4.1. The model has three main parts: precrisis, crisis, and postcrisis.

Appraisal, Assessment interpretation, perception

Conceptual Framework of the Double ABCX Model

Precrisis

how we thought of the stressor (challenging.)

The precrisis of the Double ABCX Model includes the same variables as the ABCX Formula up to the crisis. These include the variables of the stressor, resources, and definition. McCubbin and Patterson (1983a, 1983b) used lowercase letters and changed the labels of variables a little from the original ABCX Formula, however.

The *a* in the Double ABCX Model represents the initial stressor. In the population studied by McCubbin and Patterson (1983a, 1983b), it was separation from the husband/father held captive or missing during the Vietnam War. This stressor is equivalent to *A* in the ABCX Formula (Hill, 1958) while the *b* is equivalent to the *B* in the ABCX Formula. McCubbin and Patterson (1982, 1983a, 1983b) changed the label *b* from *crisis-meeting resources* (Hill, 1958) to *existing resources*. The label *existing resources* is probably a better label since families actually used the resources in Hill's (1958) formula after a stressor but prior to a crisis. In addition, McCubbin and Patterson (1982, 1983a, 1983b) expanded on resources to include psychological/ individual and social/community resources as well as intrafamilial/family resources considered by Hill. McCubbin and Patterson (1982, 1983a, 1983b) changed the label *c* from *the definition the family makes of the event* (Hill, 1958) to *perception of a*. They did not give a reason for what appears to be an arbitrary change.

developing/ establishing new resources from existing (old) resources

Crisis

In the Double ABCX Model, *x* stands for crisis. It is equivalent to *X* in Hill's (1958) ABCX Formula. While the ABCX Formula ends with the crisis, the Double ABCX Model goes on to include postcrisis variables.

Figure 4.1 The Double ABCX Model

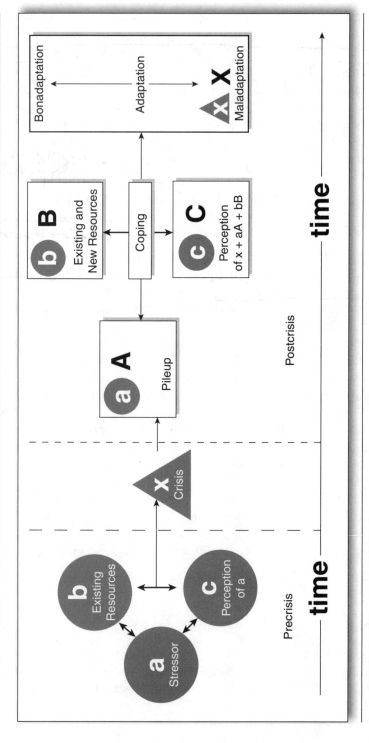

Source: McCubbin & Patterson (1983a).

86 ◀

Postcrisis

The postcrisis variables in the Double ABCX Model include pileup of stressors on top of the initial stressor (*aA*); existing and new resources (*bB*); perception (definition) of the initial stressor, pileup, and existing and new resources (*cC*); coping; and adaptation to the postcrisis variables (*xX*).

aA. *Pileup.* Pileup (*aA*) experienced by the families in the study included that resulting from five sources: (1) the initial stressor; (2) hardships of the initial stressor that increased and persisted over time to become chronic strains; (3) transitions; (4) the consequences of family efforts to cope with the separation; and (5) ambiguity within the family and within society. Hardships (demands on resources) this population experienced may have included demands on money and time. Transitions continued to occur in the family despite the absence of the husband/father. A consequence of the mothers' assuming the fathers' roles was disapproval from kin. Two types of ambiguity occurred: boundary and social. Boundary ambiguity occurred since it was unclear whether the husband/father would return. Was the husband/father still a family member? Social ambiguity is "the absence of appropriate norms and procedures for managing stressful situations" (McCubbin & Patterson, 1983a, p. 93). Wives experienced social ambiguity when their husbands' powers of attorney expired and they were unable to complete legal transactions without having legal guidelines for after the expiration.

bB. *Existing and New Resources.* In the Double ABCX Model, the *b* represents resources that existed precrisis while the *B* represents new resources that develop to be used to cope with the initial crisis. Existing resources used by the sample used to develop the model included friends, religious involvement, mental health professionals, togetherness, role flexibility, shared values and goals, and expressiveness. New resources used by the sample included educational opportunities, increased self-esteem and self-sufficiency, reallocated roles and responsibilities, new communities, new families, and community groups (counseling and church) and clubs.

cC. *Perception of* x + aA +bB. In the Double ABCX Model, the *c* is the perception/definition of the stressor that led to the crisis. The *C* is the family's perception/definition of the crisis, pileup, and existing and new resources. When the *cC* factor is positive, family members are better able to cope. The wives in the study gave positive meanings to their situations, such as "a challenge," "an opportunity for growth," or "the Lord's will" (McCubbin & Patterson, 1983a, p. 97).

Coping. Wives in the study coped by doing more things with their children, assuming stronger leadership roles in their families, encouraging the expression of feelings among family members, considering their spouses outside the family to justify behaviors such as dating while considering them inside the family to access their military wages, and forming a social network. How a family copes influences how well it adapts.

Adaptation. Adaptation can be a process or an outcome. In the Double ABCX Model, adaptation refers to an outcome as a result of change in the family system, which evolves and is intended to have long-term consequences involving changes in family roles, rules, patterns of interaction, and perceptions. It consists of a continuum of balance in functioning at two levels, the member-to-family and family-to-community levels. The positive end of the continuum, called bonadaptation, signifies balance at both the member-to-family and family-to-community levels. The negative end of the continuum, maladaptation represented by *xX*, signifies continued imbalance in one or both levels, or balance at the expense of the family's or a family member's integrity, development, or autonomy.

Critique of the Double ABCX Model

On the positive side, the Double ABCX Model includes precrisis, crisis, and postcrisis variables. The change of the label *b* from *crisis-meeting resources* to *existing resources* is a positive change since the *b* resources in the formula represent those used prior to a crisis.

On the negative side, McCubbin and Patterson (1982, 1983a, 1983b) call *c* "perception of the stressor" rather than "definition of the stressor" as Hill (1958) did—what appears to be an arbitrary change. In addition, in the Double ABCX Model, "coping does not come into play until after the family has used its resources, defined the situation, experienced crisis, and stress pile-up has occurred. It is reasonable to think that coping is constantly going on" (Burr, 1989, p. 52). Indeed, if a family uses resources precrisis, the family is coping, albeit insufficiently, when a crisis occurs.

Summary of the Double ABCX Model

In the Double ABCX Model, McCubbin and Patterson (1982, 1983a, 1983b) build on the ABCX Formula (Hill, 1958). The precrisis variables of the stressor, existing resources, and perceptions of the stressor lead to the crisis, followed by the postcrisis variables of pileup of stressors on top of the initial stressor, the use of existing and new resources, the perception of the pileup and existing and new resources, coping, and adaptation to the postcrisis variables. The major contribution of the Double ABCX Model was the addition of coping, albeit only postcrisis.

Summary

This chapter presented two family stress models, the ABCX Model and the Double ABCX Model. The ABCX Model began with the stressor and ended with the crisis, while the Double ABCX Model began with the stressor but went on to include postcrisis variables. Since the ABCX Model is the basis of most family stress models, its developer, Hill (1958), has been called the father of family stress theory. For a comparison of variables in both the ABCX and Double ABCX models with other models, see the Appendix.

EXERCISES

4.1 Outline the crisis from Exercise 2.1 using Hill's (1958) ABCX Formula/Model concepts. Following is an example of this assignment based on the case study from Chapter 2.

    I. A—The crisis-precipitating event/stressor (and its hardships)

      A. Stressor: husband's death

      B. Hardships:

        1. Demands on time to attend wake and funeral

        2. Demands on energy to grieve

        3. Demands on space to accommodate guests for funeral

    II. B—The family's crisis-meeting resources (organization) (high, medium, low): medium

      A. Integration (high, medium, low): medium

        1. Willingness to sacrifice personal interest to attain family objectives (high, medium, low): high; I sacrificed my personal interests to care for my husband and child

        2. Pride in the family tree and in the ancestral traditions (high, medium, low): medium, there was pride in the family tree from one side of the family but not the other

        3. Presence of strong patterns of emotional interdependence and unity (high, medium, low): low; we did not share our emotions very readily

        4. High participation as a family in joint activities (high, medium, low): low; other than going to doctors' visits, we did not share many activities

5. Strong affectional ties between father-mother, father-children, mother-children, and children-children (high, medium, low): medium

   a. Father-mother (high, medium, low): medium; focused on illness and child

   b. Father-children (high, medium, low): low; father was not able to pick up and hold child because of illness; he seemed to disengage

   c. Mother-children (high, medium, low): medium; child was source of emotional satisfaction

   d. Children-children (high, medium, low): only one child

B. Adaptability (high, medium, low): medium

   1. Previous success in meeting family crises (high, medium, low): medium; had recovered from other crises as when husband diagnosed with cancer but not to prior level of functioning

   2. Predominance of non-materialistic goals (high, medium, low): high; goals were within financial means for example, we lived in a mobile home at the time

   3. Flexibility and willingness to shift traditional roles of husband and wife or of father and mother, if necessary (high, medium, low): low; husband could barely perform his roles much less shift roles

   4. Acceptance of responsibility by all family members in performing family duties (high, medium, low): low; primary responsibility for all household duties and child care were mine due to husband's illness

   5. Presence of equalitarian patterns of family control and decision-making (high, medium, low): high; decisions were made as a couple

C. Marital Adjustment (poor, fair, or good): fair to good

   1. Wife (poor, fair, or good): good; there were no disagreements

   2. Husband (poor, fair, or good): fair; husband could not really participate as a marital partner in many ways

III. C—the definition the family makes of the event (challenging or crisis-provoking): challenging; I believed that I would be successful in spite of my loss

IV. X—the crisis

   1. Behavioral:

      a. Excessive activity

      b. Isolation

   2. Cognitive:

      a. Distressing dreams

      b. Slowed thinking

3. Emotional:

    a. Emotional shock

    b. Guilt

    c. Numbness

4. Physical: Sleep disturbance (insomnia)

Now complete the following outline based on your crisis.

  I. A—The crisis-precipitating event/stressor (and its hardships)

    A. Stressor

    B. Hardships

  II. B—The family's crisis-meeting resources (organization)

    A. Integration (high, medium, low)

        1. Willingness to sacrifice personal interest to attain family objectives (high, medium, low)

        2. Pride in the family tree and in the ancestral traditions (high, medium, low)

        3. Presence of strong patterns of emotional interdependence and unity (high, medium, low)

        4. High participation as a family in joint activities (high, medium, low)

        5. Strong affectional ties between father and mother, father and children, mother and children, and children and children (high, medium, low)

    B. Adaptability (high, medium, low)

        1. Previous success in meeting family crises (high, medium, low)

        2. Predominance of nonmaterialistic goals (high, medium, low)

        3. Flexibility and willingness to shift traditional roles of husband and wife or of father and mother, if necessary (high, medium, low)

        4. Acceptance of responsibility by all family members in performing family duties (high, medium, low)

        5. Presence of equalitarian patterns of family control and decision making (high, medium, low)

    C. Marital Adjustment (poor, fair, or good)

        1. Wife (poor, fair, or good)

        2. Husband (poor, fair, or good)

  III. C—The definition the family makes of the event (challenging or crisis-provoking)

  IV. X—The crisis

4.2 Outline a personal crisis or that of someone you know using the Double ABCX Model concepts. Following is an example of the assignment based on the case study in Chapter 2.

    I. Precrisis

        A. Stressor (a): husband's death

        B. Existing resources (b)

            1. Psychological/individual: did not use psychological/individual resources

            2. Intrafamilial/family: did not use intrafamily resources

            3. Social/community

                a. Persons

                    1) Coworkers

                    2) Friends

                    3) Relatives

                b. Institutions: mesoenvironmental—funeral home

        C. Perception of a (b): challenging; I believed that I would be successful in spite of my loss

    II. Crisis (x)

        A. Amount of consciousness and acceptance by each family member of his or her and others' family roles (better than average, average, below average): below average; my parents took care of my son for a period of time—a few days, I think—so I was not performing my role as parent

        B. Extent to which family members worked toward family and individual good (better than average, average, below average): below average; I was not taking care of my son, and self-care was based on what others told me to do

        C. How much family members found satisfaction with family unit (better than average, average, below average): below-average; the family unit had been redefined, and ways to find satisfaction would need to be redefined as well

        D. Whether the family had a sense of direction and was moving in that direction (better than average, average, below average): below average; family goals would need to be redefined by me as a single parent

    III. Postcrisis

        A. Pileup (aA)

            1. Initial stressor (a): husband's death

            2. A

                a. Hardships from a (initial stressor)

                    1) Demands on time to attend wake and funeral

      2) Demands on energy to grieve

      3) Demands on space to accommodate guests for funeral

    b. Transitions: not going through any transitions at the time

    c. Consequences of coping efforts: no negative consequences of coping efforts

    d. Ambiguity

      1) Family boundary: no family boundary ambiguity

      2) Social: no social ambiguity

B. Existing and new resources (bB)

  1. Existing resources (b)

    a. Psychological/individual: did not use psychological/individual resources

    b. Intrafamilial/family: did not use intrafamily resources

    c. Social/community

      1) Persons

        a) Coworkers

        b) Friends

        c) Relatives

      2) Institutions: mesoenvironmental—funeral home

  2. New resources (B)

    a. Psychological/individual: knowledge

    b. Intrafamilial/family: no new intrafamilial resources

    c. Social/community

      1) Groups—self-help

      2) Institutions

        a) Mesoenvironmental—churches

        b) Macroenvironmental—government policies

C. cC

  1. Perception of a (c): challenging; I believed that I would be successful in spite of my loss

  2. Perception of X + aA + bB (C): challenging but not insurmountable, since I had resources

D. Coping

  1. Negative: no negative coping strategies used

  2. Positive:

    a. Cognitive

      1) Accepted the situation and others

        a) Quickly accepted and confronted the situation

        b) Accepted limitations; did not try to do or be everything

        2) Gained useful knowledge
          a) Found information and facts about the situation
          b) Understood the essential nature of the situation
        3) Changed how the situation was viewed or defined
          a) Separated the stress into manageable parts
          b) Did not have false hopes but had faith in own ability to handle the situation
          c) Did not blame others or become preoccupied with blaming; instead was solution-oriented
    b. Emotional Activities
        1) Expressed feelings and affection
          a) Was honest, clear, and direct in expressing affection
    c. Relationship Activities
        1) Developed family cohesion and togetherness
          a) Did things with children and maintained stability
        2) Maintained family adaptability and flexibility
          a) Was flexible and willing to change family roles, behaviors, and attitudes
    d. Communication Activities
        1) Was open and honest
          a) Was open and honest in communications with others
    e. Community Activities
        1) Sought help and support from others
          a) Sought and accepted help from relatives when needed
          b) Sought and accepted help from community services when needed
    f. Spiritual Activities
        1) Was more involved in religious activities
        2) Increased or sought help from God
          a) Believed in God

E. Adaptation

  1. Bonadaptation
    a. Member-to-family balance: member-to-family functioning was balanced as both my and my son's individual needs were met as were those of us as a collective family
    b. Family-to-community balance: family-to-community functioning was balanced since there was no dependency on the community and roles in the community were performed
  2. Maladaptation (xX): no maladaptation
    a. Member-to-family imbalance
    b. Family-to-community imbalance

        c. Balance at expense of family member
           1) Integrity
           2) Development
           3) Autonomy

Now complete the following outline for your crisis.

  I. Precrisis
    A. Stressor (a)
    B. Existing resources (b)
      1. Psychological/individual
      2. Intrafamilial/family
      3. Social/community
    C. Perception of a (b)

  II. Crisis (x)

  III. Postcrisis
    A. Pileup (aA)
      1. Initial stressor (a)
      2. A
        a. Hardships from a (initial stressor)
        b. Transitions
          1) Individual
          2) Family
        c. Consequences of coping efforts
          1) Consequences of negative coping strategies
          2) Consequences of positive coping strategies
        d. Ambiguity
          1) Family boundary
          2) Social

    B. Existing and new resources (bB)
      1. Existing resources (b)
        a. Psychological/individual
        b. Intrafamilial/family
        c. Social/community
      2. New resources (B)
        a. Psychological/individual
        b. Intrafamilial/family
        c. Social/community
    C. cC
      1. Perception of a (c)
      2. Perception of X + aA + bB (C)

D. Coping
  1. Negative
  2. Positive

E. Adaptation
  1. Bonadaptation
    a. Member-to-family balance
    b. Family-to-community balance
  2. Maladaptation (xX)
    a. Member-to-family imbalance
    b. Family-to-community imbalance
    c. Balance at expense of family member
      1) Integrity
      2) Development
      3) Autonomy

References and Suggestions for Further Reading

Angell, R. C. (1936). *The family encounters the depression.* Gloucester, MA: Peter Smith.

Boss, P. (2002). *Family stress management: A contextual approach.* Thousand Oaks, CA: Sage.

Burr, R. G. (1989). *Reframing family stress theory: From the ABC-X Model to a Family Ecosystemic Model.* Unpublished master's thesis, Brigham Young University, Provo, UT.

Cavan, R. S., & Ranck, K. H. (1938). *The family and the depression: A study of one hundred Chicago families.* Chicago: The University of Chicago Press.

Hill, R. (1949). *Families under stress: Adjustment to the crises of war separation and reunion.* New York: Harper & Brothers.

Hill, R. (1958). Generic features of families under stress. *Social Casework, 49,* 139–150.

Koos, E. L. (1946). *Families in trouble.* Morningside Heights, NY: King's Crown.

McCubbin, H. I., & Patterson, J. M. (1982). Family adaptation to crisis. In H. I. McCubbin, A. E. Cauble, & J. M. Patterson (Eds.), *Family stress, coping, and social support.* Springfield, IL: Charles C. Thomas.

McCubbin, H. I., & Patterson, J. M. (1983a). Family stress and adaptation to crises: A Double ABCX Model of family behavior. In D. H. Olson & R. C. Miller (Eds.), *Family studies review yearbook: Vol. 1* (pp. 87–106). Beverly Hills, CA: Sage.

McCubbin, H. I., & Patterson, J. M. (1983b). The family stress process: The Double ABCX Model of family adjustment and adaptation. In H. I. McCubbin, M. Sussman, & J. M. Patterson (Eds.), *Social stress and the family: Advances and developments in family stress theory and research* (pp. 7–37). New York: Haworth.

Patterson, J. M. (1988). Families experiencing stress: I. The Family Adjustment and Adaptation Response Model II. Applying the FAAR Model to health-related issues for intervention and research. *Family Systems Medicine, 6*(2), 202–237.

CHAPTER 5

Individual Stress/ Crisis Models

The Natural History of Individual Reactions to Disaster, the Components of an Emotional Crisis, the 4 Phases in Crisis Development, and the Crisis Paradigm

T his chapter presents four individual family stress or crisis models, the Natural History of Individual Reactions to Disaster, the Components of an Emotional Crisis, the 4 Phases in Crisis Development, and the Crisis Paradigm. The models are presented in chronological order of their development. The first model considered is the Natural History of Individual Reactions to Disaster.

The Natural History of Individual Reactions to Disaster

After studying reactions to floods and fires, J. S. Tyhurst (1951, 1957a, 1957b), a psychiatrist, described what he called the Natural History of Individual Reactions to Disaster. He distinguished three overlapping periods/phases: (1) period of impact, (2) period of recoil, and (3) posttraumatic period. He characterized each period or phase according to stress, time (duration and perspective), and psychological phenomena. Tyhurst (1951) hoped that his model would be helpful in research and treatment. This model could be used to guide research and treatment after such disasters as Hurricane Katrina.

Conceptual Framework of the Natural History of Individual Reactions to Disaster

Period of Impact

According to Tyhurst (1951, 1957a, 1957b), the period of impact was the period of experiencing the maximum and most direct effect of the initial stress. Tyhurst used the term *stress* to refer to what we now define as stressors. In Tyhurst's research, the stress/stressor in the period of impact was a fire in one study and a flood in another. The observed *duration* of time of the period of impact varied from 3 minutes to 1.5 hours, but he said that it "may vary within fairly wide margins" (Tyhurst, 1951, p. 765). It began with the initial stressor and continued until the stressor was no longer operating. The time *perspective* referred to the focus of the individual at the time. The time *perspective* of the period of impact was the immediate present. Tyhurst (1951, 1957a, 1957b) observed three main reactions during the period of impact, which he labeled (1) *cool and collected*, (2) *normal*, and (3) *inappropriate*. Members of the cool and collected group ranged from 12% to 25% of the observations. They retained their awareness, assessed the situation, formulated a plan, and carried out the plan. Members of the normal group made up about 75% of the observations. They were stunned and bewildered, lacked awareness of emotions, and had physiological manifestations of fear. Members of the inappropriate group made up 10% to 25% of the observations. They showed confusion, paralyzing anxiety, hysterical crying, or screaming. After the period of impact, observed families experienced a period of recoil.

Period of Recoil

The initial stress/stressor (e.g., tornado, hurricane) is suspended in the period of recoil. Some stressors may continue during this period (e.g., from injuries incurred in the first period). The observed *duration* of the period of recoil varied as well, based more on the individual than on the nature of the stressor and lasting from several hours to 2 days (Tyhurst, 1951, 1957a, 1957b). Recoil began when the individual succeeded in avoiding the direct effect of the initial stressor and lasted until he or she felt fully secure from the initial stressor and became aware of the altered environment. The time *perspective*/focus of the period of recoil was the immediate past. The focus was still on the initial stressor. During the period of recoil, individuals gradually gained their first awareness of what they had just gone through. Some individuals gave accounts of their experiences for the first time. The majority of those observed expressed overt emotion (anxiety, fear, anger) for the first time. Tyhurst observed a childlike dependency (e.g., wanting something such as coffee or a blanket) and a need to be with others and to talk. Wanting something and needing to talk are cognitive reactions, while talking is behavioral. He claimed that the period of recoil appeared to be the most important for intervention after a disaster. Tyhurst labeled the time following the period of recoil the posttraumatic period.

Posttraumatic Period

According to Tyhurst (1951, 1957a, 1957b), the stress/stressors during the posttraumatic period were derivatives of the initial stressor in the period of impact and were based on the full awareness of the altered environment (e.g., loss of home, belongings, financial security, people) and its effect on daily living. Tyhurst (1951, 1957a, 1957b) hypothesized that the *duration* of the posttraumatic period would be the rest of a person's life. It began when the individual felt fully secure from the initial stressor and became aware of the altered environment. This period included a time of rehabilitation. The time *perspective*/focus of the posttraumatic period was the past, present, and future. Individuals during the posttraumatic period focused on the initial stressor (past), the altered environment (present), and the effects the altered environment would have on daily living (future). Tyhurst (1951, 1957a, 1957b) observed anxiety, fatigue, recurrent catastrophic dreaming, and depression during the posttraumatic period. Besides emotional disturbances, Tyhurst observed physical complaints. These included such things as nausea, gastric upset, and headaches. He suggested that the physical complaints were the outcomes of the emotional disturbances and could become "persistent if not recognized and treated appropriately" (1957a, p. 387). A discussion of appropriate "treatment" appears in Part III of this book; however, family scientists may use the term *management* rather than *treatment*. Tyhurst used the word *treatment* because he was a psychiatrist and approached stress from a medical perspective.

Critique of the Natural History
of Individual Reactions to Disaster

Tyhurst's (1951, 1957a, 1957b) model provides a framework for understanding the effects on individuals of disasters and is not as helpful for understanding other types of stressors. The time covered by Tyhurst's model begins at the onset of the stressor and does not take into account any prestressor variables. In the model, the term *stress* was used to refer to what we now call stressors. In addition, the term *psychological phenomena* was used to refer to physical as well as emotional reactions. Despite the limitations of the model, it is helpful in understanding crises from catastrophic stressors.

Summary of the Natural History of Individual Reactions to Disaster

Tyhurst's model is an individual versus a family model. It provides a framework for understanding the effects of disasters on individuals. After observing individuals who experienced disasters (floods and fires), Tyhurst (1951, 1957a, 1957b) reported three periods/phases of what he called the Natural History of Individual Reactions to Disaster—impact, recoil, and posttraumatic. He characterized each period according to stress/stressor, time (duration and perspective), and psychological phenomena. There are some problems in the model, such as use of the terms *stress* for *stressor* and *psychological phenomena* for *physical* as well as *emotional reactions*, but despite those limitations, the model is useful for understanding crises resulting from natural disasters. Tyhurst's choice of terms can be attributed to his background as a psychiatrist. Another psychiatrist, Peter Sifneos, developed the Components of an Emotional Crisis.

The Components of an Emotional Crisis

From his study of individuals he saw at a mental health agency, Peter Sifneos (1960), a psychiatrist, identified components of what he called an emotional crisis (a hazardous event or situation, vulnerability, a precipitating factor or incident, and an acute crisis state). Sifneos directed the psychiatric clinic at Massachusetts General Hospital and was associated with the Harvard Medical School Department of Psychiatry at the time. The Components of an Emotional Crisis (see Figure 5.1) are useful in guiding assessment of individuals to determine whether or not they are in crisis.

Conceptual Framework of the Components of an Emotional Crisis

Hazardous Event or Situation

Sifneos (1960) defined a hazardous event or situation as a "difficult or dangerous situation that becomes stressful to some individuals and not to

Figure 5.1 Components of an Emotional Crisis

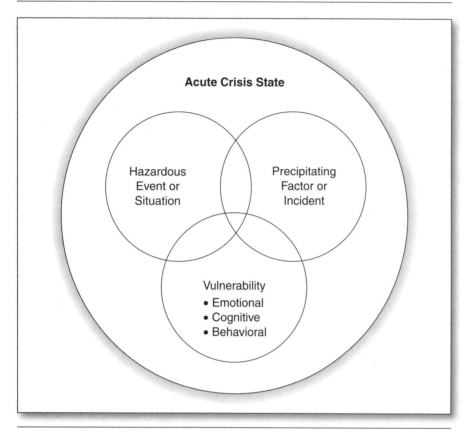

Source: Hoff (2001).

others" (p. 176); thus hazardous events or situations are stressors. Sifneos identified hazardous events as situations originating from changes in the environment and from changes in the individual. Environmental hazardous situations or events in the study conducted by Sifneos included loss of a family member by separation, illness, or death; disturbed behavior (excessively passive or aggressive) of a family member, usually a child; disabling physical or mental illness of a family member; new arrival in the family by birth or return from armed services; change in civil status such as marriage; moving; forced change in roles; change in work status (new job, retirement, or unemployment); entering school; and family isolation from the community. Individual hazardous situations included physical illness, incapacitating injury, puberty, climacteric, pregnancy, and the onset of mental illness. Once the hazardous event or situation occurred, Sifneos (1960) observed, individuals entered a state of vulnerability.

Vulnerability

Vulnerability (Hoff, 1989, 1995, 2001), or vulnerable state (Golan, 1969), referred to the individual's painful, unpleasant state (Sifneos, 1960) in reaction to the hazardous event or situation. The hazardous event or situation led to a person becoming vulnerable to/at risk for a crisis developing. Hoff (1989, 1995, 2001) suggested identifying how vulnerable a person is by assessing *emotional, cognitive,* and *behavioral* manifestations/symptoms of the vulnerable state. A person may recover from the vulnerable state quickly or may be in a vulnerable state for years, or at any time after a person becomes vulnerable, a precipitating factor or incident may occur, leading to an acute crisis state.

Precipitating Factor or Incident

According to Sifneos (1960), a precipitating factor or incident was an event that brought about the change from a vulnerable state to a crisis state, a state of disequilibrium. The precipitating factor or incident could be minor (Golan, 1969). It was the "straw that broke the camel's back" that led a person to the acute crisis state (Golan, 1969). Precipitating factors or incidents identified in Sifneos's research included a talk with a doctor, teacher, clergyman, lawyer, nurse, job supervisor, police officer, friend, psychiatrist, or social worker; impending school or physical exams; fights; new jobs; admission to or discharge from a hospital; meetings; engagements; trips; and the possibility of a child's school expulsion. If a crisis was experienced immediately following a hazardous event, the hazardous event and the precipitating factor were said to be the same stressor. The precipitating factor or incident led to the crisis state.

Acute Crisis State

The acute crisis state was the state of active crisis. Golan (1969) suggested appraising "the four primary areas of reaction" (p. 393)—affective (emotional), perceptive–cognitive, behavioral, and biophysiological (physical)—to determine whether a person was in an acute crisis state. See Chapter 2 for examples of each type of crisis manifestation. The Components of an Emotional Crisis ended at the crisis and did not address what happened to an individual after the crisis.

Critique of the Components of an Emotional Crisis

The Components of an Emotional Crisis illustrate only from the time of a stressor/hazardous event to the time of a crisis. It does not cover any factors after the crisis, which is appropriate for its stated purpose of assessment of whether an individual is in crisis. The Components of an Emotional Crisis help us to understand that often what tips an individual into a crisis state is a minor event. Although Sifneos (1960) did not use the term *pileup*, the hazardous event and the precipitating factor suggest a pileup of stressors.

Summary of the Components of an Emotional Crisis

Sifneos (1960) presented the Components of an Emotional Crisis: the hazardous event or situation (first stressor), vulnerability (state of distress), the precipitating factor or incident (second stressor), and the acute crisis state. The hazardous event or situation, which can be environmental or individual, leads to a person being in a vulnerable state that can last for years. A precipitating factor or incident can then lead that person into an acute crisis state. Although the model is a useful tool for assessment of crisis, a weakness of the Components of an Emotional Crisis is that they do not go further than the crisis as the 4 Phases in Crisis Development, which was contributed to stress/crisis theory by another psychiatrist.

The 4 Phases in Crisis Development

Gerald Caplan, a psychiatrist, was involved in the early stages of the preventive mental health movement, a community approach. The preventive, community approach was based on the assumption that "many mental health disorders resulted from maladaptation or maladjustment" (Caplan, 1964, p. 28) to crises. Caplan was the first to conclude that poorly managed crises led to mental illness (a negative crisis outcome). Caplan's phases apply more to crises occurring as gradual processes and to less catastrophic stressors, such as physical disease, than to crises occurring after natural disasters or emotional stressors (Hoff, 1984, 1989, 1995, 2001). Caplan's (1964) 4 Phases began with the stressor and interwove with each other. The phases were intended to be guidelines for practitioners as well as researchers.

Conceptual Framework of the 4 Phases in Crisis Development

Phase 1

Phase 1 of Caplan's 4 Phases in Crisis Development began with the initial rise in tension/stress from the impact of the stressor. In Phase 1, the task was to act on the stressor to reduce it, to reduce its consequences, and/or to find ways of physically escaping it. "Goal-directed, problem-solving behavior in a world of reality" (Caplan, 1981, p. 414) was necessary to complete this task. In reaction to the stressor, however, the individual manifestations of stress in this phase made accomplishing the task difficult. Caplan (1981) suggested that the magnitude of cognitive manifestations affected the intensity of the emotions. He believed that the emotions led to physical (neuroendocrine) processes, which improved cognitive functioning temporarily but led to increasing disorganization. He concluded that interpretation (definition) of the stressor led to behavioral manifestations. The individual responded with "habitual" problem-solving responses/coping strategies (Caplan, 1964) to maintain homeostasis or balance in this phase. Based on this conclusion, Caplan (1981) suggested intervening at the cognitive level, particularly with a support group or social network of relatives, friends, neighbors, and community caregivers. He contended that social support complemented and supplemented aspects of individual functioning weakened by the stressor. If habitual problem solving failed to solve the problem, the individual moved to Phase 2 of the model.

Phase 2

Since, in Phase 1 of Caplan's 4 Phases in Crisis Development, the habitual, usual problem solving failed to accomplish the task of reducing or escaping the stressor or reducing the stressor's consequences, the individual moved to Phase 2. This failure led to a rise in tension/stress (Caplan, 1964). If the tension or stress rose further, the individual moved to Phase 3 of the model.

Phase 3

In Phase 3, tension/stress rose further stimulating the use of "novel"/ new resources to cope (Caplan, 1964). Based on the work of other researchers (Sachar, Mackenzie, Binstock, & Mack, 1968, and Wolff, Freidman, Hofer, & Mason, 1964, cited in Caplan, 1981), Caplan contended that individuals used their "customary defense mechanisms" (p. 416), such as denial, selective inattention, and withdrawal during this phase. Because of the use of defense mechanisms or novel/new resources to cope, "the problem may be solved" (Caplan, 1964) in this phase, and the person would not move to Phase 4. It was in this third phase that the family was most likely to consider seeking outside assistance from a crisis interventionist as part of new or novel resources.

Phase 4

In Phase 4 of Caplan's 4 Phases in Crisis Development, the "problem"/stressor continued and the "tension"/stress rose resulting in major disorganization or what Chapter 2 defines as crisis. This phase is equivalent to Tyhurst's (1951, 1957a, 1957b) Phase 3, the posttraumatic period, and Sifneos's (1960) acute crisis state in the Components of an Emotional Crisis.

Critique of the 4 Phases in Crisis Development

On the positive side, Caplan's (1964) 4 Phases in Crisis Development are useful for crises occurring as gradual processes, less catastrophic stressors, and physical disease. On the negative side, this model is not as applicable for emotional stressors or catastrophic events such as natural disasters. In addition, it does not include prestressor variables, nor does it include postcrisis variables.

Summary of the 4 Phases in Crisis Development

Caplan's (1964, 1981) interwoven 4 Phases in Crisis Development began in an individual when a "problem"/stressor occurred. The problem/stressor led to emotional, physical, cognitive, and behavioral changes related to the interpretation/definition of the problem/stressor. In Phase 1, individuals reacted with habitual/usual problem solving/coping to attempt to relieve the tension/stress. When the habitual/usual problem solving failed to relieve the tension/stress, the individual entered Phase 2 of crisis development with its concomitant increase in tension/stress. In Phase 3, the tension/stress increased further, leading to attempts to reduce the tension/stress by using customary defense mechanisms or novel/new resources to cope. Although a useful model for explaining crises with gradual onsets, such as physical illnesses, the model is less useful in understanding crises from emotional or catastrophic stressors. It is also limited in its scope, beginning at the stressor and ending with the crisis. The Crisis Paradigm (Hoff, 1984, 1989, 1995, 2001) goes beyond the crisis.

The Crisis Paradigm

Lee Ann Hoff (1984, 1989, 1995, 2001) received degrees in social science (anthropology and medical sociology) and psychiatric–mental health nursing. Drawing from psychology, nursing, sociology, psychiatry, anthropology, philosophy, and political science, she developed a research-based crisis paradigm to explain what happens from a sociopsychocultural perspective when individuals experience crises and to help assist individuals with managing crises (see Figure 5.2). The intertwined circles of the crisis origins and aids to positive resolution signify the distinct yet interrelated origins of crisis and aids to resolution. The solid lines from origins to manifestations to aids to positive resolution illustrate the opportunity for positive resolution when appropriate aids to resolution are used. The broken line from manifestations to negative resolutions illustrates the potential danger of negative resolution in the absence of appropriate aids/resources.

Conceptual Framework of the Crisis Paradigm

Crisis Origins

Hoff (1984, 1989, 1995, 2001) identified three broad categories of crisis origins: situational, transitional, and social/cultural. Hoff (1984) included crisis origins in her paradigm because she assumed that "insight into how a problem begins enhances our chances of dealing effectively with the problem" (p. 37).

She pointed out that the origin of a crisis could be simple (have one origin) or multifaceted/interrelated (have multiple origins). She contended that crises with simple origins might be easier to handle with greater possibilities of a positive outcome than those with multifaceted origins because crisis intervention is also more complex for crises with multifaceted origins. Since crisis intervention flows from the crisis origin, a crisis with a multifaceted origin requires a multifaceted approach. In addition, Hoff (1984, 1989, 1995, 2001) contends that crises developing from situational and transitional origins are easier to cope with successfully than crises originating from social or cultural origins because those having social or cultural origins "are less amenable to control by individuals" (Hoff, 1989, p. 42). Identification of the primary origin of a crisis is also important to providing appropriate intervention, as some crises originate from all three broad categories, and although intervention is required to address each of the origins, the intervention would address the primary origin first.

Situational

According to Hoff (1984, 1989, 1995, 2001), situational origins are those that are usually unanticipated; therefore, individuals can prepare for them only indirectly. Examples of indirect preparation for crises of situational origin include using careful driving habits, which can reduce auto accident risk;

Figure 5.2 Crisis Paradigm

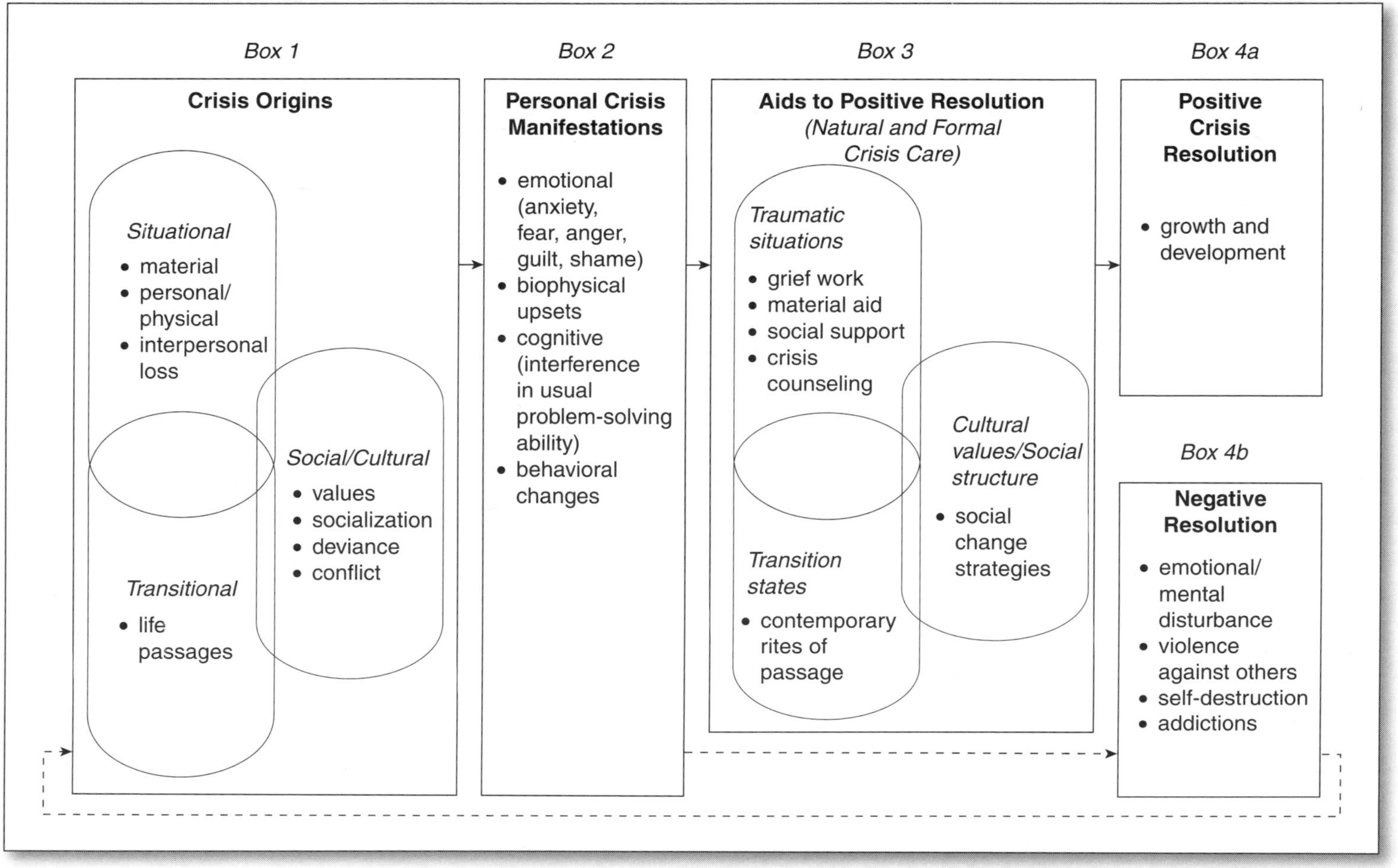

Box 1

Crisis Origins

Situational
- material
- personal/physical
- interpersonal loss

Social/Cultural
- values
- socialization
- deviance
- conflict

Transitional
- life passages

Box 2

Personal Crisis Manifestations
- emotional (anxiety, fear, anger, guilt, shame)
- biophysical upsets
- cognitive (interference in usual problem-solving ability)
- behavioral changes

Box 3

Aids to Positive Resolution
(Natural and Formal Crisis Care)

Traumatic situations
- grief work
- material aid
- social support
- crisis counseling

Cultural values/Social structure
- social change strategies

Transition states
- contemporary rites of passage

Box 4a

Positive Crisis Resolution
- growth and development

Box 4b

Negative Resolution
- emotional/mental disturbance
- violence against others
- self-destruction
- addictions

Source: Hoff (2001).

having a healthy lifestyle by not smoking, maintaining a healthy diet, and exercising, which can reduce risk of heart attack or cancer; practicing open communication, which may lessen the chance of divorce; and changing sexual behavior, which can reduce risk of AIDS. Family life educators and psychoeducators (counselors and therapists) can help reduce the risk of situational crises through their educational programs.

Hoff (1984, 1989, 1995, 2001) divided situational origins into the three subcategories of material, personal/physical, and interpersonal loss. Hoff (1984, 1989, 1995, 2001) defined *material* origins as environmental origins such as fires or natural disasters. Examples of *personal/physical* origins are things that happen to individuals such as heart attacks, diagnoses with fatal illnesses, losses of limbs, and other body disfigurements. Personal/physical origins often relate to personal life choices such as choosing to smoke and eat unhealthfully. Hoff (1984, 1989, 1995, 2001) defined *interpersonal loss* as social loss. Examples of interpersonal loss include death of loved ones, separation, and divorce.

Transitional. Hoff (1984, 1989, 1995, 2001) defined the second broad category of crisis origins, *transitional* origins, as anticipated life passages. Hoff (1984, 1989, 1995, 2001) did not consider unanticipated transitions such as changing from being an employee to being unemployed because of a layoff. Refer back to Chapter 2 for a more complete discussion of transitions.

Social/Cultural. The next broad category of crisis origins proposed by Hoff (1984, 1989, 1995, 2001) was s*ocial/cultural.* It included the subcategories of *values, socialization, deviance,* and *conflict.* Stressors because of discrimination originate from cultural values, such as valuing different ages, races, genders, or classes more. Deviant acts (behaviors that violate accepted social norms) can be acts of others, as when others victimize us, or acts of self, as when one commits a crime (Hoff, 1989, 1995, 2001). We cannot usually anticipate deviant acts of others while we can anticipate deviant acts of ourselves.

Personal Crisis Manifestations

Personal crisis manifestations, the subjective reactions of a person to a stressor, appear in Box 2 of the Crisis Paradigm (Figure 5.2). Hoff (1984, 1989, 1995, 2001) divided the crisis manifestations into four categories: *emotional, biophysical, cognitive,* and *behavioral.* See Chapter 2 of this book for a detailed discussion of these individual crisis manifestations.

Aids to Positive Resolution
(Natural and Formal Crisis Care)

Aids to positive resolution include both natural and formal crisis care. Natural crisis care is crisis care/management performed by those other than professionals (i.e., family, friends). Formal crisis care, also called institutional crisis care/management, is crisis care/management performed by paraprofessionals or professionals. Hoff's (1984, 1989, 1995, 2001) Crisis Paradigm illustrates the relationship between crisis origins and aids to positive resolutions of crises. Part III of this book presents a detailed discussion of aids to positive crisis resolution.

Traumatic Situations. Hoff's (1984, 1989, 1995, 2001) suggestions for appropriate aids to positive resolution for crises with situational origins include *grief work, material aid, social support,* and/or *crisis counseling.* Grief work is appropriate for any loss whether it is material, personal/ physical, or interpersonal. Part III of this book addresses grief work. Material aid in the form of such things as housing or financial assistance is particularly appropriate for material losses. Social support and crisis counseling are appropriate for crises originating from any traumatic situation. Part III of this book addresses crisis counseling.

Transition States. Hoff (1984, 1989, 1995, 2001) suggested the appropriate aid to positive resolution from crises with transitional origins was *contemporary rites of passage* (rituals). She suggested that we evaluate traditional rituals that may be harmful, such as hazing rituals and some bachelor parties. In addition, it may be appropriate to form new, contemporary rituals for such things as divorce to ease that transition.

Cultural Values/Social Structure. Hoff (1984, 1989, 1995, 2001) suggested the appropriate aid to positive resolution from crises with social/cultural origins was *social change strategies.* Social change strategies include such things as protesting and advocacy in attempts to effect changes in society. The formation of Mothers Against Drunk Driving (MADD) illustrates a social change strategy. Protesting against war after a child dies in the military is another example of a social change strategy.

Crisis Resolution

The Crisis Paradigm (Hoff, 1984, 1989, 1995, 2001) shows that crisis resolution may be positive or negative. The paradigm does not take into account the possibility of a neutral resolution. Positive crisis resolution is considered first.

Positive Crisis Resolution. Positive crisis resolution occurs when the individual experiences *growth and development* because of the crisis. Ways in which an individual may grow include acquiring new resources and acquiring new ways of solving problems (new coping strategies). A person who learns new communication skills because of a crisis would be considered to have had a positive crisis resolution. In the Crisis Paradigm, if one does not experience positive crisis resolution, he or she is said to experience negative crisis resolution.

Negative Crisis Resolution. Individuals who experience negative crisis resolution, according to Hoff (1984, 1989, 1995, 2001), will experience such things as *emotional/mental disturbance, violence against others, self-destruction,* and/or *addiction.* An example of an emotional/mental disturbance includes developing neuroses. Neuroses include disorders characterized by anxieties, compulsions, obsessions, phobias, and/or tics. Violence against others includes such things as abuse and homicide. Self-destruction includes suicide as well as such things as cutting behavior. Addiction includes not only alcohol and drug addiction but also addiction to other things such as shopping, sex, work, pornography, video games, and gambling. The Crisis Paradigm ends with the crisis resolution; thus it includes no other postcrisis variables.

Critique of the Crisis Paradigm

A weakness of the Crisis Paradigm (Hoff, 1984, 1989, 1995, 2001) is that it changes terminology from Box 1, Crisis Origins, to Box 3, Aids to Positive Resolution. See Figure 5.2. *Situational* in Box 1 becomes *traumatic situations* in Box 3. *Transitional* in Box 1 becomes *transition states* in Box 3. *Social/cultural* in Box 1 becomes *cultural values/social structure* in Box 3. In addition, only anticipated transitions are considered in the model. Another negative of the Crisis Paradigm is that it does not allow for a neutral crisis resolution in which an individual experiences neither growth and development nor emotional/mental disturbance, violence, self-destruction, or addiction. Lastly, the Crisis Paradigm includes no postcrisis variable beyond resolution. On the positive side, the paradigm includes a variable that appears only in this stress model, aids to positive resolution, making it very helpful for both natural/informal and institutional/formal crisis managers. Thus, the model is useful for both assessment and intervention.

Table 5.1 Comparison of Individual Stress Models

Natural History of Individual Reactions to Disaster	Components of an Emotional Crisis	4 Phases of Crisis Development	Crisis Paradigm
Period of Impact: Stress	Hazardous Event or Situation	Phase 1: Problem	Crisis Origin
		Phase 1: Interpretation of Problem	
Period of Impact: Psychological Phenomena		Phase 1: Tension	
		Phase 1: Habitual Problem Solving	
Period of Recoil: Stress		Phase 2: Problem Continues	
Period of Recoil: Psychological Phenomena	Vulnerability	Phase 2: Rise in Tension	
		Phase 3: Problem Continues	
		Phase 3: Tension Rises Further	
		Phase 3: Tries to Reduce Tension	
Posttraumatic Period: Stress	Precipitating Factor	Phase 4: Problem Continues	
Posttraumatic Period: Psychological Phenomena	Acute Crisis State	Phase 4: Tension Rises Resulting in Major Disorganization	Personal Crisis Manifestations
Posttraumatic Period: Rehabilitation			Aids to Positive Resolution
			Resolution

Summary of the Crisis Paradigm

Hoff (1984, 1989, 1995, 2001), a nurse, developed the Crisis Paradigm from a sociopsychocultural perspective to explain crises and to assist in crisis care/management for individuals. The paradigm consists of four boxes showing the relationship among crisis origins, personal crisis manifestations, aids to positive resolution, and resolution. Although there are some inconsistencies in terminology from Box 1 to Box 3 in the paradigm, the fact that the Crisis Paradigm is the only stress model to include aids to positive resolution outweighs the inconsistencies, making the paradigm useful to both natural/informal and institutional/formal crisis managers.

Summary

This chapter presented four individual stress/crisis models—the Natural History of Individual Reactions to Disaster, the Components of an Emotional Crisis, the 4 Phases in Crisis Development, and the Crisis Paradigm—in chronological order of their development. Although each model uses different terminology, there are similarities across some of the models as illustrated in Table 5.1, which compares the models. Despite some overlap, each model has unique features. The choice of model to use depends on the purpose and the type of stressor. If working with people who experienced a disaster or catastrophic event, the Natural History of Individual Reactions to Disaster might be most useful. If working with someone who presents after what seems like a minor event, use the Components of an Emotional Crisis. If someone experiences a stressor of a physical illness, the 4 Phases of Crisis Development might best explain what he or she experiences. If we need help determining what interventions to use with someone in crisis, the Crisis Paradigm is useful.

EXERCISES

5.1 Outline the crisis from Exercise 2.1 using Tyhurst's (1951, 1957a, 1957b) Natural History of Individual Reactions to Disaster concepts. Following is an example of this assignment based on the case study from Chapter 2.

 I. Period of Impact

 A. Stress (initial stressor): husband's death

 B. Time

 1. Duration: a few minutes

 2. Perspective (immediate present): focused on watching my husband take his last breath

    C. Psychological Phenomena (cool and collected, normal, inappropriate): cool and collected

       1. Cool and collected

         a. Retained awareness: I was aware of what was happening and what I needed to do

         b. Assessed the situation: I sat with my husband a while

         c. Formulated a plan: While sitting with my husband, I planned to call the nurse to report that he had died

         d. Carried out the plan: I called the nurse

       2. Normal

         a. Stunned and bewildered: no

         b. Lacked awareness of emotions: no

         c. Had physiological manifestations: no

       3. Inappropriate

         a. Confused: no

         b. Paralyzed with anxiety: no

         c. Cried hysterically: no

         d. Screamed: no

II. Period of Recoil

    A. Stress: funeral

    B. Time

       1. Duration: 2 days

       2. Perspective (immediate past): focus of thoughts was on death of husband

    C. Psychological Phenomena

       1. Behavioral: no behavioral phenomena

       2. Cognitive

         a. Distressing dreams

         b. Slowed thinking

       3. Emotional

         a. Emotional shock

         b. Guilt

         c. Numbness

       4. Physical: sleep disturbance (insomnia)

III. Posttraumatic Period

    A. Stress (altered environment): awareness that I no longer had a husband and had to make all decisions on my own

    B. Time

       1. Duration: rest of life

       2. Perspective

        a. Past: focused thoughts on death of husband

        b. Present: focused thoughts on making decisions alone

        c. Future: focused thoughts on never being married again

  C. Psychological Phenomena

    1. Behavioral

        a. Excessive activity

        b. Isolation

    2. Cognitive

        a. Distressing dreams

        b. Slowed thinking

    3. Emotional

        a. Emotional shock

        b. Guilt

        c. Numbness

    4. Physical: sleep disturbance (insomnia)

  D. Rehabilitation

Now complete the following outline about your crisis.

  I. Period of Impact

    A. Stress (initial stressor)

    B. Time

      1. Duration

      2. Perspective (immediate present)

    C. Psychological Phenomena (cool and collected, normal, inappropriate)

      1. Cool and collected

        a. Retained awareness

        b. Assessed the situation

        c. Formulated a plan

        d. Carried out the plan

      2. Normal

        a. Stunned and bewildered

        b. Lacked awareness of emotions

        c. Had physiological manifestations

      3. Inappropriate

        a. Confused

        b. Paralyzed with anxiety

      c. Cried hysterically

      d. Screamed

II. Period of Recoil

    A. Stress

    B. Time

      1. Duration

      2. Perspective (immediate past)

    C. Psychological Phenomena

      1. Behavioral

      2. Cognitive

      3. Emotional

      4. Physical

III. Posttraumatic Period

    A. Stress (altered environment)

    B. Time

      1. Duration

      2. Perspective

        a. Past

        b. Present

        c. Future

    C. Psychological Phenomena

      1. Behavioral

      2. Cognitive

      3. Emotional

      4. Physical

    D. Rehabilitation

5.2   Outline the crisis from Exercise 2.1 using Sifneos's (1960) Components of an Emotional Crisis concepts. Following is an example based on the case study from Chapter 2.

    I. Hazardous event or situation (environmental or individual): husband's death (environmental)

    II. Vulnerability

      A. Behavioral: no behavioral phenomena

      B. Cognitive

        1. Distressing dreams

        2. Slowed thinking

      C. Emotional
         1. Emotional shock
         2. Guilt
         3. Numbness

  III. Precipitating factor or incident: funeral

  IV. Acute crisis state

      A. Behavioral
         1. Excessive activity
         ★ 2. Isolation

      B. Cognitive
         1. Distressing dreams
         2. Slowed thinking

      C. Emotional
         1. Emotional shock
         2. Guilt
         3. Numbness

      D. Biophysiological: sleep disturbance (insomnia)

Now complete the outline below based on your crisis.

    I. Hazardous event or situation (environmental or individual)

   II. Vulnerability (indicate how long vulnerability lasted)

      A. Behavioral
      B. Cognitive
      C. Emotional

  III. Precipitating factor or incident

  IV. Acute crisis state

      A. Behavioral
      B. Cognitive
      C. Emotional
      D. Biophysiological

5.3   Use Caplan's (1964) 4 Phases in Crisis Development to evaluate the crisis from Exercise 2.1. Following is an example of this assignment based on the case study from Chapter 2.

    I. Phase 1

      A. Problem (stressor): husband's death

    B. Interpretation/definition of problem: challenging; I believed that I would be successful in spite of my loss

    C. Tension/stress manifestations

        1. Behavioral: no behavioral phenomena

        2. Cognitive

            a. Distressing dreams

            b. Slowed thinking

        3. Emotional

            a. Emotional shock

            b. Guilt

            c. Numbness

        4. Physical: sleep disturbance (insomnia)

    D. Habitual problem solving/coping

        1. Reduce stressor: there was no way to reduce the stressor

        2. Reduce stressor consequences: I reduced the stressor consequences by

            a. Depending on parents to care for child

            b. Depending on brother- and sister-in-law to plan funeral

        3. Escape stressor: there was no way to escape stressor

II. Phase 2

    A. Problem (stressor) continues: husband is still dead

    B. Rise in tension/stress

        1. Behavioral: no behavioral phenomena

        2. Cognitive

            a. Distressing dreams

            b. Slowed thinking

        3. Emotional

            a. Emotional shock

            b. Guilt

            c. Numbness

        4. Physical: sleep disturbance (insomnia)

III. Phase 3

    A. Problem (stressor) continues: husband is still dead

    B. Tension/stress rises further

        1. Behavioral: no behavioral phenomena

  2. Cognitive

   a. Distressing dreams

   b. Slowed thinking

  3. Emotional

   a. Emotional shock

   b. Guilt

   c. Numbness

  4. Physical: sleep disturbance (insomnia)

 C. Tries to reduce tension/stress by using

  1. Customary defense mechanisms

   a. Denial: did not use denial

   b. Selective attention: used selective attention by not giving much attention to meal preparation

   c. Withdrawal: did not use withdrawal

   d. Other: did not use other defense mechanisms

  2. Novel/new resources: did not use novel/new resources

IV. Phase 4

 A. Problem (stressor) continues: husband is still dead

 B. Tension/stress rises resulting in major disorganization (crisis)

  1. Behavioral

   a. Excessive activity

   b. Isolation

  2. Cognitive

   a. Distressing dreams

   b. Slowed thinking

  3. Emotional

   a. Emotional shock

   b. Guilt

   c. Numbness

  4. Physical: sleep disturbance (insomnia)

Now complete the following outline based on your crisis.

 I. Phase 1

 A. Problem (stressor)

 B. Interpretation/definition of problem

    C. Tension/stress manifestations

      1. Behavioral

      2. Cognitive

      3. Emotional

      4. Physical

    D. Habitual problem solving/coping

      1. Reduce stressor

      2. Reduce stressor consequences

      3. Escape stressor

II. Phase 2

    A. Problem (stressor) continues

    B. Rise in tension/stress

      1. Behavioral

      2. Cognitive

      3. Emotional

      4. Physical

III. Phase 3

    A. Problem (stressor) continues

    B. Tension/stress rises further

      1. Behavioral

      2. Cognitive

      3. Emotional

      4. Physical

    C. Tries to reduce tension/stress by using

      1. Customary defense mechanisms

        a. Denial

        b. Selective attention

        c. Withdrawal

        d. Other

      2. Novel/new resources

IV. Phase 4

    A. Problem (stressor) continues

    B. Tension/stress rises, resulting in major disorganization (crisis)

    1. Behavioral

    2. Cognitive

    3. Emotional

    4. Physical

5.4   Use the Crisis Paradigm (Hoff, 1984, 1989, 1995, 2001) to describe the crisis from Exercise 2.1. If the origin is multifaceted, identify the primary origin. Also indicate whether the aids to positive resolution used were natural or formal aids. Following is an example of this assignment based on the case presented in Chapter 2.

I. Crisis origins (simple/one or complex/multiple): complex/multiple

   A. Situational (unanticipated; therefore can only prepare indirectly)

      1. Material (environmental): husband's death was not material origin

      2. Personal/physical (individual): husband's death was not personal/physical origin

      3. Interpersonal (social): husband's death was interpersonal origin (primary)

   B. Transitional (anticipated life passages): husband's death was normative transition to widowhood but out of time sequence

   C. Social/cultural

      1. Values: husband's death was not values origin

      2. Socialization: husband's death was not socialization origin

      3. Deviance

         a. Act of others (unanticipated): husband's death was not deviant act of others' origin

         b. Act of self: husband's death was not deviant act of self origin

      4. Conflict: husband's death was not conflict origin

II. Personal Crisis Manifestations

   A. Behavioral

      1. Excessive activity

      2. Isolation

   B. Cognitive

      1. Distressing dreams

      2. Slowed thinking

   C. Emotional

      1. Emotional shock

2. Guilt

3. Numbness

D. Physical: sleep disturbance (insomnia)

III. Aids to Positive Resolution (Natural and Formal Crisis Care)

A. Traumatic Situations

1. Grief work: used grief work (natural)

2. Material aid

a. Used material aid from parents in the form of meals (natural)

b. Used material aid from Veterans Administration in the form of tombstone (formal)

c. Used material aid from Social Security Administration in the form of dependent benefits (formal)

3. Social support: used social support in the form of widows groups (formal)

4. Crisis counseling: used crisis counseling in the form of a psychologist (formal)

B. Transitions: contemporary rites of passage—used rites of passage in the form of the wake and funeral (formal)

C. Cultural values/social structure: social change strategies: did not use social change strategies

IV. Resolution: positive

A. Positive Crisis Resolution: growth and development—became more interdependent and less independent

B. Negative Crisis Resolution: did not have negative resolution

1. Emotional/mental disturbance: did not have emotional/mental disturbance

2. Violence against others: was not violent against others

3. Self-destruction: was not self-destructive

4. Addiction: did not develop addiction

Now complete the following outline based on your crisis.

I. Crisis origins (simple/one or complex/multiple)

A. Situational (unanticipated; therefore can only prepare indirectly)

1. Material (environmental)

2. Personal/physical (individual)

3. Interpersonal (social)

B. Transitional (anticipated life passages)

C. Social/cultural

1. Values

2. Socialization

3. Deviance

    a. Act of others (unanticipated)

    b. Act of self

4. Conflict

II. Personal Crisis Manifestations

A. Behavioral

B. Cognitive

C. Emotional

D. Physical

III. Aids to Positive Resolution (Natural and Formal Crisis Care)

A. Traumatic Situations

1. Grief work

2. Material aid

3. Social support

4. Crisis counseling

B. Transitions: contemporary rites of passage

C. Cultural values/social structure: social change strategies

IV. Resolution

A. Positive Crisis Resolution: growth and development

B. Negative Crisis Resolution

1. Emotional/mental disturbance

2. Violence against others

3. Self-destruction

4. Addiction

References and Suggestions for Further Reading

Caplan, G. (1964). *Principles of preventive psychiatry.* New York: Basic Books.

Caplan, G. (1981). Mastery of stress: Psychosocial aspects. *The American Journal of Psychiatry, 138*(4), 413–420.

Golan, N. (1969). When is a client in crisis? *Social Casework, 50,* 389–394.

Hoff, L. A. (1984). *People in crisis: Understanding and helping* (2nd ed.). Menlo Park, CA: Addison Wesley.

Hoff, L. A. (1989). *People in crisis: Understanding and helping* (3rd ed.). Menlo Park, CA: Addison Wesley.

Hoff, L. A. (1995). *People in crisis: Understanding and helping* (4th ed.). San Francisco: Jossey-Bass.

Hoff, L. A. (2001). *People in crisis: Clinical and public health perspectives* (5th ed.). San Francisco: Jossey-Bass.

Sifneos, P. E. (1960). A concept of "emotional crisis." *Mental Hygiene, 44,* 169–179.

Tyhurst, J. S. (1951). Individual reactions to community disaster: The natural history of psychiatric phenomena. *American Journal of Psychiatry, 107,* 764–769.

Tyhurst, J. S. (1957a). Psychological and social aspects of civilian disaster. *Canadian Medical Association Journal, 76,* 385–393.

Tyhurst, J. S. (1957b). The role of transition states—including disasters—in mental illness. In *Symposium on preventive and social psychiatry.* Washington, DC: Walter Reed Army Institute of Research and the National Research Council.

CHAPTER 6

The Family Adjustment and Adaptation Response (FAAR) Model

The Family Adjustment and Adaptation Response (FAAR) Model developed by Hamilton McCubbin and Joan Patterson (1983) is an expansion of the Double ABCX Model in an attempt to describe the process by which families achieve precrisis adjustment and postcrisis adaptation based on longitudinal observations of families under stress from a husband/father held captive or unaccounted for in the Vietnam War. It is a multivariate model that addresses psychological (individual), intrafamilial, and social (community) variables identified from prior family stress studies. According to the model, families go through cycles of adjustment, crisis, and adaptation. "Families do not always progress in a direct, linear fashion through all the FAAR processes" (McCubbin & Patterson, 1983, p. 32). They may be stuck in one phase or return to an earlier phase. They may return to crisis from restructuring, consolidation, or maladaptation of the adaptation phase.

It appears that McCubbin and Patterson parted ways after 1983, with Patterson (1988, 1989, 1993, 2002) continuing the development of the FAAR Model and McCubbin going on to collaborate with his wife, Marilyn, to develop the Typology Model of Family Adjustment and Adaptation (McCubbin, Thompson, Pirner, & McCubbin, 1988; McCubbin & McCubbin, 1987) and the Resiliency Model of Family Stress, Adjustment, and Adaptation (McCubbin & McCubbin, 1991, 1993). See later chapters for the Typology and Resiliency models. Based on additional research, Patterson revised the FAAR Model in 1988, 1989, 1993, and 2002. She suggested that her revisions made "the model more salient for biopsychosocial research" (Patterson, 1988, p. 208).

Conceptual Framework of the Family Adjustment and Adaptation Response (FAAR) Model

Figure 6.1 illustrates the original FAAR Model (McCubbin & Patterson, 1983) since this early illustration is more detailed than later figures. The two main phases of the model include the adjustment phase and the adaptation phase separated by a crisis. Family adjustment and family adaptation are outcomes of a family's efforts to achieve balanced functioning and are on a continuum from good (bonadjustment and bonadaptation) to poor (maladjustment and maladaptation). The adjustment phase is a relatively stable period when the family meets demands with little change in the system. A crisis state occurs when the family cannot meet demands and becomes imbalanced or in disequilibrium. During the adaptation phase, the family tries to restore balance/homeostasis.

Adjustment Phase

The adjustment phase in the FAAR Model (McCubbin & Patterson, 1983) includes demands, resources, and resistance. Multiple arrows show the interrelationship among the variables. "During the adjustment phase, the patterns of family interaction, family roles, and rules of relationship have been established and guide day-to-day activity so that things are fairly predictable and members generally know what to expect from each other" (Patterson, 1988, p. 227). In this stable period, families always undergo minor changes but overtly or covertly resist major changes in the family.

Demands

Demands of *prior strains* (unresolved stressors), the *stressor (a),* and *hardships* from the stressor appear first in the model. Patterson (1988) said that there were three sources of demands: individual family members, the family unit, and the community. The variable of demands of hardships is redundant, as the definition of hardships is demands on resources. Patterson removed hardships from the FAAR Model in 1988. Later Patterson (2002) added *daily hassles* (minor disruptions of daily life) to the list of demands.

Existing Resources (b)

Existing resources (*b*) are used in the adjustment phase of the FAAR Model. Patterson (1988) said that just as there are three sources of demands,

Figure 6.1 The Family Adjustment and Adaptation Response (FAAR) Model

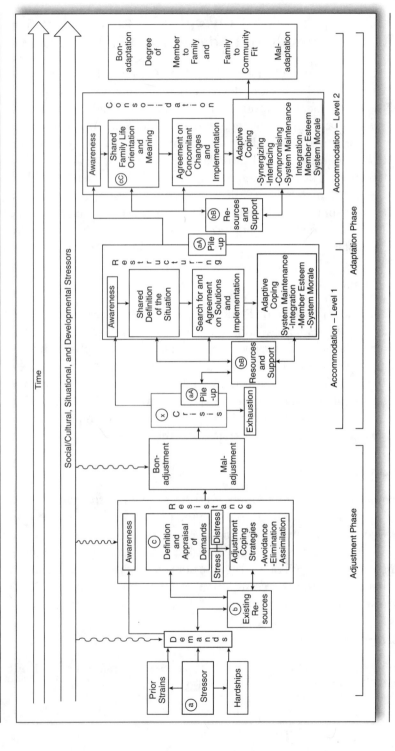

Source: McCubbin & Patterson (1983).

there are "three potential sources of resources: individual family members, the family unit, and the community" (p. 215). She added the concept of *capabilities* to the FAAR Model in 1988. She defined capabilities as resources and coping. See Chapter 2 for examples of resources.

Resistance

Resistance, according to McCubbin and Patterson (1983), refers to resistance to change. It includes awareness, definition and appraisal of demands with positive or negative stress, and adjustment coping strategies. *Awareness* refers to the family becoming aware of the demands of the prior strains, the stressor, the hardships, and daily hassles.

The *definition and appraisal of demands (c)* is analogous to *C* in the ABCX Formula. The definition may be positive or negative, leading to positive stress (eustress) or negative stress (distress). Figure 6.1 shows *stress or distress.* The use of the terms *eustress* and *distress* in the model might be more appropriate here.

In later versions of the FAAR Model, Patterson (1988, 1993, 2002) dropped stress and distress from the model. She also changed the term *definition* to *meanings* and expanded it to include definitions at three levels: Level 1 or situational, Level 2 or family identity (how members see themselves as a family unit)/global, and Level 3 or worldview (how members see their family in relation to systems outside the family). Patterson (2002) contends that these meanings shape the nature and extent of risk for crisis and the protective capacity of a family. The *Level 1* of meanings, *situational,* is arrived at individually and includes a primary and secondary appraisal. According to Patterson (1993), each individual family member makes a *primary appraisal* of the stressor and demands and a *secondary appraisal* of capabilities for managing demands. She found that families may *converge* in their appraisals and have a consensus or they may *diverge* and have a discrepancy in meanings. She suggested that consensus is not always necessary for a family to function well, but it is important when a coordinated response is necessary for effective functioning, as when deciding whether to take an asthmatic child to the hospital.

The *Level 2* of meanings has been called *family identity* (Patterson, 2002) and *global meanings* (Patterson, 1988). The term *family identity/ global meanings,* also called the family schema, refers to how the family members see themselves as a unit (Patterson, 2002) and how the family views the relationship of family members to each other and the relationship of the family to the community (Patterson, 1988). *Family schema,* based on Piaget's (1952) *cognitive schema,* an individual cognitive structure, describes a shared cognitive structure. Family schemas, although changeable, usually change only in response to crises.

In 1988, Patterson referred to global meanings as the degree of shared purpose (common family goals), collectivity (identity with family, community, and nation), framability (optimism with realism), relativism (setting limits and accepting less-than-perfect solutions), and shared control (control midway between personal control and fatalism/no control). In 2002, Patterson referred to family identity as family rules that are usually implicit about (1) definitions of external (who is in or out of the family) and internal boundaries (encouraging or discouraging family subsystems), (2) role assignments for accomplishing tasks (earning income, child care, meal preparation, household maintenance, etc.), and (3) rules for interaction. Implicit rules are rules that, although not talked about, family members follow. During crises, implicit rules may become explicit. Family members talk about explicit rules. Patterson (1993) referred to Boss's (1987, 1988) work on boundary ambiguity when discussing external family boundaries.

Labeling family schema as Level 2 contradicts Burr's (1989) characterization of levels of abstraction. According to Burr, rules are Level I, metarules (rules about rules) are Level II, and the family schema/paradigm is Level III. Refer to Chapter 2. Patterson (1993, 2002) used Sluzki's (1983) definitions of the three levels of abstraction in which Level 1 is process, Level 2 is structure, and Level 3 is worldview, in which case both Level 2, structure, and Level 3, worldview, are part of the family paradigm.

Level 3 of meanings, *worldview,* according to Patterson (1993), refers to individually held beliefs about existential issues (the purpose of life). The concern is whether there is a consensus among family members regarding these beliefs. An example of a worldview is seeing the world as benevolent or malevolent.

The *adjustment coping strategies* used in the adjustment phase are avoidance, elimination, and/or assimilation, terms borrowed from Piaget (1952). According to McCubbin and Patterson (1983), the changes that take place in the adjustment phase are Level I or first-order changes. Thus, we can say that the coping strategies of avoidance, elimination, and/or assimilation used in the adjustment phase are Level I coping strategies. *Avoidance* refers to efforts to deny or ignore the stressor and demands. An example of avoidance in the study by McCubbin and Patterson (1983) was families clinging "to maintaining their existing lifestyle and family structure as confirmation that nothing was different" (p. 21). These families made only minimal changes in family routines. *Elimination* is the effort to rid the family of demands by changing or removing the stressor or by altering the definition of the stressor. An example of elimination from the study by McCubbin and Patterson (1983) was families defining the situation as temporary. These families resisted making any substantial change in structure or function. *Assimilation* means efforts to accept demands into the structure and interaction patterns by using or reallocating resources or making minor changes in structure. Assimilation occurs when a family uses money saved for a down payment on a home to buy food when family income is reduced. Patterson used the term *resistance capabilities* to categorize coping and resources in her revision of the FAAR Model in 1988.

Bonadjustment to Maladjustment

Levels of adjustment from bonadjustment to maladjustment are the outcome of the adjustment phase. That is, the level of adjustment varies on a continuum. When the level of family adjustment is good (bonadjustment), the family is characterized by positive physical and mental health of members, optimal role functioning, and a family unit that accomplishes life cycle tasks (Patterson, 1988). The family deals with the new *demands* of *stressors* and *strains* by using its *resistance capabilities* of *resources* and *coping* to cope through continuous first-order (Level I) changes, such as avoidance (denying or ignoring the demand), elimination (getting rid of or redefining the demand), and assimilation (accepting the demand with minor changes in structure). If coping by using the adjustment processes of avoidance, elimination, and/or assimilation is insufficient to meet the demands to which families are exposed or if the family chooses to produce a structural change in the family unit as a way of promoting growth, the outcome is poor (maladjustment), and the family enters a state of crisis.

Crisis

When the outcome of the adjustment phase is *maladjustment,* the family goes into a state of crisis. According to Patterson (1988), crises occur when there is a demand–capability imbalance (when there are not enough resources and coping strategies to meet the demands of the stressor). See Chapter 2 for discussion of family crisis manifestations.

Adaptation Phase

The adaptation phase consists of two levels—Accommodation Level 1 and Accommodation Level 2. Sometimes a family never does successfully adapt and moves to exhaustion.

Exhaustion

Exhaustion refers to the crisis outcome when the family is unable or chooses not to resolve the crisis through structural changes especially if family resources are depleted because members had few to begin with or were unable to acquire or activate additional ones. Families may go directly from crisis to exhaustion, but families are apt to move toward exhaustion if they have repeated adaptation phases several times and have been unsuccessful at restructuring and consolidation. The illustration of the FAAR Model does not clearly indicate these alternative possibilities (see Figure 6.1). The family ending often happens with exhaustion. McCubbin and Patterson (1983) suggested "that extended lack of attention to system maintenance may be a major contributor to family exhaustion" (p. 32). If the family does not end, it begins the process of structural change, and the adaptation phase begins either for the first time or again.

Accommodation Level 1

Accommodation Level 1 of the adaptation phase consists of the *aA* factor of pileup, the *bB* factor of resources and support, and restructuring, the first stage of adaptation. Restructuring consists of awareness, shared definition, search for and agreement on solutions and implementation of them, and the adaptive coping of system maintenance. The adaptation phase of the FAAR Model is analogous to recovery in the Truncated Roller Coaster Profile of Adjustment (Hill, 1949).

Pileup (aA) of strains, stressors, and daily hassles is experienced at this point. Pileup in the FAAR Model is equivalent to pileup in the Double ABCX Model. Pileup is defined in Chapter 2 of this book.

Resources and support (bB) refer to resources used by the family to buffer the impact of pileup. The family uses resources to resolve problems. Resources and support (*bB*) in the FAAR Model are equivalent to existing and new resources in the Double ABCX Model. See Chapter 2 of this book for a detailed discussion of resources.

Restructuring. In Accommodation Level 1 of the adaptation phase, one or more family members reach *awareness* that the existing family structure and interaction patterns are not adequate to meet demands of the pileup. It is not necessary that all members become aware. Then efforts to come up with a *shared definition of the situation (cC),* which is not always possible, follow awareness. A *search for and agreement on solutions and implementation* of those solutions follow. These solutions involve Level II or second-order changes such as changes in metarules and/or changes in interaction/behavior patterns (structural changes). A family defining the problem as not enough income and agreeing on the solution of the stay-at-home mom getting a job illustrates this process. The *adaptive coping* of *system maintenance,* designed for maintaining *family integration, member esteem,* and *system morale,* occurs as well. System maintenance keeps the family functioning as a unit. Continuing to show affection illustrates efforts to maintain member esteem. During restructuring, part or all of the family could either not decide on major structural change or not implement the change. In either case, the family may return to a crisis state rather than moving to consolidation of Accommodation Level 2.

Accommodation Level 2

Accommodation Level 2 consists of the *aA* factor of pileup, the *bB* factor of resources and support, and consolidation. *Pileup (aA)* of demands, strains, stressors, and daily hassles may be reduced due to the restructuring from Accommodation Level 1. *Resources and social support (bB)* used at this point may be different from those used previously.

According to McCubbin and Patterson (1983), once a family makes a second-order change, the family begins the second level of accommodation consisting of consolidation. In this phase, the family makes additional changes to support and complement the new behavior patterns from Accommodation Level 1.

Consolidation. Consolidation consists of awareness that the family has made change that does not fit prior structure and patterns, the *cC* factor of a shared family life orientation and meaning, agreement on concomitant changes and implementation of the changes, and adaptive coping strategies. At Accommodation Level 2, it is important that the family share awareness, unlike at Level 1 when shared awareness is not necessary. The shared awareness supports shared meaning, which supports agreement on concomitant (accompanying) changes and their implementation. A family sharing the belief that an absent father would want the family to move on facilitates changes in the family (McCubbin & Patterson, 1983).

The adaptive coping strategies of synergizing, interfacing, compromising, and system maintenance facilitate consolidation efforts. The family makes second-order efforts to restore balance at the two levels of intrafamily (through synergizing) and community (through interfacing). *Synergizing* is coordinating and pulling together perceptions, needs, and resources (lifestyle). These efforts are intrafamily (internal to the family). The family tries to restore balance through second-order change (structural change in roles, rules, interaction patterns, and/or meanings) and possibly third-order change (changes in family schemas). Intrafamily second-order efforts include "(1) altering or expanding their definitions and meanings to take into account their changed circumstances; (2) reducing the pileup of demands; (3) developing and acquiring new resources (called adaptive resources); and/or (4) developing new coping strategies for dealing with demands" (Patterson, 1988, p. 229).

Interfacing refers to relating to the community through new rules and transactions. An example of interfacing is moving. *Compromising* refers to supporting less-than-perfect solutions. *System maintenance* was discussed under Accommodation Level 1.

If the family does not care for the changes required because of restructuring, it may return to the restructuring phase, or if the family does not make the changes necessary to achieve congruence with the new family patterns from restructuring, the family may return to a crisis state. When a stay-at-home mother enters the workforce during restructuring but the family refuses to share household chores (refuses to consolidate), the family may return to restructuring in which the mother may choose to work part-time, or she may not continue bringing in the extra income, leading the family back into a crisis state (McCubbin & Patterson, 1983).

Bonadaptation or Maladaptation

Determined by the degree of balance of demands and capabilities at the member-to-family and the family-to-community level, the outcome of the adaptation phase is family adaptation on a continuum from *bonadaptation to maladaptation*. In maladaptation there may be an imbalance of demands to capabilities or a balance at a price to a family member or to the family unit. When a family balances demands and capabilities at the expense of a family member, that family member may experience deterioration in health or development. He or she becomes the scapegoat or family symptom carrier (Patterson, 1988). When a family balances demands and capabilities at the expense of the family unit, the unit deteriorates in integrity, autonomy, or ability to accomplish life cycle tasks. Even though a family makes changes during consolidation, the outcome may be on the maladaptation end of the continuum, leaving the family vulnerable to another crisis (McCubbin & Patterson, 1983). The family may return to restructuring after maladaptation.

According to Patterson (1988), *bonadaptation* occurs when there is minimal discrepancy between demands and capabilities at two levels of interaction: individual-to-family and family-to-individual. A family with bonadaptation has positive physical and mental health, promotion of member development, optimal role functioning, accomplishment of life cycle tasks, and family integrity and sense of control.

Critique of the Family Adjustment and Adaptation Response (FAAR) Model

The FAAR Model (McCubbin & Patterson, 1983) covers both pre- and postcrisis periods. In the adjustment phase of the original model, a demand of hardships appears redundant, as hardships are demands on resources. Patterson (1988) later removed hardships from this part of the model. The figure of the FAAR Model (McCubbin & Patterson, 1983) (Figure 6.1) shows stress and distress. The use of the terms *eustress* and *distress* would have been more appropriate here. Instead the continuum was dropped from later models. Labeling family schema (Patterson, 1988, 1989, 1993, 2002) as Level 2 contradicts Burr's (1989) characterization of levels of abstraction, in which the family schema/paradigm is Level III, metarules (rules about rules) are Level II, and rules are Level I. In addition, according to McCubbin and Patterson (1983), families go through three stages of adaptation, which they called resistance, restructuring, and consolidation. This is a little confusing as resistance takes place during the adjustment phase and restructuring and consolidation take place during the adaptation phase.

Summary of the Family Adjustment and Adaptation Response (FAAR) Model

According to the Family Adjustment and Adaptation Response (FAAR) Model (McCubbin & Patterson, 1983), families go through cycles of adjustment, crisis, and adaptation. These phases cover the pre- and postcrisis periods, eliminating limitations of some earlier models. Patterson revised the FAAR Model in 1988 to include situational and global meanings. In 2002, she changed global meanings to family identity and added worldview meanings. She also added the component of daily hassles at that time.

EXERCISE

6.1   Outline the crisis from Exercise 2.1 using the FAAR Model concepts. Following is an example of the assignment based on the case study presented in Chapter 2.

I.   Adjustment phase (ABCX)

A. Demands

1. Prior strains (unresolved stressors)

   a. Individual: new job

      1) Demanded time for class preparation
      2) Demanded energy for class preparation

   b. Family: illness of husband

      1) Demanded time to care for husband
      2) Demanded energy to care for husband
      3) Demanded money to pay medical bills

   c. Community: none

2. Stressor (a)

   a. Individual: not an individual stressor
   b. Family: husband's death

      1) Demands on time to attend wake and funeral
      2) Demands on energy to grieve
      3) Demands on space to accommodate guests for funeral

   c. Community: not a community stressor

3. Hardships (removed by Patterson, 1988)

   a. Individual

      1) Demands on time to attend wake and funeral
      2) Demands on energy to grieve
      3) Demands on space to accommodate guests for funeral

   b. Family: no hardships for family
   c. Community: no hardships for community

4. Daily hassles (added by Patterson, 2002)

   a. Individual

      1) Single parenting
      2) Getting to work
      3) Taking care of house

   b. Family: no family hassles
   c. Community: no community hassles

B. Existing resources (*b*; called resistance capabilities along with coping by Patterson, 1988)

   1. Individual: did not use individual resources

   2. Family: did not use family recourses

3. Community

   a. Persons

      1) Coworkers

      2) Friends

      3) Relatives

   b. Institutions: mesoenvironmental—funeral home

C. Resistance

   1. Awareness: I was aware that my husband had died and that things would never be the same as before his death

   2. Definition and appraisal/meaning (c) (Patterson, 1988) of demands

      a. Level 1/situational (individual) (Patterson, 1988) (family convergence/consensus or divergence/discrepancy)

         1) Primary appraisal of stressor and demands: challenging; I believed that I would be successful in spite of my loss

         2) Secondary appraisal of capabilities for managing demands: I believed that I had the capabilities to manage the demands

      b. Level 2/family identity (Patterson, 2002)/global meanings (Patterson, 1988)

         1) Definitions of boundaries

            a) External (ambiguity) (who is in and who is out of the family system): There was not ambiguity as to who was in or out of the family; my son and I were the only members of my family of procreation

            b) Internal (encouraging or discouraging family subsystems): There were no subsystems since there was only my child and I

         2) Role assignments for accomplishing tasks (segregated or egalitarian): egalitarian

         3) Rules for interactional behavior

      c. Level 3/worldview (Patterson, 1993) (family convergence/consensus or divergence/discrepancy): family convergence/consensus

   3. Stress-distress: I experienced distress at the death of my husband

   4. Adjustment coping strategies (called resistance capabilities along with resources by Patterson, 1988) (Level I, first-order changes)

      a. Avoidance: avoidance was not used

      b. Elimination: elimination was not used

      c. Assimilation: I assimilated the death of my husband into my family life

D. Bonadjustment-Maladjustment: maladjustment

   1. Positive physical and mental health: I had positive mental health

2. Optimal role functioning: I was not functioning optimally in my roles of worker, as I missed work, and of mother, as I depended on my parents to care for my child

3. Accomplishment of life cycle tasks: I was not accomplishing the life cycle tasks associated with motherhood

II. Crisis (x)

A. Amount of consciousness and acceptance by each member of his or her and others' family roles (better than average, average, below average): below average; my parents took care of my son for a period of time—a few days, I think—so I was not performing my role as parent

B. Extent to which family members worked toward family and individual good (better than average, average, below average): below average; I was not taking care of my son, and self-care was based on what others told me to do

C. How much family members found satisfaction with family unit (better than average, average, below average): below average; the family unit had been redefined, and ways to find satisfaction would need to be redefined as well

D. Whether the family had a sense of direction and was moving in that direction (better than average, average, below average): below average; family goals would need to be redefined by me as a single parent

III. Adaptation phase (Double ABCX)

A. Exhaustion: did not experience exhaustion

B. Accommodation—Level 1

1. Pileup (aA; demands of)

a. Strains

1) Individual: new job demanded time and energy for class preparation
2) Family: illness of husband; the demands of the strain of my husband's illness actually were removed with his death
3) Community: none

b. Stressor

1) Individual: not an individual stressor
2) Family: husband's death

a) Demands on time to attend wake and funeral
b) Demands on energy to grieve
c) Demands on space to accommodate guests for funeral

3) Community: not a community stressor

c. Daily hassles

1) Individual

a) Single parenting

b) Getting to work

c) Taking care of house

2) Family: no family hassles

3) Community: no community hassles

2. Resources and support (bB; capabilities)

a. Existing resources (b)

1) Psychological/individual: did not use psychological/individual resources

2) Intrafamilial/family: did not use intrafamily resources

3) Social/community

a) Persons

i. Coworkers

ii. Friends

iii. Relatives

a) Institutions: mesoenvironmental—funeral home

b. New resources (B)

1) Psychological/individual: knowledge

2) Intrafamilial/family: no new intrafamilial resources

3) Social/community

a) Groups—self-help

b) Institutions

1) Mesoenvironmental—churches

2) Macroenvironmental—government policies

3. Restructuring

a. Awareness: awareness that existing family structure and interaction patterns were not adequate to meet demands of pileup

b. Shared definition of the situation (cC): challenging but not insurmountable since I had resources

c. Search for and agreement on solutions and implementation

1) Role changes: no longer had role of caretaker

2) Rule changes: I became the only rule maker in the family

3) Goal changes: goals did not change

4) Interaction changes: interaction with child increased as no longer had to care for husband

d. Adaptive coping/system maintenance (capabilities)

        1) Integration: maintained integration through parental sacrifice to attain family objectives, high participation in joint activities, and strong affectional ties between mother and child.

        2) Member esteem: no activities to maintain member esteem

        3) System morale: no activities to maintain system morale

  4. Pileup (aA)

    a. Strains

        1) Individual: new job demanded time and energy for class preparation

        2) Family: illness of husband; the demands of the strain of my husband's illness actually were removed with his death

        3) Community: none

    b. Stressor

        1) Individual: not an individual stressor

        2) Family: husband's death demanded energy to grieve

        3) Community: not a community stressor

    c. Daily hassles

        1) Individual

          a) Single parenting

          b) Getting to work

          c) Taking care of house

        2) Family: no family hassles

        3) Community: no community hassles

C. Accommodation—Level 2

  1. Resources and support (bB; capabilities)

    a. Existing resources (b)

        1) Psychological/individual: did not use psychological/individual resources

        2) Intrafamilial/family: did not use intrafamily resources

        3) Social/community

          a) Persons

            i. Coworkers

            ii. Friends

            iii. Relatives

          b) Institutions: mesoenvironmental—funeral home

    b. New resources (B)

        1) Psychological/individual: knowledge

        2) Intrafamilial/family: no new intrafamilial resources

        3) Social/community

           a) Groups—self-help

           b) Institutions

               i. Mesoenvironmental—churches

               ii. Macroenvironmental—government policies

2. Consolidation

    a. Awareness: I was aware that I now needed to make all decisions and rules on my own without my husband

    b. Shared family life orientation and meaning (cC): since I was the only adult in the family, there was no one with which to share meaning

    c. Agreement on concomitant changes and implementation: since I was the only adult in the family, there was no one with which to agree on changes and implementations

    d. Adaptive coping (capabilities)

        1) Synergizing (coordinating and pulling together perceptions, needs, and resources): did not synergize

        2) Interfacing (relating to community through new rules and transactions): interfaced with community in that began receiving Social Security benefits for child

        3) Compromising (supporting less-than-perfect solutions): compromised in that supported solution of being a single parent as was needed at the time

        4) System maintenance

           a) Integration: maintained integration through parental sacrifice to attain family objectives, high participation in joint activities, and strong affectional ties between mother and child

           b) Member esteem: no activities to maintain member esteem

           c) System morale: no activities to maintain system morale

D. Bonadaptation or maladaptation (continuum of balance of demands and capabilities): bonadpaptation

    1. Bonadaptation (balance of demands and capabilities) (Patterson, 1988)

        a. Positive physical and mental health: neither my son nor I was physically or mentally ill

        b. Promotion of member development: my son's development was promoted, evidenced by normal development patterns

        c. Optimal role functioning: I was functioning in my roles of mother and worker

      d. Accomplishment of life cycle tasks: the tasks of the family life cycle stage of child rearing were being accomplished

      e. Family integrity: the family's integrity was maintained as the family remained intact

      f. Sense of control: I maintained a sense of control over things within the realm of my control such as where we lived

  2. Maladaptation (Patterson, 1988)

      a. Imbalanced (demands outweigh capabilities): demands did not outweigh capabilities

        1) Member-to-family: demands did not outweigh capabilities

        2) Family-to-community: demands did not outweigh capabilities

      b. Balanced at both levels, but at a price

        1) Deterioration of member health and/or development (scapegoat/symptom carrier): there was no deterioration of member health or development

        2) Deterioration of family unit

          a) Integrity: there was no deterioration of family integrity

          b) Autonomy: there was no deterioration of autonomy

          c) Ability to accomplish life cycle tasks: there was no deterioration in ability to accomplish life cycle tasks

Now complete the following outline based on your crisis.

  I. Adjustment phase (ABCX)

    A. Demands

      1. Prior strains (unresolved stressors)

        a. Individual

        b. Family

        c. Community

      2. Stressor (a)

        a. Individual

        b. Family

        c. Community

      3. Hardships (removed by Patterson, 1988)

        a. Individual

        b. Family

        c. Community

      4. Daily hassles (added by Patterson, 2002)

   a. Individual
   b. Family
   c. Community

B. Existing resources (b; called resistance capabilities along with coping by Patterson, 1988)

   1. Individual
   2. Family
   3. Community

C. Resistance

   1. Awareness
   2. Definition and appraisal/meaning (c) (Patterson, 1988) of demands
      a. Level 1/situational (individual) (Patterson, 1988) (family convergence/consensus or divergence/discrepancy)

         1) Primary appraisal of stressor and demands
         2) Secondary appraisal of capabilities for managing demands

      b. Level 2/family identity (Patterson, 2002)/global meanings (Patterson, 1988)

         1) Definitions of boundaries

            a) External (ambiguity) (who is in and who is out of the family system)
            b) Internal (encouraging or discouraging family subsystems)

         2) Role assignments for accomplishing tasks (segregated or egalitarian)
         3) Rules for interactional behavior

      c. Level 3/worldview (Patterson, 1993) (family convergence/consensus or divergence/discrepancy)

   3. Stress-distress
   4. Adjustment coping strategies (called resistance capabilities along with resources by Patterson, 1988) (Level I, first-order changes)

      a. Avoidance
      b. Elimination
      c. Assimilation

D. Bonadjustment-Maladjustment

   1. Positive physical and mental health
   2. Optimal role functioning
   3. Accomplishment of life cycle tasks

II. Crisis (x)

III. Adaptation phase (Double ABCX)

A. Exhaustion

   B. Accommodation—Level 1

      1. Pileup (aA; demands of)

         a. Strains

         b. Stressors

         c. Daily hassles

      2. Resources and support (bB; capabilities)

         a. Personal

         b. Family

         c. Community

      3. Restructuring

         a. Awareness

         b. Shared definition of the situation (cC)

         c. Search for and agreement on solutions and implementation

            1) Role changes

            2) Rule changes

            3) Goal changes

            4) Interaction changes

         d. Adaptive coping/system maintenance (capabilities)

            1) Integration

            2) Member esteem

            3) System morale

      4. Pileup (aA)

   C. Accommodation—Level 2

      1. Resources and support (bB; capabilities)

         a. Personal

         b. Family

         c. Community

      2. Consolidation

         a. Awareness

         b. Shared family life orientation and meaning (cC)

         c. Agreement on concomitant changes and implementation

         d. Adaptive coping (capabilities)

            1) Synergizing (coordinating and pulling together perceptions, needs, and resources)

            2) Interfacing (relating to community through new rules and transactions)

            3) Compromising (supporting less-than-perfect solutions)

4) System maintenance

   a) Integration

   b) Member esteem

   c) System morale

D. Bonadaptation or maladaptation (continuum of balance of demands and capabilities)

   1. Bonadaptation (balance of demands and capabilities) (Patterson, 1988)

     a. Positive physical and mental health

     b. Promotion of member development

     c. Optimal role functioning

     d. Accomplishment of life cycle tasks

     e. Family integrity

     f. Sense of control

   2. Maladaptation (Patterson, 1988)

     a. Imbalanced (demands outweigh capabilities)

       1) Member-to-family

       2) Family-to-community

     b. Balanced at both levels, but at a price

       1) Deterioration of member health and/or development (scapegoat/symptom carrier)

       2) Deterioration of family unit

         a) Integrity

         b) Autonomy

         c) Ability to accomplish life cycle tasks

References and Suggestions for Further Reading

Boss, P. (1987). Family stress. In M. Sussman & S. Steinmetz (Eds.), *Handbook of marriage and the family* (pp. 695–723). New York: Plenum Press.

Boss, P. (1988). *Family stress management.* Newbury Park, CA: Sage.

Burr, R. G. (1989). *Reframing family stress theory: From the ABC-X Model to a Family Ecosystemic Model.* Unpublished master's thesis, Brigham Young University, Provo, UT.

Hill, R. (1949). *Families under stress.* New York: Harper & Brothers.

McCubbin, H. I., & McCubbin, M. A. (1987). Family stress theory and assessment: The Resiliency Model of Family Stress, Adjustment, and Adaptation. In H. I. McCubbin & A. I. Thompson (Eds.), *Family assessment inventories for research and practice* (pp. 2–32). Madison: University of Wisconsin.

McCubbin, H. I., & Patterson, J. M. (1983). The family stress process: The Double ABCX Model of family adjustment and adaptation. In H. I. McCubbin, M. Sussman, & J. M. Patterson (Eds.), *Social stress and the family: Advances and developments in family stress theory and research* (pp. 7–37). New York: Haworth.

McCubbin, H. I., Thompson, A. I., Pirner, P. A., & McCubbin, M. A. (1988). *Family types and strengths.* Edina, MN: Burgess International Group.

McCubbin, M. A., & McCubbin, H. I. (1987). Family stress theory and assessment: The T-Double ABCX Model of family adjustment and adaptation. In H. I. McCubbin & A. Thompson (Eds.), *Family assessment inventories for research and practice* (pp. 3–32). Madison: University of Wisconsin.

McCubbin, M. A., & McCubbin, H. I. (1991). Family stress theory and assessment: The Resiliency Model of Family Stress Adjustment and Adaptation. In H. I. McCubbin & A. Thompson (Eds.), *Family assessment inventories for research and practice* (pp. 3–31). Madison: University of Wisconsin.

McCubbin, M. A., & McCubbin, H. I. (1993). Families coping with illness: The Resiliency Model of Family Stress, Adjustment, and Adaptation. In C. Danielson, B. Hamel-Bissell, & P. Winstead-Fry (Eds.), *Families, health & illness: Perspectives on coping and intervention* (pp. 21–764). St. Louis, MO: Mosby.

Patterson, J. M. (1988). Families experiencing stress: I. The Family Adjustment and Response Model, II. Applying the FAAR Model to health-related issues for intervention and research. *Family Systems Medicine, 6*(2), 202–237.

Patterson, J. M. (1989). A family stress model: The Family Adjustment and Adaptation Response. In C. Ramsey (Ed.), *The science of family medicine* (pp. 95–117). New York: Guilford Press.

Patterson, J. M. (1993). The role of family meanings in adaptation to chronic illness and disability. In J. M. Patterson, A. P. Turnbull, S. K. Behr, D. L. Murphy, & J. G. Marquis (Eds.), *Cognitive coping, families, and disability* (pp. 221–238). Baltimore: Brookes.

Patterson, J. M. (2002). Integrating family resilience and family stress theory. *Journal of Marriage and Family, 64,* 349–360.

Piaget, J. (1952). *The origins of intelligence in children.* New York: International University Press.

Reiss, D. (1981). *The family's construction of reality.* Cambridge, MA: Harvard University Press.

Sluzki, C. E. (1983). Process, structure and world views: Toward an integrated view of systemic models in family therapy. *Family Process, 22,* 469–476.

CHAPTER 7

The Typology Model of Family Adjustment and Adaptation

Expanding on the Double ABCX Model of Family Adjustment (McCubbin & Patterson, 1982, 1983a, 1983b), Marilyn McCubbin and her husband Hamilton McCubbin (1987) developed the Typology Model of Family Adjustment and Adaptation to add the component of family types. It emphasizes "the importance of the family's established patterns of functioning, referred to as Typologies, as buffers against family dysfunction and as targets for change as the family adapts to a crisis" (McCubbin, McCubbin, Thompson, & Thompson, 1995, p. 5) and thus can serve as a guide for intervention as well as research. The Typology Model appears to combine the components of the Double ABCX Model (McCubbin & Patterson, 1982, 1983a, 1983b) with the two phases of adjustment and adaptation from the FAAR Model (McCubbin & Patterson, 1983b).

Conceptual Framework of the Typology Model of Family Adjustment and Adaptation

Adjustment Phase

The adjustment phase consists of the A, B, C, PSC, V, and T factors interacting with each other to produce the outcome of the X factor. See Figures 7.1 and 7.2. Adjustment refers to a short-term response that is adequate to manage most demands.

Figure 7.1 Outline of Adjustment Phase of Typology Model

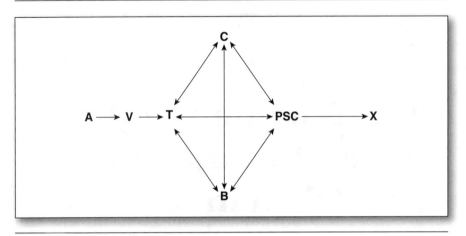

Source: McCubbin, Thompson, Pirner, & McCubbin (1988).

The level of family adjustment and/or the family's transition into a crisis situation (X) (and into the adaptation phase or exhaustion) in response to a stressor event or transition is determined by—**A** (the stressor event or transition and its level of severity)—interacting with the **V** (the family's vulnerability determined, in part, by the concurrent pileup of **demands**— stressors, transitions, and strains and by the family's life cycle stage), interacting with **T** (the family's typology—regenerative, resilient, rhythmic, balanced, etc.), interacting with **B** (the family's resistance resources)—interacting with **C** (the appraisal the family makes of the event) and—interacting with **PSC** (the family's problem solving and coping responses to the family situation, including the demands created by the stressor as well as the stressor event/transition itself). (McCubbin, Thompson, Pirner, & McCubbin, 1988, pp. 5–6)

A *Factor*

In the Typology Model, the *A* factor refers to the stressor event or transition on the detailed figure, Figure 7.2. The level of severity of the stressor helps determine the amount of stress experienced by the family. The level of severity is determined by the degree to which the stressor threatens or disrupts the family's stability or places demands on the family's resources.

Figure 7.2 Components of Adjustment Phase of Typology Model

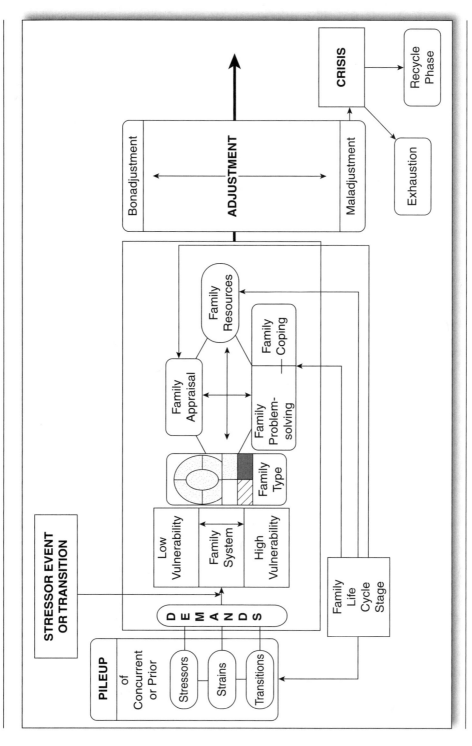

Source: McCubbin, Thompson, Pirner, & McCubbin (1988).

V *Factor*

The *V* factor equals family system vulnerability. It refers to the "interpersonal and organizational condition of family" (McCubbin et al., 1988, p. 6). Family system vulnerability includes *pileup of concurrent or prior stressors, strains, and transitions;* their *demands;* and the *family life cycle stage* and its demands.

T *Factor*

The *T* factor, labeled *family type* in the detailed figure (7.2), and the new contribution of the Typology Model, consists of characteristics of the family system and explains "how it typically appraises, operates, and/or behaves" (McCubbin et al., 1988, p. 6). Based on the Circumplex Model (Olson & McCubbin, 1982), an alternative family typology was developed, including the family types of regenerative, resilient, rhythmic, and traditionalistic (McCubbin & McCubbin, 1987; McCubbin et al., 1988). This alternative typology is used in this model. Regenerative, resilient, rhythmic, and traditionalistic family types are each determined by two levels (high and low) of two dimensions (McCubbin et al., 1988). See Figure 7.3.

The Typology of Regenerative Families consists of the two dimensions of family of *family hardiness* (sense of control and meaningfulness in life, involvement in activities, commitment to learn and explore new experiences) and *family coherence* (emphasis on acceptance, loyalty, pride, faith, trust, respect, caring, and shared values). The four types of family systems based on the regenerative typology are *vulnerable* (low coherence and hardiness), *durable* (high coherence and low hardiness), *secure* (low coherence and high hardiness), and *regenerative* (high coherence and high hardiness). The authors hypothesized that, in crises, regenerative families would experience more positive family adjustment than durable, secure, and vulnerable families.

The Typology of Resilient Families consists of the two dimensions of *family bonding* (open to discussion, feeling close, desirous of connection, doing things together) and *family flexibility* (open communication, compromise, willingness to shift responsibilities, and participation in decision making). The four types of family systems based on the regenerative typology are *fragile* (low flexibility and bonding), *pliant* (high flexibility and low bonding), *bonded* (low flexibility and high bonding), and *resilient* (high flexibility and high bonding). The authors hypothesized that, in crises, resilient families would experience more positive family adjustment than fragile, pliant, and bonded families.

Figure 7.3 Family Types

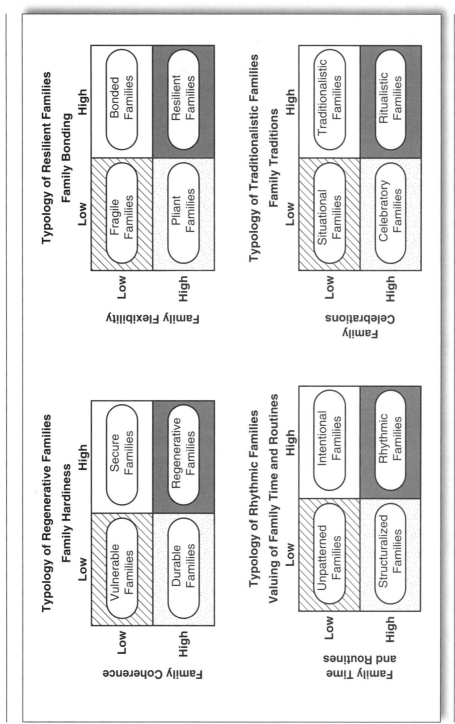

Source: McCubbin, Thompson, Pirner, & McCubbin (1988).

The Typology of Rhythmic Families consists of the dimensions of *time and routines* and *valuing*. Routines promote parent–child, husband–wife, family unit, and family–relative togetherness. Valuing refers to the degree of importance of family time and routines. The four types of family systems based on the rhythmic typology are *unpatterned* (low family time and routines and low valuing), *structuralized* (high family time and routines and low valuing), *intentional* (low family time and routines and high valuing), and *rhythmic* (high family time and routines and high valuing). The authors hypothesized that, in crises, rhythmic families would experience more positive family adjustment than structuralized, intentional, and unpatterned families.

The Typology of Traditionalistic Families consists of the dimensions of celebrations (spouse's birthday, special occasions, and major holidays) and traditions (holiday decorating, special experiences around changes, special rules around religious occasions, and which members participate in special events). The four types of family systems based on the traditionalistic typology are *situational* (low celebrations and traditions), *celebratory* (high celebrations and low traditions), *traditionalistic* (low celebrations and high traditions), and *ritualistic* (high celebrations and traditions). The authors hypothesized that, in crises, traditionalistic families would experience more positive family adjustment than celebratory, ritualistic, and situational families.

B *Factor*

In the detailed model of family typology, the *B* factor appears as *family resources*. The authors of the model call these adjustment or resistance resources because they can help families adjust to stressors and thus resist crises. They say that family resistance resources include family strengths, rituals that "capture and perpetuate the family's way of dealing with the outside world" (McCubbin et al., 1988, pp. 10–11), and routines that "act as guidelines for how things should be done and enhance the family's conception of themselves and their social world" (p. 11).

C *Factor*

The *C* factor in the detailed figure (7.2) of the Typology Model appears as *family appraisal* (of seriousness of stressor, its hardships, and effect on family). The *C* factor is analogous to *C* in the ABCX Formula (Hill, 1958) and in the Double ABCX Model (McCubbin & Patterson, 1982, 1983a, 1983b).

PSC *Factor*

The *PSC* factor in the detailed figure (7.2) of the Typology Model of Family Adjustment and Adaptation appears as problem solving and coping, which is the family's management of the stressful situation. The authors define family problem solving as the family's skills in defining the stressor as manageable, identifying alternative courses of action, and initiating steps to resolve the discrete issues. In their research, the authors found that coping skills used in the adjustment phase were *avoidance* (efforts to deny or ignore the stressor and demands), *elimination* (efforts to rid self of demands by changing or removing stressor, or altering the definition), and *assimilation* (efforts to accept demands created by stressor by making minor changes in family). These skills are analogous to the adjustment/resistance coping strategies of the FAAR Model (McCubbin & Patterson, 1983). In the FAAR Model, family problem solving refers to the skill of using a decision-making process to determine which coping strategies to use, while family coping refers to skills used to reduce distress.

X *Factor*

The *X* factor appears as *maladjustment* and *crisis* in the detailed figure (7.2). When family coping is insufficient to meet demands, the family becomes maladjusted. This situation is likely to occur when the nature of the stressor involves structural change in the family; the nature, number, and duration of demands deplete resources; the number and persistence of strains tax resources; and/or the family seizes opportunity to produce change by allowing or facilitating demand–capability imbalance.

According to the authors, disorganization and demand for change in family roles, rules, boundaries, and/or behavior patterns characterize a crisis. Some stressors do not lead to crisis. In these situations, the family has a positive outcome involving minor adjustments/changes in the family. Family members experience bonadjustment rather than maladjustment and the resulting state of crisis.

Family Adaptation Phase

The adaptation phase consists of the *AA, BB, BBB, CC, CCC, PSC, R, T, X,* and *XX* factors (see Figure 7.4).

Figure 7.4   Outline of Adaptation Phase of Typology Model

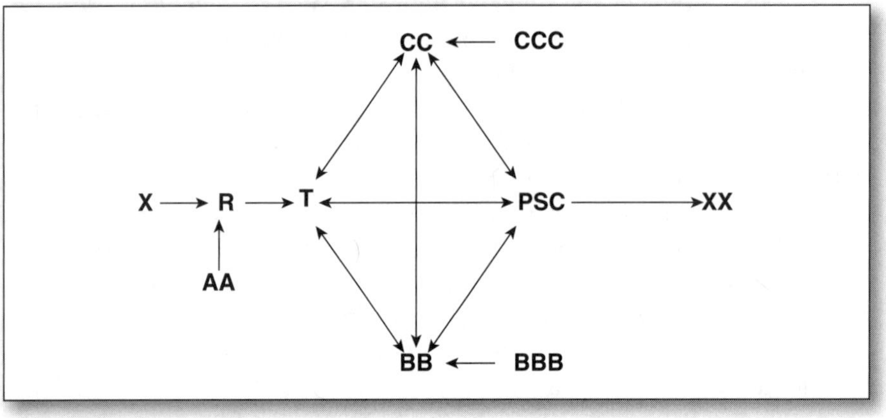

Source: McCubbin, Thompson, Pirner, & McCubbin (1988).

The level of family adaptation (XX) and/or the family's transition back into a crisis situation (or exhaustion) in response to a crisis situation is determined by—**AA** the pile-up of demands on or in the family system created by the crisis situation, Life Cycle changes and unresolved strains—interacting with the **R** the family's level of regenerativity determined in part by the concurrent pile-up of demands—stressors, transitions, and strains—interacting with **T** the family's typology—(resilient, rhythmic, balanced etc.),—interacting with **BB** the family's strengths (the family's adaptive strengths, capabilities and resources)—interacting with **CC** the family's appraisal of the situation (the meaning the family attaches to the total situation) and **CCC** the family's schema (i.e. world view and sense of coherence which shapes the family's situational appraisal and meaning)—interacting with **BBB** the support from friends and the community (social support), interacting with **PSC** the family's problem solving and coping responses to the total family situation. (McCubbin et al., 1988, p. 15)

X *Factor*

In Figure 7.5, the *X* factor is referred to as *situational or transitional crisis.*

Figure 7.5 Components of Adaptation Phase of Typology Model

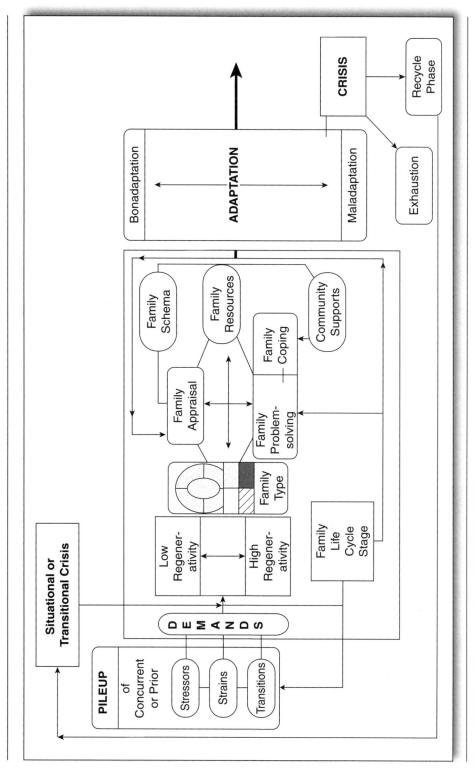

Source: McCubbin, Thompson, Pirner, & McCubbin (1988).

AA *Factor*

In the detailed figure (7.5), the *AA* factor appears as *pileup of the concurrent or prior stressors, strains, or transitions and demands.* The authors say that concurrent stressors and strains result from coping efforts. Common concurrent stressors are intrafamily ambiguity and social ambiguity.

R *Factor*

The *R* factor is represented by *regenerativity* (low or high) in the detailed figure (7.5). This appears to be redundant in that the family typology represented by the factor *T* also addresses regenerativity.

T *Factor*

As in the adjustment phase, in the detailed figure (7.5) of the adaptation phase, the *T* factor appears as *family type* based on the alternative version of the Circumplex Model.

BB *Factor*

In the detailed figure (7.5), *family resources* (characteristics, traits, or competencies) represent the *BB* factor. These resources may be tangible or intangible. The authors acknowledge that individual family members might use their personal resources as well as the family using family resources.

BBB *Factor*

In the detailed figure (7.5), *community supports* (persons, groups, and institutions outside the family) represent the *BBB* factor. The authors address community supports at both the mesoenvironmental level (services of schools, churches, employers, and the medical community) and the macroenvironmental level (government policies).

CC *Factor*

The *CC* factor appears as the *family appraisal* in the detailed diagram. It refers to the situational appraisal (definition of demands, capabilities, and relationship of family members to each other/balance or imbalance). Capabilities are the potentiality of resources, strengths, and coping strategies.

CCC *Factor*

The *CCC* factor appears as the *family schema* in the detailed diagram. It refers to the global (supra) appraisal (view of the relationship of family members to each other and the family to the community). Patterson (1988) discussed five dimensions of the family schema: shared purpose, collectivity, frameabiity, relativism, and shared control.

PSC *Factor*

Family problem solving and *coping* (covert or overt effort/process of acquiring and allocating resources to maintain or restore balance between demands and resources) represent the *PSC* factor in the detailed figure (7.5). The authors consider both individual and family system coping when assessing family coping.

XX *Factor*

XX represents the family's level of adaptation and the possible transition back into a crisis. *XX* also represents the possibility of exhaustion or recycling of the adaptation phase after that crisis. If the family does not experience another crisis, it moves back into the adjustment phase.

Critique of the Typology Model of Family Adjustment and Adaptation

On the positive side, in the discussion of the Typology Model, both individual family members and the family system are considered. On the negative side, however, individuals do not appear in the diagram of the model. There also appears to be some redundancy in the model, as the *R* factor is represented by *regenerativity* in the detailed figure (7.5). This appears to be redundant in that the family typology represented by the factor *T* also addresses regenerativity. A confusing aspect of the detailed diagram is the fact that when the text refers to maladjustment, the detailed diagram actually has maladaptation. In addition, the Typology Model uses the term *appraisal* rather than *definition* as in the ABCX Model (Hill, 1958) or *perception* as in the Double ABCX Model (McCubbin & Patterson, 1982, 1983a, 1983b).

Summary of the Typology Model of Family Adjustment and Adaptation

The Typology Model of Family Adjustment and Adaptation (McCubbin & McCubbin, 1987; McCubbin et al., 1988) is a very complex model of family stress. It adds the component of family types to the Double ABCX Model. It also includes the adjustment and adaptation phases of the FAAR Model. The model, in its complexity, adds to stress theory and addresses the apparent complexity of family stress.

EXERCISE

7.1   Using the Typology of Family Adjustment and Adaptation (McCubbin et al., 1988) concepts, evaluate the crisis from Exercise 2.1. Following is an example of this assignment based on the case study presented in Chapter 2.

I. Adjustment phase

A. A factor

1. Stressor event or transition: husband's death
2. Level of severity: husband's death was severe because of its nature, but not as severe as it would have been had we not already made adjustments as he became sicker and had we not had insurance

a. Degree threatens or disrupts the family's stability: husband's death required some changes in family roles, routines, and responsibilities but not to a great degree since many of these changes had been made before he died; did not threaten existence of family

b. Degree places demands on the family's resources: husband's death did not place demands on family resources since he had some life insurance to cover funeral costs

B. V factor: family system vulnerability (interpersonal and organizational condition of family) (high or low): high

1. Pileup of concurrent or prior stressors, strains, or transitions (and their demands)

a. Prior

1) Stressors: no prior stressors
2) Strains

a) Individual: new job

i.   Demanded time for class preparation
ii. Demanded energy for class preparation

b) Family: illness of husband

i.   Demanded time to care for husband
ii.   Demanded energy to care for husband
iii. Demanded money to pay medical bills

c) Community: no prior community strains

      3) Transitions: no prior transitions

   b. Concurrent

      1) Stressors: no concurrent stressors

      2) Strains: no concurrent strains

         a) Individual: no concurrent individual strains

         b) Family: no concurrent family strains

         c) Community: no concurrent community strains

   c. Transition: no concurrent transitions

  2. Family life cycle stage (and its demands): child rearing

    a) Demanded time to care for child

    b) Demanded energy to care for child

    c) Demanded space for child

    d) Demanded money to care for child

C. T factor: family type (set of basic attributes about the family system, which characterizes and explains how a family system typically appraises, operates, and/or behaves)

  1. Regenerative (vulnerable, durable, secure, or regenerative): durable to regenerative

   a. Hardiness (high or low): low to high

      1) Sense of control: high

      2) Meaningfulness in life: low

      3) Involvement in activities: low

      4) Commitment to learn and explore new experiences: high

   b. Coherence (high or low): high

      1) Acceptance: low

      2) Loyalty: high

      3) Pride: high

      4) Faith: low

      5) Trust: low

      6) Respect: high

      7) Caring: high

      8) Shared values: high

  2. Resilient (fragile, pliant, bonded, or resilient): fragile, pliant, bonded, or resilient

   a. Bonding (high or low): low to high

      1) Open to discussion: low

      2) Feeling close: high

      3) Desirous of connection: high

      4) Doing things together: low

    b. Flexibility (high or low): low to high

       1) Open communication: low

       2) Compromise: high

       3) Willingness to shift responsibilities: low

       4) Participation in decision making: high

3. Rhythmic (unpatterned, structuralized, intentional, or rhythmic): intentional

    a. Family time and routines (high or low): low

       1) Routines to promote parent–child togetherness: low

       2) Routines to promote husband–wife togetherness: low

       3) Routines to promote family unit togetherness: low

       4) Routines to promote family–relative togetherness: high

    b. Valuing family time and routines (high or low): high

       1) Degree of importance of routines to promote parent–child togetherness: high

       2) Degree of importance of routines to promote husband–wife togetherness: high

       3) Degree of importance of routines to promote family unit togetherness: high

       4) Degree of importance of routines to promote family–relative togetherness: high

4. Traditionalistic (situational, celebratory, traditionalistic, or ritualistic): situational

    a. Traditions (high or low): low

       1) Holiday decorating: low

       2) Special experiences around changes: low

       3) Special rules around religious occasions: low

       4) Members participate in special events: low

    b. Celebrations (high or low): low

       1) Spouse's birthday: low

       2) Special occasions: low

       3) Major holidays: low

D. B factor: family resources (resistance)

  1. Family strengths: did not use family strengths

  2. Rituals ("captures and perpetuates the family's way of dealing with the outside world," McCubbin et al., 1988, pp. 10–11): wake and funeral

  3. Routines ("act as guidelines for how things should be done and enhance the family's conception of themselves and their social world," McCubbin et al., 1988, p. 11): did not use routines since had to establish new routines

E. Factor C: family appraisal (of seriousness of stressor, its hardships, and effect on family): challenging; I believed that I would be successful in spite of my loss
F. PSC factor: family management of the stressful situation through its problem solving and coping

1. Problem solving (skills)
   a. Define the stressor as manageable: defined husband's death as challenge that was manageable
   b. Identify alternative courses of action: did not identify alternative courses of action
   c. Initiate steps to resolve the discrete issues: did not initiate steps to resolve discrete issues
   d. Resolve the problem: did not resolve the problem

2. Coping
   1. Avoidance (efforts to deny or ignore the stressor and demands): avoidance was not used
   2. Elimination (effort to rid self of demands by changing or removing stressor, or altering the definition): elimination was not used
   3. Assimilation (efforts to accept demands created by stressor by making minor changes in family): I assimilated the death of my husband into my family life

G. X factor
   A. Maladjustment
      1. Nature of stressor involves structural change in family: nature of stressor required structural change
      2. Nature, number, and duration of demands depletes resources: demands did not deplete resources
      3. Number and persistence of strains tax resources: number and persistence of strains taxed resources of time and energy
      4. Family seizes opportunity to produce change by allowing or facilitating demand–capability imbalance: did not seize opportunity to produce change
   B. Crisis
      1. Amount of consciousness and acceptance by each family member of his or her and others' family roles (better than average, average, below average): below average; my parents took care of my son for a period of time—a few days, I think—so I was not performing my role as parent
      2. Extent to which family members worked toward family and individual good (better than average, average, below average): below average; I was not taking care of my son, and self-care was based on what others told me to do

3. How much family members found satisfaction with family unit (better than average, average, below average): below average; the family unit had been redefined, and ways to find satisfaction would need to be redefined as well

4. Whether the family had a sense of direction and was moving in that direction (better than average, average, below average): below average; family goals would need to be redefined by me as a single parent

II. Family adaptation phase

A. X factor (situational or transitional crisis): transitional

1. Amount of consciousness and acceptance by each family member of his or her and others' family roles (better than average, average, below average): below average; my parents took care of my son for a period of time—a few days, I think—so I was not performing my role as parent

2. Extent to which family members worked toward family and individual good (better than average, average, below average): below average; I was not taking care of my son, and self-care was based on what others told me to do

3. How much family members found satisfaction with family unit (better than average, average, below average): below average; the family unit had been redefined, and ways to find satisfaction would need to be redefined as well

4. Whether the family had a sense of direction and was moving in that direction (better than average, average, below average): below average; family goals would need to be redefined by me as a single parent

B. AA factor: pileup

1. Situational or transitional crisis

a. Amount of consciousness and acceptance by each family member of his or her and others' family roles (better than average, average, below average): below average; my parents took care of my son for a period of time—a few days, I think—so I was not performing my role as parent

b. Extent to which family members worked toward family and individual good (better than average, average, below average): below average; I was not taking care of my son, and self-care was based on what others told me to do

c. How much family members found satisfaction with family unit (better than average, average, below average): below average; the family unit had been redefined, and ways to find satisfaction would need to be redefined as well

d. Whether the family had a sense of direction and was moving in that direction (better than average, average, below average): below average; family goals would need to be redefined by me as a single parent

2. Concurrent or prior (and their demands)

  a. Stressors

  1) Intrafamily ambiguity: ambiguity about husband's roles as he was able to perform some roles and not others (prior)

  2) Social ambiguity: no social ambiguity

  b. Strains

  1) Individual: new job

  a) Demanded time for class preparation

  b) Demanded energy for class preparation

  2) Family: illness of husband

  a) Demanded time to care for husband

  b) Demanded energy to care for husband

  c) Demanded money to pay medical bills

  3) Community: no concurrent or prior community strains

  c. Transition: no prior or concurrent transitions

C. R factor: regenerativity (pileup of demands interacting with family typology) (low or high): high

D. T factor: family type

  1. Regenerative (vulnerable, durable, secure, or regenerative): regenerative

  a. Hardiness (high or low): high

  1) Sense of control: high

  2) Meaningfulness in life: high

  3) Involvement in activities: low

  4) Commitment to learn and explore new experiences: high

  b. Coherence (high or low): high

  1) Acceptance: high

  2) Loyalty: high

  3) Pride: high

  4) Faith: low

  5) Trust: high

  6) Respect: high

  7) Caring: high

  8) Shared values: high

  2. Resilient (fragile, pliant, bonded, or resilient): bonded

  a. Bonding (high or low): high

  1) Open to discussion: low

  2) Feeling close: high

  3) Desirous of connection: high

  4) Doing things together: high

      b. Flexibility (high or low): low

        1) Open communication: low
        2) Compromise: low
        3) Willingness to shift responsibilities: low
        4) Participation in decision making: low

  3. Rhythmic (unpatterned, structuralized, intentional, or rhythmic): rhythmic
      a. Family time and routines (high or low): high

        1) Routines to promote parent–child togetherness: high
        2) Routines to promote husband–wife togetherness: low
        3) Routines to promote family unit togetherness: high
        4) Routines to promote family–relative togetherness: high

      b. Valuing family time and routines (high or low): high

        1) Degree of importance of routines to promote parent–child togetherness: high
        2) Degree of importance of routines to promote husband–wife togetherness: low
        3) Degree of importance of routines to promote family unit togetherness: high
        4) Degree of importance of routines to promote family–relative togetherness: high

  4. Traditionalistic (situational, celebratory, traditionalistic, or ritualistic): situational
      a. Traditions (high or low): low
        1) Holiday decorating: low
        2) Special experiences around changes: low
        3) Special rules around religious occasions: low
        4) Members participate in special events: low

      b. Celebrations (high or low): low

        1) Spouse's birthday: low
        2) Special occasions: low
        3) Major holidays: low

E. BB factor: family resources (tangible or intangible)

  1. Personal resources: knowledge (intangible)

  2. Family system resources: did not use family system resources

F. BBB factor: community supports

  1. Mesoenvironmental level
    a. Persons
      1) Coworkers (tangible)
      2) Friends (tangible)
      3) Relatives (tangible)

   b. Groups: self-help (tangible)

   c. Institutions

     1) Funeral home (tangible)

     2) Church (tangible)

  2. Macroenvironmental level (government policies)

   a. Veterans Administration (VA) provided tombstone (tangible)

   b. Social Security Administration (SSA) provided dependent benefits (tangible)

G. Family appraisal

  1. CC factor: situational appraisal (definition of demands, capabilities, and relationship of family members to each other/balance or imbalance): challenging but not insurmountable since I had resources

  2. CCC factor: global (supra) appraisal (family schema for how it views the relationship of family members to each other and the family to the community) five dimensions

   a. Shared purpose (degree of common family goals): low

   b. Collectivity (degree of identity)

     1) Family: high

     2) Community: low

     3) Nation: low

   c. Framability (degree of optimism with realism): low

   d. Relativism (degree of)

     1) Setting limits: high

     2) Accepting less-than-perfect solutions: high

   e. Shared control (degree of control midway between personal control and fatalism/no control): high

H. PSC factor: adaptive coping

  1. Family problem solving: I did all of the family problem solving as the only adult in the family

  2. Family coping (covert or overt)

   a. Individual

     1) Grief work (overt)

     2) Material aid

       a) Used material aid from parents in the form of meals (overt)

       b) Used material aid from Veterans Administration in the form of tombstone (overt)

       c) Used material aid from Social Security Administration in the form of dependent benefits (overt)

     3) Used social support in the from of widows' groups (overt)

     4) Used crisis counseling in the form of psychologist visits (overt)

     5) Used rites of passage in the form of the wake and funeral (overt)

      b. Family system

        1) To maintain or restore balance between demands and resources

          a) Direct action to reduce the number and/or intensity of demands: ate supper at parents' house on weeknights and lunch on Saturdays to reduce need to shop for food, cook, and wash dishes

          b) Direct action to acquire additional resources: went to VA and SSA to get benefits

          c) Maintaining existing resources: continued to work at present job

          d) Managing tension associated with strains: managed tension associated with job by bringing son to babysitter's when had day off so could catch up on work

          e) Changing appraisal: did not change appraisal

        2) To ease the strains of restructuring (adaptive coping strategies)

          a) Synergizing (efforts to share lifestyle orientation): did not synergize

          b) Interfacing (new rules for and transactions with community interaction): interfaced with community in that began receiving Social Security benefits for child

          c) Compromising (supporting less-than-perfect solutions): compromised in that supported solution of being a single parent as was needed at the time

  I. Adaptation: Bonadaptation

    1. Bonadaptation

    2. Maladaptation and crisis (exhaustion or recycling of phase)

Now complete the following outline for your crisis.

  I. Adjustment phase

  A. A factor

    1. Stressor event or transition

    2. Level of severity

      a. Degree threatens or disrupts the family's stability

      b. Degree places demands on the family's resources

  B. V factor: family system vulnerability (interpersonal and organizational condition of family) (high or low)

    1. Pileup of concurrent or prior stressors, strains, or transitions (and their demands)

      a. Prior

        1) Stressors

        2) Strains

        3) Transitions

      b. Concurrent

        1) Stressors

        2) Strains

        3) Transitions

    2. Family life cycle stage (and its demands)

C. T factor: family type (set of basic attributes about the family system, which characterizes and explains how a family system typically appraises, operates, and/ or behaves)

    1. Regenerative (vulnerable, durable, secure, or regenerative)

        a. Hardiness (high or low)

            1) Sense of control

            2) Meaningfulness in life

            3) Involvement in activities

            4) Commitment to learn and explore new experiences

        b. Coherence (high or low)

            1) Acceptance

            2) Loyalty

            3) Pride

            4) Faith

            5) Trust

            6) Respect

            7) Caring

            8) Shared values

    2. Resilient (fragile, pliant, bonded, or resilient)

        a. Bonding (high or low)

            1) Open to discussion

            2) Feeling close

            3) Desirous of connection

            4) Doing things together

        b. Flexibility (high or low)

            1) Open communication

            2) Compromise

            3) Willingness to shift responsibilities

            4) Participation in decision making

    3. Rhythmic (unpatterned, structuralized, intentional, or rhythmic)

        a. Family time and routines (high or low)

            1) Routines to promote parent–child togetherness

            2) Routines to promote husband–wife togetherness

            3) Routines to promote family unit togetherness

            4) Routines to promote family–relative togetherness

        b. Valuing family time and routines (high or low)

            1) Degree of importance of routines to promote parent–child togetherness

        2) Degree of importance of routines to promote husband–wife togetherness

        3) Degree of importance of routines to promote family unit togetherness

        4) Degree of importance of routines to promote family–relative togetherness

    4. Traditionalistic (situational, celebratory, traditionalistic, or ritualistic)

      a. Traditions (high or low)

        1) Holiday decorating

        2) Special experiences around changes

        3) Special rules around religious occasions

        4) Members participate in special events

      b. Celebrations (high or low)

        1) Spouse's birthday

        2) Special occasions

        3) Major holidays

D. B factor: family resources (adaptation/resistance)

  1. Family strengths

  2. Rituals ("captures and perpetuates the family's way of dealing with the outside world," McCubbin et al., 1988, pp. 10–11)

  3. Routines ("act as guidelines for how things should be done and enhance the family's conception of themselves and their social world," McCubbin et al., 1988, pp. 11)

E. Factor C: family appraisal (of seriousness of stressor, its hardships, and effect on family)

F. PSC factor: family management of the stressful situation

  1. Problem solving (skills)

    a. Define the stressor as manageable

    b. Identify alternative courses of action

    c. Initiate steps to resolve the discrete issues

    d. Resolve the problem

  2. Coping

    a. Avoidance (efforts to deny or ignore the stressor and demands)

    b. Elimination (effort to rid self of demands by changing or removing stressor, or altering the definition)

    c. Assimilation (efforts to accept demands created by stressor by making minor changes in family)

G. X factor

  1. Maladjustment

    a. Nature of stressor involves structural change in family

    b. Nature, number, and duration of demands deplete resources

   c. Number and persistence of strains tax resources

   d. Family seizes opportunity to produce change by allowing or facilitating demand–capability imbalance

  2. Crisis

II. Family adaptation phase

 A. X factor (situational or transitional crisis)

 B. AA factor: pileup

  1. Situational or transitional crisis

  2. Concurrent (resulting from coping efforts) or prior stressors, strains, or transitions (and demands)

   a. Stressor

    1) Intrafamily ambiguity

    2) Social ambiguity

   b. Strain

   c. Transition

 C. R factor: regenerativity (pileup of demands interacting with family typology) (low or high)

 D. T factor: family type

  1. Regenerative (vulnerable, durable, secure, or regenerative)

   a. Hardiness (high or low)

    1) Sense of control

    2) Meaningfulness in life

    3) Involvement in activities

    4) Commitment to learn and explore new experiences

   b. Coherence (high or low)

    1) Acceptance

    2) Loyalty

    3) Pride

    4) Faith

    5) Trust

    6) Respect

    7) Caring

    8) Shared values

  2. Resilient (fragile, pliant, bonded, or resilient)

   a. Bonding (high or low)

    1) Open to discussion

2) Feeling close

3) Desirous of connection

4) Doing things together

b. Flexibility (high or low)

1) Open communication

2) Compromise

3) Willingness to shift responsibilities

4) Participation in decision making

3. Rhythmic (unpatterned, structuralized, intentional, or rhythmic)

a. Family time and routines (high or low)

1) Routines to promote parent–child togetherness

2) Routines to promote husband–wife togetherness

3) Routines to promote family unit togetherness

4) Routines to promote family–relative togetherness

b. Valuing family time and routines (high or low)

1) Degree of importance of routines to promote parent–child togetherness

2) Degree of importance of routines to promote husband–wife togetherness

3) Degree of importance of routines to promote family unit togetherness

4) Degree of importance of routines to promote family–relative togetherness

4. Traditionalistic (situational, celebratory, traditionalistic, or ritualistic)

a. Traditions (high or low)

1) Holiday decorating

2) Special experiences around changes

3) Special rules around religious occasions

4) Members participate in special events

b. Celebrations (high or low)

1) Spouse's birthday

2) Special occasions

3) Major holidays

E. BB factor: family resources (tangible or intangible)

1. Personal resources

2. Family system resources

F. BBB factor: community supports

1. Mesoenvironmental level

a. Persons

b. Groups

c. Institutions

    2. Macroenvironmental level

G. Family appraisal

    1. CC factor: situational appraisal (definition of demands, capabilities, and relationship of family members to each other/balance or imbalance)

    2. CCC factor: global (supra) appraisal (family schema for how it views the relationship of family members to each other and the family to the community) five dimensions

      a. Shared purpose (degree of common family goals)

      b. Collectivity (degree of identity)

        1) Family

        2) Community

        3) Nation

      c. Framabiity (degree of optimism with realism)

      d. Relativism (degree of)

        1) Setting limits

        2) Accepting less-than-perfect solutions

      e. Shared control (degree of control midway between personal control and fatalism/no control)

H. PSC factor: adaptive coping

    1. Family problem solving

    2. Family coping (covert or overt effort/process of acquiring and allocating resources to maintain or restore balance between demands and resources)

      a. Individual

      b. Family system

        1) To maintain or restore balance between demands and resources

          a) Direct action to reduce the number and/or intensity of demands

          b) Direct action to acquire additional resources

          c) Maintaining existing resources

          e) Managing tension associated with strains

          f) Changing appraisal

        2) To ease the strains of restructuring (adaptive coping strategies)

          a) Synergizing (efforts to share lifestyle orientation)

          b) Interfacing (new rules for and transactions with community interaction)

          c) Compromising (supporting less-than-perfect solutions)

I. Adaptation: Bonadaptation

    1. Bonadaptation

    2. Maladaptation and crisis (exhaustion or recycling of phase)

References and Suggestions for Further Reading

Hill, R. (1958). Generic features of families under stress. *Social Casework, 49,* 139–150.

McCubbin, H. I., McCubbin, M. A., Thompson, A. I., & Thompson, E. A. (1995). *Resiliency in ethnic minority families: A conceptual model for predicting family adjustment and adaptation.* Madison: University of Wisconsin System Center for Excellence in Family Studies.

McCubbin, H. I., & Patterson, J. M. (1982). Family adaptation to crisis. In H. I. McCubbin, A. E. Cauble, & J. M. Patterson (Eds.), *Family stress, coping, and social support.* Springfield, IL: Charles C. Thomas.

McCubbin, H. I., & Patterson, J. M. (1983a). Family stress and adaptation to crises: A Double ABCX Model of family behavior. In D. H. Olson & R. C. Miller (Eds.), *Family studies review yearbook: Vol. 1* (pp. 87–106). Beverly Hills, CA: Sage.

McCubbin, H. I., & Patterson, J. M. (1983b). The family stress process: The Double ABCX Model of Family Adjustment and Adaptation. In H. I. McCubbin, M. Sussman, & J. M. Patterson (Eds.), *Social stress and the family: Advances and developments in family stress theory and research* (pp. 7–37). New York: Haworth.

McCubbin, H. I., Thompson, A. I., Pirner, P. A., & McCubbin, M. A. (1988). *Family types and strengths.* Edina, MN: Burgess International Group.

McCubbin, M. A., & McCubbin, H. I. (1987). Family stress theory and assessment: The T-Double ABCX Model of Family Adjustment and Adaptation. In H. I. McCubbin & A. Thompson (Eds.), *Family assessment inventories for research and practice* (pp. 3–32). Madison: University of Wisconsin.

Olson, D., & McCubbin, H. (1982). Circumplex Model of marital and family systems V: Application to family marital and family stress and crisis intervention. In H. I. McCubbin, A. Cauble, & J. Patterson (Eds.), *Family stress, coping, and social support* (pp. 33–45). Springfield, IL: Charles C. Thomas.

Patterson, J. M. (1988). Families experiencing stress: I. The Family Adjustment and Response Model; II. Applying the FAAR Model to health-related issues for intervention and research. *Family Systems Medicine, 6*(2), 202–237.

The Resiliency Model of Family Stress, Adjustment, and Adaptation

T he Resiliency Model of Family Stress, Adjustment, and Adaptation, developed by McCubbin and Associates (McCubbin, McCubbin, Thompson, & Thompson, 1995; McCubbin, Thompson, & McCubbin, 2001; McCubbin & McCubbin, 1991, 1993, 1996), expands on the work of Reuben Hill (1949, 1958), the Double ABCX Model (McCubbin & Patterson, 1981, 1983a, 1983b), and the Typology Model of Family Adjustment and Adaptation (McCubbin, Thompson, Pirner, & McCubbin, 1988; McCubbin & McCubbin, 1987, 1989). According to Marilyn McCubbin and Hamilton McCubbin (1993), the Resiliency Model emphasizes the postcrisis, adaptation phase. It attempts to explain why some families are "resilient" and recover from crises while others stay vulnerable or deteriorate after crises (McCubbin & McCubbin, 1996). It includes components that help explain cultural differences (family paradigms, schemas, and coherence).

Conceptual Framework of the Resiliency Model of Family Stress, Adjustment, and Adaptation

In the first version of the Resiliency Model (McCubbin & McCubbin, 1991), little change occurred from the Typology Model (McCubbin et al., 1988; McCubbin & McCubbin, 1987, 1989). Later versions of the Resiliency Model saw more distinct changes (McCubbin et al., 1995; McCubbin et al., 2001; McCubbin & McCubbin, 1993, 1996).

Initially, it appeared that the Resiliency Model was so called because resiliency was the jargon of the time. Resiliency appears in the original Resiliency Model as only one of the family types. The Typology Model of Family Adjustment and Adaptation seemed to be a more appropriate name for the model since the Resiliency Model did not appear to add much to that model. It appeared to be a refinement of the Typology Model rather than a new model; however, subsequent research and refinement of the model instituted other distinctive changes. The addition of newly instituted patterns of functioning was a positive change to the adaptation phase. Marilyn McCubbin and Hamilton McCubbin (1993) said that the greater the degree to which the new patterns address hardships and are congruent with the schema, the more positive the level of adaptation. Although initially diagramed almost identically to the Typology Model, the later diagram of the Resiliency Model appears very different. See Figures 8.1 and 8.2. Within the Resiliency Model of Family Stress and Adaptation (McCubbin et al., 1995; McCubbin & McCubbin, 1993, 1996), resilience includes two related processes, adjustment and adaptation.

Adjustment Phase

The first phase of the Resiliency Model, the adjustment phase, consists of the variables of the stressor, vulnerability, established patterns of functioning, family resources, stressor appraisal, problem solving and coping, and the outcome of adjustment. The components of the adjustment phase interact to determine the type of adjustment.

Stressor (A)

The stressor in the Resiliency Model is the same as the *A* factor in the Typology Model. See Table 8.1. It includes the level of severity of the stressor defined as the degree to which a stressor threatens family stability, disrupts family functioning, and/or places demands in excess of family capabilities.

Vulnerability (V)

The family's vulnerability in the Resiliency model is equivalent to the *V* factor in the Typology Model and ranges from high to low. The *pileup* of *stressors, strains,* and *transitions* and their demands shape the family's vulnerability. Vulnerability interacts with *established patterns of functioning (*T*)*, family typology.

Figure 8.1 The Adjustment Phase of the Resiliency Model

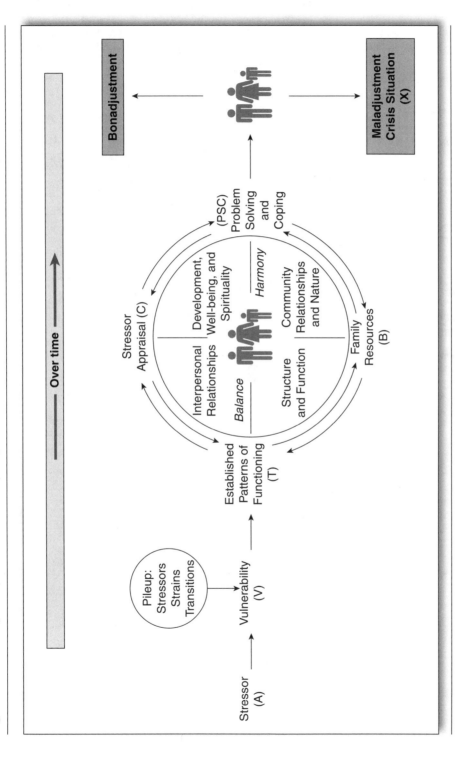

Source: McCubbin, H., Thompson, A. & McCubbin, M. A. (1996) Resiliency in families: A conceptual model of family adjustment and adaptation in response to stress and crises. In H. McCubbin, A.,Thompson, & M. A. McCubbin, *Family assessment: Resiliency, coping and adaptation* (p.15), copyright 1996 by Hamilton McCubbin, Anne Thompson, Marilyn A. McCubbin, and the Board of Regents, University of Wisconsin System. Reprinted by Permission of Hamilton McCubbin.

Table 8.1 Comparison of the Family Adjustment and Adaptation Response (FAAR) Model, the Typology Model of Family Adjustment and Adaptation, and the Resiliency Model of Family Stress, Adjustment, and Adaptation

Family Adjustment and Adaptation Response (FAAR) Model	Typology Model of Family Adjustment and Adaptation	Resiliency Model of Family Stress, Adjustment, and Adaptation
Adjustment Phase	*Adjustment Phase*	*Adjustment Phase*
Stressor (*a*)	*A* Factor	Stressor (*A*)
Demands	*V* Factor	Vulnerability (*V*)
	T Factor	Established Patterns of Functioning (*T*) (Family Typology)
Existing Resources (*b*)	*B* Factor	Family Resources (B)
Definition and Appraisal of Demands (*c*)	*C* Factor	Stressor Appraisal (*C*)
Adjustment Coping Strategies	*PSC* Factor	Problem Solving and Coping (*PSC*)
Bonadjustment or Maladjustment	Adjustment	Bonadjustment or Maladjustment/Crisis Situation (*X*)
Crisis (**x**)	**X** *Factor*	*Crisis Situation* (**X**) *(Maladjustment)*
Exhaustion	Exhaustion	Inadequate and/or Deterioration in Family Patterns of Functioning (*T*)
Adaptation Phase	*Adaptation Phase*	*Adaptation Phase*
Pileup (*aA*)	*AA* Factor	Pileup of Demands (*AA*)
	X Factor	Maladjustment Crisis Situation (*X*)
	R Factor	
	T Factor	Retained Patterns of Functioning (*T*)
	T Factor	Restored Patterns of Functioning (*T*)
	T Factor	Newly Initiated Patterns of Functioning (*TT*)

Family Adjustment and Adaptation Response (FAAR) Model	*Typology Model of Family Adjustment and Adaptation*	*Resiliency Model of Family Stress, Adjustment, and Adaptation*
Resources and Support (*bB*)	*BB* Factor	Family Resources (*BB*): Family Support
Resources and Support (*bB*)	*BBB* Factor	Family Resources (*BB*): Social Support
Resources and Support (*bB*)	*BBB* Factor	Family Resources (*BB*): Kin Support
Resources and Support (*bB*)	*BBB* Factor	Family Resources (*BB*): Community Support
Awareness		
Shared Definition of the Situation (*cC*)	*CC* Factor	Situational Appraisal (*CC*)
Search for and Agreement on Solutions and Implementation		
Adaptive Coping: System Maintenance—Integration, Member Esteem, System Morale	*PSC* Factor	Problem Solving and Coping (*PSC*)
		Paradigms (*CCC*)
		Coherence (*CCCC*)
Shared Family Life Orientation and Meaning (*cC*)	*CCC* Factor: Global Appraisal	Schema (*CCCCC*)
Agreement on Concomitant Changes and Implementation	*PSC* Factor	Problem Solving and Coping (*PSC*)
Adaptive Coping: Synergizing, Interfacing, Compromising, System Maintenance	*PSC* Factor	Problem Solving and Coping (*PSC*)
Bonadaptation/ Maladaptation	*XX* Factor	Family Adaptation (*XX*)

Established Patterns of Functioning (T)

The family's established patterns of functioning in the Resiliency Model are equivalent to the *T* factor, the family typology (regenerative, resilient, rhythmic, or traditionalistic), in the Typology Model. The family's typology interacts with the family's resistance resources.

Family Resources (B)

Family resources (*B*) in the Resiliency Model are equivalent to the *B* factor, resistance resources, in the Typology Model. Adjustment involves resistance resources or family protective factors (FPF) in facilitating a family's ability and efforts to maintain integrity and functioning and to fulfill developmental tasks despite being at risk, called elasticity (McCubbin, McCubbin, Thompson, Han, & Allen, 1997). Resources interact with the family's appraisal of the stressor.

Stressor Appraisal (C)

The stressor appraisal (*C*) in the Resiliency Model is equivalent to Factor *C* in the Typology Model. It refers to the appraisal of the seriousness of the stressor and its hardships as to whether it is a setback or a catastrophe. The appraisal interacts with the family's problem-solving and coping strategies.

Problem Solving and Coping (PSC)

Problem solving and coping (*PSC*) in the Resiliency Model are equivalent to the *PSC* factor in the Typology Model. According to the Resiliency Model, the family's problem-solving skills include the family's ability to define the stressor as manageable, identify alternative courses of action, initiate steps to resolve discrete and interpersonal issues, and resolve the problem. Coping includes behaviors to maintain or strengthen family, maintain emotional stability and well-being, obtain or use resources, and initiate efforts to resolve hardships.

Adjustment

Adjustment refers to the outcome of the adjustment phase, which can be *bonadjustment (balance and harmony)* or *maladjustment/crisis situation (X)*. In bonadjustment there is balance and harmony in the family's *development, well-being, and spirituality; community relationships and nature; structure and function;* and *interpersonal relationships. Maladjustment/crisis situation (X)* refers to imbalance and disharmony in the same factors. A family lives in the adjustment phase until there is a maladjustment/crisis situation. From the crisis, the family moves into the adaptation phase.

Adaptation Phase

The adaptation phase in the Resiliency Model (Figure 8.2) is equivalent to the family adaptation phase in the Typology Model. It adds several new interacting components, including *inadequate and/or deterioration in family patterns of functioning (T), retained patterns of functioning (T), restored patterns of functioning (T),* or *newly instituted patterns of functioning (TT)*; *coherence (CCCC)*; and *schemas (CCCCC)*, discussed in the following sections.

Inadequate and/or Deterioration in Family Patterns of Functioning (T)

In the Resiliency Model, *inadequate and/or deterioration in family patterns of functioning (T)* means that the family's stabilized patterns of functioning were inadequate prior to the stressor and/or the patterns deteriorated in response to the stressor. These patterns interact with the pileup of demands.

Pileup of Demands (AA)

The pileup of demands *(AA)* is equivalent to the *AA* factor in the adaptation phase of the Typology Model. See Table 8.1. The pileup of demands interacts with the crisis.

Maladjustment/Crisis Situation (X)

The maladjustment/crisis situation *(X)* is equivalent to the *X* factor in the adaptation phase of the Typology Model. See Table 8.1.

Patterns of Functioning

The Resiliency Model adds patterns of functioning after the crisis to indicate whether there are *retained patterns of functioning (T), restored patterns of functioning (T),* or *newly instituted patterns of functioning (TT).*

Figure 8.2 The Adaptation Phase of the Resiliency Model of Family Stress, Adjustment, and Adaptation

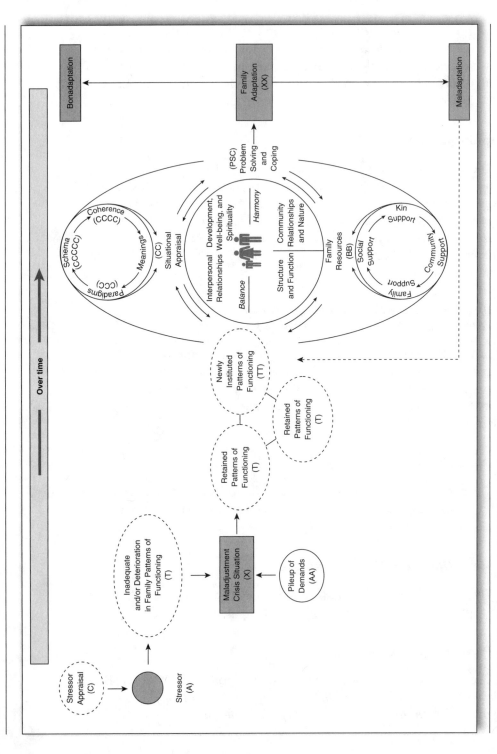

Source: McCubbin, H., Thompson, A. & McCubbin, M. A. (1996) Resiliency in families: A conceptual model of family adjustment and adaptation in response to stress and crises. In H. McCubbin, A. Thompson, & M. A. McCubbin, *Family Assessment: Resiliency; coping and adaptation* (p.25), copyright 1996 by Hamilton McCubbin, Anne Thompson, Marilyn A. McCubbin, and the Board of Regents, University of Wisconsin System. Reprinted by Permission of Hamilton McCubbin.

This part of the model shows that during a crisis, family patterns of function-ing may stay the same, change but go back to precrisis patterns, or change and remain in the new pattern. Alterations in patterns of functioning may help alleviate stress, may lead to further stress, or both. When a mother enters the workforce, it may relieve stress from financial difficulties but add stress because the family needs to alter routines related to running the household to facilitate her new role.

Family Resources (BB) (Family Recovery Factors)

Family resources (*BB*) in the Resiliency Model are equivalent to the *BB* and *BBB* factors (family and community resources, respectively) in the Typology Model. See Table 8.1. Adaptation involves family regenerative/recovery factors (FRF) to facilitate buoyancy, the family's ability to "bounce back" from crises. The Resiliency Model lists four specific types of resources including *social support, kin support, community support, and family sup-port* as part of family resources. The resources interact with the situational appraisal.

Situational Appraisal (CC)

Situational appraisal (*CC*) in the Resiliency Model is equivalent to the *CC* factor in the Typology Model and *cC*, shared definition of the situation, in the FAAR Model. See Table 8.1. Influences on the situational appraisal in the Resiliency Model are *paradigms (CCC), coherence (CCCC),* and *schema (CCCCC).*

Paradigms (CCC). *Paradigms (CCC),* in the Resiliency Model, refer to specific views, expectations, and patterns of functioning affecting specific domains of family life, such as child rearing, work, and education, which vary by culture (McCubbin et al., 1995). Child rearing may be community focused, in which kin and/or community members share responsibility or nuclear family focused, in which the nuclear family is responsible. Work roles may be for the present and for others, in which the fruits of labor are shared, or for the present and/or future and the self, in which fruits of labor are used or saved by the individual or nuclear family. Education may be informal, formal (schools bear the responsibility for education), or both. Coherence influences paradigms.

Coherence (CCCC). *Coherence (CCCC)* in the Resiliency Model means the worldview "that expresses the family's sense of order" (McCubbin et al.,

1995, p. 12). Coherence explains the cognitive basis for using potential resources to cope. When the world is viewed as comprehensible, the family believes that internal and external environments are structured, predictable, and explicable. When the world is viewed as manageable, the family believes that resources are available to meet demands. When the world is viewed as meaningful, the family believes that life demands are challenges worthy of investment. The family schema influences its coherence.

***Schema* (CCCCC).** *Schema* (CCCCC) in the Resiliency Model refers to shared values, beliefs, and expectations about family structure, self-/group orientation, spiritual beliefs, land/nature, and time orientation (McCubbin et al., 1995). In the Resiliency Model, the schema (*CCCCC*) is similar to the *CCC* factor or global appraisal, which was defined as the family schema (how the family viewed the relationship of family members to each other and the family to the community) in the Typology Model. Families may expect an extended or a nuclear family structure, expect a self- (individualism) or a group (familism) orientation, share spiritual or religious beliefs, and believe that land and nature should be preserved or used without regard to the future. Their time orientation may be present-oriented, future-oriented, or both. A family's instituted patterns of function, resources, and appraisal influence and are influenced by the family's problem solving and coping.

Problem Solving and Coping (PSC)

Problem solving and coping (*PSC*) in the Resiliency Model is equivalent to the *PSC* factor, problem solving and coping, in the Typology Model and adaptive coping in the FAAR Model. See Table 8.1. As in the adjustment phase, *problem solving* refers to the family's ability to define the stressor as manageable, identify alternative courses of action, initiate steps to resolve discrete and interpersonal issues, and resolve the problem. *Coping* refers to behaviors to maintain or strengthen family, maintain emotional stability and well-being, obtain or use resources, and initiate efforts to resolve hardships. A family's problem solving and coping interacting with the other variables in the adaptation phase influences the family's adaptation.

Family Adaptation (XX)

Family adaptation (*XX*) in the Resiliency Model is equivalent to the *XX* factor, the level of family adaptation, in the Typology Model. See Table 8.1. In the Resiliency Model, *bonadaptation* represents *balance* and *harmony* in the family's *development, well-being, and spirituality; community relationships and nature; structure and function;* and *interpersonal relationships,* while *maladaptation* refers to *imbalance* and *disharmony* in those areas. When a family experiences bonadaptation, the family returns to the adjustment phase, while when a family experiences maladaptation, the family returns to crisis and begins the adaptation process again.

Critique of the Resiliency Model of Family Stress, Adjustment, and Adaptation

In its first version, so little change occurred from the Typology Model (McCubbin et al., 1988; McCubbin & McCubbin, 1987, 1989) to the Resiliency Model (McCubbin & McCubbin, 1991) that it appeared to be the same model. Later versions (McCubbin et al., 1995; McCubbin & McCubbin, 1993, 1996) saw changes that were more distinctive, such as the addition of several new interacting components, including *inadequate and/or deterioration in family patterns of functioning (T), retained patterns of functioning (T), restored patterns of functioning (T),* or *newly instituted patterns of functioning (TT)*; *coherence (CCCC)*; and *schema (CCCCC)*.

Summary of the Resiliency Model of Family Stress, Adjustment, and Adaptation

Expanding on the Typology Model, the Resiliency Model emphasizes the postcrisis adaptation phase in an attempt to explain why some families are resilient and remain free from crisis while others do not. See Table 8.1 for a comparison of the Typology and Resiliency models with the FARR Model. The Resiliency Model adds several new factors to that phase, including *inadequate and/or deterioration in family patterns of functioning (T), retained patterns of functioning (T), restored patterns of functioning (T),* or *newly instituted patterns of functioning (TT)*; *coherence (CCCC)*; and *schema (CCCCC)*. Family paradigms, coherence and schema help to explain cultural differences in response to stressors.

EXERCISE

8.1 Outline the crisis from Exercise 2.1 using the Resiliency Model of Family Stress, Adjustment, and Adaptation concepts. Following is an example of the assignment based on the case study presented in Chapter 2.

   I. Adjustment Phase

      A. Stressor (A): husband's death

      1. Level of severity: degree to which stressor

         a. Threatens family stability: low

         b. Disrupts family functioning: high

         c. Places demands on family capabilities: low

B. Vulnerability (V) (high to low) Shaped by Pileup of

      1. Stressors and demands: no stressors

      2. Strains and demands

         a. Individual: new job

            1) Demanded time for class preparation

            2) Demanded energy for class preparation

         b. Family: illness of husband

            1) Demanded time to care for husband

            2) Demanded energy to care for husband

            3) Demanded money to pay medical bills

         c. Community: no concurrent or prior community strains

      3. Transitions and demands: no transitions

C. Established Patterns of Functioning (T) (Family Typology)

      1. Regenerative (vulnerable, secure, durable, or regenerative): durable to regenerative

         a. Hardiness (high or low): low to high

            1) Sense of control: high

            2) Meaningfulness in life: low

            3) Involvement in activities: low

            4) Commitment to learn and explore new experiences: high

         b. Coherence (high or low): high

            1) Acceptance: low

            2) Loyalty: high

            3) Pride: high

            4) Faith: low

            5) Trust: low

            6) Respect: high

            7) Caring: high

            8) Shared values: high

      2. Resilient (fragile, bonded, pliant, or resilient): fragile, bonded, pliant, or resilient

         a. Bonding (high or low): low to high

            1) Open to discussion: low

   2) Feeling close: high

   3) Desirous of connection: high

   4) Doing things together: low

  b. Flexibility (high or low): low to high

   1) Open communication: low

   2) Compromise: high

   3) Willingness to shift responsibilities: low

   4) Participation in decision making: high

 3. Rhythmic (unpatterned, intentional, structuralized, or rhythmic): intentional

  a. Family time and routines (high or low): low

   1) Routines to promote parent–child togetherness: low

   2) Routines to promote husband–wife togetherness: low

   3) Routines to promote family unit togetherness: low

   4) Routines to promote family–relative togetherness: high

  b. Valuing family time and routines (high or low): high

   1) Degree of importance of routines to promote parent–child togetherness: high

   2) Degree of importance of routines to promote husband–wife togetherness: high

   3) Degree of importance of routines to promote family unit togetherness: high

   4) Degree of importance of routines to promote family–relative togetherness: high

 4. Traditionalistic (situational, traditionalistic, celebratory, or ritualistic): situational

  a. Traditions (high or low): low

   1) Holiday decorating: low

   2) Special experiences around changes: low

   3) Special rules around religious occasions: low

   4) Members participate in special events: low

  b. Celebrations (high or low): low

   1) Spouse's birthday: low

   2) Special occasions: low

   3) Major holidays: low

D. Family Resources (B) [Family Protective Factors (FPF)]

 1. Family strengths: did not use family strengths

 2. Rituals ("captures and perpetuates the family's way of dealing with the outside world," McCubbin et al., 1988, pp. 10–11): wake and funeral

    3. Routines ("act as guidelines for how things should be done and enhance the family's conception of themselves and their social world," McCubbin et al., 1988, p. 11): did not use routines since had to establish new routines

E. Stressor Appraisal (C) (of seriousness of stressor and its hardships as setback or catastrophe): challenging; I believed that I would be successful in spite of my loss

F. Problem Solving and Coping (PSC)

    1. Problem-solving skills

        a. Define the stressor as manageable: defined husband's death as challenge that was manageable

        b. Identify alternative courses of action: did not identify alternative courses of action

        c. Initiate steps to resolve issues

            1) Discrete: did not initiate steps to resolve discrete issues

            2) Interpersonal: did not initiate steps to resolve interpersonal issues

        d. Resolve the problem: did not resolve the problem

    2. Coping (strategies, patterns, and behaviors)

        a. Maintain or strengthen family: did not use

        b. Maintain emotional stability and well-being: did not use

        c. Obtain or use resources: did not use

        d. Initiate efforts to resolve hardships: did not use

G. Adjustment

    1. Bonadjustment (balance and harmony): did not have bonadjustment

        a. Development, well-being, and spirituality

        b. Community relationships and nature

        c. Structure and function

        d. Interpersonal relationships

    2. Maladjustment/crisis situation (imbalance and disharmony)

        a. Development well-being, and spirituality: imbalance; developmental needs and spirituality were ignored

        b. Community relationships and nature: imbalance; functions in the community were not performed

        c. Structure and function: imbalance; family functions, such as caring for child, were not performed by family members

        d. Interpersonal relationships: imbalance; interpersonal relationships were not nurtured

II. Adaptation Phase

A. Stressor (A): husband's death

B. Stressor Appraisal (C) (setback or catastrophe): setback

C. Inadequate and/or Deterioration in Family Patterns of Functioning (7): deterioration

1. Regenerative (vulnerable, secure, durable, or regenerative): durable
   a. Hardiness (high or low): low
      1) Sense of control: low
      2) Meaningfulness in life: low
      3) Involvement in activities: low
      4) Commitment to learn and explore new experiences: high
   b. Coherence (high or low): high
      1) Acceptance: low
      2) Loyalty: high
      3) Pride: high
      4) Faith: low
      5) Trust: low
      6) Respect: high
      7) Caring: high
      8) Shared values: high

2. Resilient (fragile, bonded, pliant, or resilient): fragile
   a. Bonding (high or low): low
      1) Open to discussion: low
      2) Feeling close: low
      3) Desirous of connection: high
      4) Doing things together: low
   b. Flexibility (high or low): low
      1) Open communication: low
      2) Compromise: low
      3) Willingness to shift responsibilities: low
      4) Participation in decision making: low

3. Rhythmic (unpatterned, intentional, structuralized, or rhythmic): unpatterned to intentional
   a. Family time and routines (high or low): low
      1) Routines to promote parent–child togetherness: low
      2) Routines to promote husband–wife togetherness: low
      3) Routines to promote family unit togetherness: low
      4) Routines to promote family–relative togetherness: high
   b. Valuing family time and routines (high or low): low to high
      1) Degree of importance of routines to promote parent–child togetherness: high
      2) Degree of importance of routines to promote husband–wife togetherness: low

3) Degree of importance of routines to promote family unit togetherness: low

4) Degree of importance of routines to promote family–relative togetherness: high

4. Traditionalistic (situational, traditionalistic, celebratory, or ritualistic): situational

a. Traditions (high or low): low

1) Holiday decorating: low

2) Special experiences around changes: low

3) Special rules around religious occasions: low

4) Members participate in special events: low

b. Celebrations (high or low): low

1) Spouse's birthday: low

2) Special occasions: low

3) Major holidays: low

D. Pileup of Demands (AA)

1. Stressors: no other stressors at that time

2. Strains: new job

a. Demanded time for class preparation

b. Demanded energy for class preparation

3. Transitions: no transitions

E. Maladjustment/Crisis Situation (X)

1. Amount of consciousness and acceptance by each family member of his or her and others' family roles (better than average, average, below average): below average; my parents took care of my son for a period of time—a few days, I think—so I was not performing my role as parent

2. Extent to which family members worked toward family and individual good (better than average, average, below average): below average; I was not taking care of my son, and self-care was based on what others told me to do

3. How much family members found satisfaction with family unit (better than average, average, below average): below average; the family unit had been redefined, and ways to find satisfaction would need to be redefined as well

4. Whether the family had a sense of direction and was moving in that direction (better than average, average, below average): below average; family goals would need to be redefined by me as a single parent

F. Patterns of Functioning

1. Retained patterns of functioning (T): instituted new patterns of functioning

2. Restored patterns of functioning (T): instituted new patterns of functioning

3. Newly instituted patterns of functioning (TT): instituted new patterns of functioning
    a. Regenerative (vulnerable, durable, secure, or regenerative): regenerative
        1) Hardiness (high or low): high
            a) Sense of control: high
            b) Meaningfulness in life: high
            c) Involvement in activities: low
            d) Commitment to learn and explore new experiences: high
        2) Coherence (high or low): high
            a) Acceptance: high
            b) Loyalty: high
            c) Pride: high
            d) Faith: low
            e) Trust: high
            f) Respect: high
            g) Caring: high
            h) Shared values: high
    b. Resilient (fragile, pliant, bonded, or resilient): bonded
        1) Bonding (high or low): high
            a) Open to discussion: low
            b) Feeling close: high
            c) Desirous of connection: high
            d) Doing things together: high
        2) Flexibility (high or low): low
            a) Open communication: low
            b) Compromise: low
            c) Willingness to shift responsibilities: low
            d) Participation in decision making: low
    c. Rhythmic (unpatterned, structuralized, intentional, or rhythmic): rhythmic
        1) Family time and routines (high or low): high
            a) Routines to promote parent–child togetherness: high
            b) Routines to promote husband–wife togetherness: low
            c) Routines to promote family unit togetherness: high
            d) Routines to promote family–relative togetherness: high
        2) Valuing family time and routines (high or low): high
            a) Degree of importance of routines to promote parent–child togetherness: high
            b) Degree of importance of routines to promote husband–wife togetherness: low

         c) Degree of importance of routines to promote family unit togetherness: high

         d) Degree of importance of routines to promote family–relative togetherness: high

     d. Traditionalistic (situational, celebratory, traditionalistic, or ritualistic): situational

       1) Traditions (high or low): low

         a) Holiday decorating: low

         b) Special experiences around changes: low

         c) Special rules around religious occasions: low

         d) Members participate in special events: low

       2) Celebrations (high or low): low

         a) Spouse's birthday: low

         b) Special occasions: low

         c) Major holidays: low

G. Family Resources (BB) (Family Recovery Factors)

  1. Social support: self-help group

  2. Kin support: parents cared for son

  3. Community support

    a. Funeral home provided wake and service

    b. Church provided priest for service

    c. Veterans Administration (VA) provided tombstone

    d. Social Security Administration (SSA) provided dependent benefits

  4. Family support: no family support

H. Situational Appraisal (CC)

  1. Paradigms (CCC)

    a. Child rearing (community focused vs. nuclear family focused): nuclear focused

    b. Work roles (for present and others vs. for present and/or future and self): for present and/or future and self

    c. Education (informal, formal, or both): both

  2. Coherence (CCCC); the degree the world is

    a. Comprehensible: internal and external environments are

      1) Structured: yes

      2) Predictable: yes

      3) Explicable: yes

    b. Manageable (resources are available to meet demands): yes

    c. Meaningful (life demands are challenges worthy of investment): yes

3. Schema (CCCCC) (shared values)
   a. Family structure (extended vs. nuclear family): extended
   b. Self-/group orientation (we vs. I): we
   c. Spiritual beliefs (spiritual vs. religious): spiritual
   d. Land/nature (preserved vs. used): preserved
   e. Time orientation (present vs. future): future

I. Problem Solving and Coping (PSC)
1. Problem-solving skills
   a. Define the stressor as manageable: identified stressor as a challenge
   b. Identify alternative courses of action: identified ways to live without husband
   c. Initiate steps to resolve issues: did not initiate steps to resolve issues
      1) Discrete
      2) Interpersonal
   d. Resolve the problem: did not resolve the problem

2. Coping (strategies, patterns, and behaviors)
   a. Maintain or strengthen family
      1) Parental sacrifice to attain family objectives
      2) High participation in joint activities
      3) Strong affectional ties between mother and child
   b. Maintain emotional stability and well-being: used crisis counseling from psychologist
   c. Obtain or use resources: went to VA and SSA to get benefits
   d. Initiate efforts to resolve hardships: did not initiate efforts to resolve hardships

J. Family Adaptation (XX): Bonadaptation
1. Bonadaptation (balance and harmony)
   a. Development, well-being, and spirituality: balanced; my son's development was promoted evidenced by normal development patterns
   b. Community relationships and nature: balanced; returned to work
   c. Structure and function: balanced; I was functioning in my roles of mother and worker
   d. Interpersonal relationships: balanced; depended on parents less

2. Maladaptation (imbalance and disharmony)
   a. Development, well-being, and spirituality
   b. Community relationships and nature
   c. Structure and function
   d. Interpersonal relationships

Now complete the following outline for your crisis.

I. Adjustment Phase
  A. Stressor (A)
    1. Level of severity: degree to which stressor
      a. Threatens family stability
      b. Disrupts family functioning
      c. Places demands on family capabilities
  B. Vulnerability (V) (high to low) Shaped by Pileup of
    1. Stressors and demands
    2. Strains and demands
    3. Transitions and demands
  C. Established Patterns of Functioning (T) (Family Typology)
    1. Regenerative (vulnerable, durable, secure, or regenerative)
      a. Hardiness (high or low)
        1) Sense of control
        2) Meaningfulness in life
        3) Involvement in activities
        4) Commitment to learn and explore new experiences
      b. Coherence (high or low)
        1) Acceptance
        2) Loyalty
        3) Pride
        4) Faith
        5) Trust
        6) Respect
        7) Caring
        8) Shared values

    2. Resilient (fragile, pliant, bonded, or resilient)
      a. Bonding (high or low)
        1) Open to discussion
        2) Feeling close
        3) Desirous of connection
        4) Doing things together
      b. Flexibility (high or low)
        1) Open communication
        2) Compromise
        3) Willingness to shift responsibilities
        4) Participation in decision making

3. Rhythmic (unpatterned, structuralized, intentional, or rhythmic)
   a. Family time and routines (high or low)
      1) Routines to promote parent–child togetherness
      2) Routines to promote husband–wife togetherness
      3) Routines to promote family unit togetherness
      4) Routines to promote family–relative togetherness
   b. Valuing family time and routines (high or low)
      1) Degree of importance of routines to promote parent–child togetherness
      2) Degree of importance of routines to promote husband–wife togetherness
      3) Degree of importance of routines to promote family unit togetherness
      4) Degree of importance of routines to promote family–relative togetherness

4. Traditionalistic (situational, celebratory, traditionalistic, or ritualistic)
   a. Traditions (high or low)
      1) Holiday decorating
      2) Special experiences around changes
      3) Special rules around religious occasions
      4) Members participate in special events
   b. Celebrations (high or low)
      1) Spouse's birthday
      2) Special occasions
      3) Major holidays

D. Family Resources (B) [Family Protective Factors (FPF)]
E. Stressor Appraisal (C) (of seriousness of stressor and its hardships as setback or catastrophe)
F. Problem Solving and Coping (PSC)

1. Problem-solving skills: family's ability to
   a. Define the stressor as manageable
   b. Identify alternative courses of action
   c. Initiate steps to resolve issues
      1) Discrete
      2) Interpersonal
   d. Resolve the problem

2. Coping (strategies, patterns, and behaviors)
   a. Maintain or strengthen family
   b. Maintain emotional stability and well-being
   c. Obtain or use resources
   d. Initiate efforts to resolve hardships

G. Adjustment
1. Bonadjustment (balance and harmony)
   a. Development, well-being, and spirituality
   b. Community relationships and nature
   c. Structure and function
   d. Interpersonal relationships
2. Maladjustment/crisis situation (imbalance and disharmony)
   a. Development, well-being, and spirituality
   b. Community relationships and nature
   c. Structure and function
   d. Interpersonal relationships

II. Adaptation Phase
A. Stressor (A)
B. Stressor Appraisal (C) (setback or catastrophe)
C. Inadequate and/or Deterioration in Family Patterns of Functioning (T)
1. Regenerative (vulnerable, durable, secure, or regenerative)
   a. Hardiness (high or low)
      1) Sense of control
      2) Meaningfulness in life
      3) Involvement in activities
      4) Commitment to learn and explore new experiences
   b. Coherence (high or low)
      1) Acceptance
      2) Loyalty
      3) Pride
      4) Faith
      5) Trust
      6) Respect
      7) Caring
      8) Shared values
2. Resilient (fragile, pliant, bonded, or resilient)
   a. Bonding (high or low)
      1) Open to discussion
      2) Feeling close
      3) Desirous of connection
      4) Doing things together
   b. Flexibility (high or low)
      1) Open communication
      2) Compromise

            3) Willingness to shift responsibilities

            4) Participation in decision making

    3. Rhythmic (unpatterned, structuralized, intentional, or rhythmic)

       a. Family time and routines (high or low)

            1) Routines to promote parent–child togetherness

            2) Routines to promote husband–wife togetherness

            3) Routines to promote family unit togetherness

            4) Routines to promote family–relative togetherness

       b. Valuing family time and routines (high or low)

            1) Degree of importance of routines to promote parent–child togetherness

            2) Degree of importance of routines to promote husband–wife togetherness

            3) Degree of importance of routines to promote family unit togetherness

            4) Degree of importance of routines to promote family–relative togetherness

    4. Traditionalistic (situational, celebratory, traditionalistic, or ritualistic)

       a. Traditions (high or low)

            1) Holiday decorating

            2) Special experiences around changes

            3) Special rules around religious occasions

            4) Members participate in special events

       b. Celebrations (high or low)

            1) Spouse's birthday

            2) Special occasions

            3) Major holidays

D. Pileup of Demands (AA)

   1. Stressors

   2. Strains

   3. Transitions

E. Maladjustment/Crisis Situation (X)

F. Patterns of Functioning

   1. Retained patterns of functioning (T)

   2. Restored patterns of functioning (T)

   3. Newly instituted patterns of functioning (TT)

G. Family Resources (BB) (Family Recovery Factors)

   1. Social support

   2. Kin support

   3. Community support

   4. Family support

H. Situational Appraisal (CC)

1. Paradigms (CCC)
   a. Child rearing (community focused vs. nuclear family focused)
   b. Work roles (for present and others vs. for present and/or future and self)
   c. Education (informal, formal, or both)

2. Coherence (CCCC); the degree the world is
   a. Comprehensible: internal and external environments are
      1) Structured
      2) Predictable
      3) Explicable
   b. Manageable (resources are available to meet demands)
   c. Meaningful (life demands are challenges worthy of investment)

3. Schema (CCCCC) (shared values)
   a. Family structure (extended vs. nuclear family)
   b. Self-/group orientation (we vs. I)
   c. Spiritual beliefs (spiritual vs. religious)
   d. Land/nature (preserved vs. used)
   e. Time orientation (present vs. future)

I. Problem Solving and Coping (PSC)

1. Problem-solving skills: family's ability to
   a. Define the stressor as manageable
   b. Identify alternative courses of action
   c. Initiate steps to resolve issues
      1) Discrete
      2) Interpersonal
   d. Resolve the problem

2. Coping (strategies, patterns, and behaviors)
   a. Maintain or strengthen family
   b. Maintain emotional stability and well-being
   c. Obtain or use resources
   d. Initiate efforts to resolve hardships

J. Family Adaptation (*XX*)

1. Bonadaptation (balance and harmony)
   a. Development, well-being, and spirituality
   b. Community relationships and nature
   c. Structure and function
   d. Interpersonal relationships

2. Maladaptation (imbalance and disharmony)
   a. Development, well-being, and spirituality
   b. Community relationships and nature
   c. Structure and function
   d. Interpersonal relationships

References and Suggestions for Further Reading

Hill, R. (1949). *Families under stress.* New York: Harper & Row.

Hill, R. (1958). Generic features of families under stress. *Social Casework, 49,* 139–150.

McCubbin, H. I., & McCubbin, M. A. (1991). Family stress theory and assessment: The Resiliency Model of Family Stress, Adjustment, and Adaptation. In H. I. McCubbin & A. I. Thompson (Eds.), *Family assessment inventories for research and practice* (pp. 3–32). Madison: University of Wisconsin.

McCubbin, H. I., McCubbin, M. A., Thompson, A. I., Han, S., & Allen, C. T. (1997). Families under stress: What makes them resilient. *Journal of Family and Consumer Sciences, 89*(3), 2–11.

McCubbin, H. I., McCubbin, M. A., Thompson, A. I., & Thompson, E. A. (1995). *Resiliency in ethnic minority families: A conceptual model for predicting family adjustment and adaptation.* Madison: University of Wisconsin System.

McCubbin, H. I., & Patterson, J. M. (1981). *Systematic assessment of family stress, resources, and coping: Tools for research, education, and clinical intervention.* St. Paul, MN: Department of Family Social Science.

McCubbin, H. I., & Patterson, J. M. (1983a). The family stress process: The Double ABCX Model of adjustment and adaptation. In H. McCubbin, M. Sussman, & J. Patterson (Eds.), *Social stress and the family: Advances and developments in family stress theory and research* (pp. 7–37). New York: Haworth.

McCubbin, H. I., & Patterson, J. M. (1983b). Family transitions: Adaptation to stress. In H. I. McCubbin & C. R. Figley (Eds.), *Stress and the family: Coping with normative transitions* (pp. 5–25). New York: Brunner/Mazel.

McCubbin, H. I., Thompson, A., & McCubbin, M. A. (2001). *Family measures: Stress, coping and resiliency—Inventories for research and practice.* Honolulu: Kamechamecha Schools.

McCubbin, H. I., Thompson, A., Pirner, P., & McCubbin, M. A. (1988). *Family types and family strengths: A life cycle and ecological perspective.* Edina, MN: Burgess International Group.

McCubbin, M. A., & McCubbin, H. I. (1987). Family stress theory and assessment: The T-Double ABCX Model of family adjustment and adaptation. In H. I. McCubbin & A. Thompson (Eds.), *Family assessment inventories for research and practice* (pp. 3–32). Madison: University of Wisconsin.

McCubbin, M. A., & McCubbin, H. I. (1989). Theoretical orientations to family stress and coping. In C. R. Figley (Ed.), *Treating stress in families* (pp. 3–43). New York: Brunner/Mazel.

McCubbin, M. A., & McCubbin, H. I. (1991). Family stress theory and assessment: The Resiliency Model of Family Stress Adjustment and Adaptation. In H. I. McCubbin & A. Thompson (Eds.), *Family assessment inventories for research and practice* (pp. 3–31). Madison: University of Wisconsin.

McCubbin, M. A., & McCubbin, H. I. (1993). Families coping with illness: The Resiliency Model of Family Stress, Adjustment, and Adaptation. In C. Danielson, B. Hamel-Bissell, & P. Winstead-Fry (Eds.), *Families, health & illness: Perspectives on coping and intervention* (pp. 21–64). St. Louis, MO: Mosby.

McCubbin, M. A., & McCubbin, H. I. (1996). Resiliency in families: A conceptual model of family adjustment and adaptation in response to stress and crises. In H. I. McCubbin, A. I. Thompson, & M. A. McCubbin (Eds.), *Family assessment: Resiliency, coping and adaptation—Inventories for research and practice* (pp. 1–64). Madison: University of Wisconsin System.

CHAPTER 9

The Family Distress Model and the Contextual Model of Family Stress

The Family Distress Model

Cornille, a marriage and family therapist, and Boroto, a psychologist (1992), developed the Family Distress Model (FDM) "as a guide to understanding the process families go through to confront and accommodate change" (p. 182). The authors proposed that the model, heavily influenced by family systems medicine, has utility for guiding both research and intervention with families dealing with stressors (Cornille & Boroto, 1992).

Conceptual Framework of the Family Distress Model

The Family Distress Model consists of five phases (Cornille, Mullis, & Mullis, 2006) originally termed stages (Cornille & Boroto, 1992). Figure 9.1 illustrates the five phases of the model, and a discussion of each of the phases follows.

Phase I: Family's Stable (Predictable) Pattern

According to the FDM, families have predictable (Cornille et al., 2006), originally called stable (Cornille & Boroto, 1992), patterns that fit their resources, identity, values, and goals. Families believe that their patterns are the "normal and preferable ways of living" (Cornille & Boroto,

Figure 9.1 The Family Distress Model

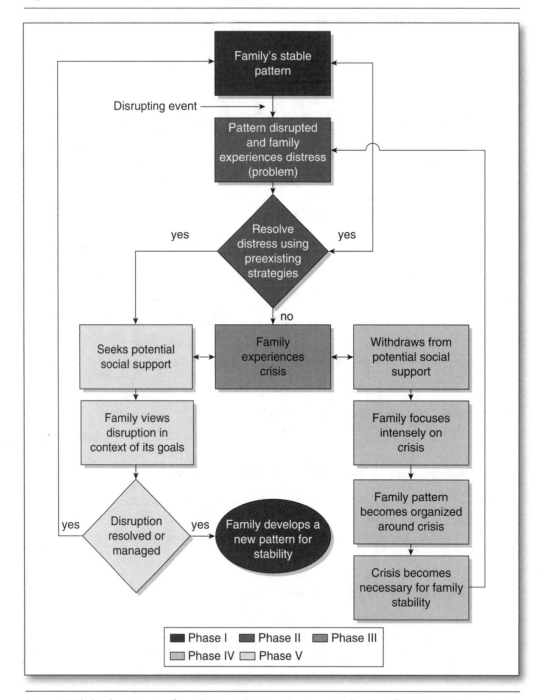

Source: With kind permission from Springer Science+Business Media: Cornille, T. A., & Boroto, D. R. (1992). The Family Distress Model: A conceptual and clinical application of Reiss' strong bonds finding. *Contemporary Family Therapy, 14*(3), 181–198.

1992, p. 187). These patterns include routines, roles, rituals, and rules on which the family bases decisions about day-to-day life, such as when and where to have dinner. These decisions are made to support the family's identity, values, and goals. The family's predictable pattern in the FDM is similar to the *T* factor in the Typology Model (McCubbin, Thompson, Pirner, & McCubbin, 1988; McCubbin & McCubbin, 1987, 1989), and the established patterns of functioning in the Resiliency Model (McCubbin, McCubbin, Thompson, & Thompson, 1995; McCubbin & McCubbin, 1991, 1993, 1996).

Disrupting Event

The disrupting event appears between Phases I and II of the FDM (Cornille & Boroto, 1992; Cornille, Boroto, Barnes, & Hall, 1996; Cornille et al., 2006). The disrupting event of the FDM (Cornille & Boroto, 1992; Cornille et al., 1996; Cornille et al., 2006) is the stressor in other stress models. The authors of the FDM acknowledge that disrupting events originate from both external and internal sources.

Phase II: Problems

In Phase II of the FDM, normal family patterns are disrupted, and the family experiences distress. The family resolves the distress using preexisting patterns in this phase.

Pattern disrupted and family experiences distress (problem). In this part of Phase II, the authors define distress as the problem while, in their discussion, they define the disrupting event as the problem (Cornille et al., 1996), leading to confusion in understanding the model. The disrupting event disrupts the family's predictable pattern of routines, roles, rituals, and rules, leading to distress. This part of the model is similar to family system vulnerability in the Typology Model (McCubbin et al., 1988; McCubbin & McCubbin, 1987, 1989).

Resolve distress using preexisting strategies. Generally, disruptions in patterns are minor inconveniences that the family addresses without much thought or conscious attention by using preestablished, simple strategies (first-order or Level 1 changes). If preestablished strategies successfully reestablish the family pattern, the family returns to Phase I, its predictable pattern; however, if preestablished strategies fail to reestablish the family pattern, the family may try different strategies. If the different strategies fail to reestablish the family pattern, the family moves into Phase III and experiences a crisis. Families alternatively move to Phase 5 and seek support and avoid a crisis.

Phase III: Family Experiences Crisis

The authors of the FDM define a crisis as "a problem for which the family believes no solution is available" (Cornille et al., 1996, p. 440). In Chapter 2 of this book, however, crisis refers to a state of being, which is consistent with most of the latest stress literature (e.g., Boss, 1988). When a family experiences a crisis, according to the FDM, its members may go to either Phase IV in which they withdraw from potential support or Phase V in which they seek potential support.

Phase IV: Patterns Organized Around the Crisis

In Phase IV of the FDM (Cornille & Boroto, 1992; Cornille et al., 1996; Cornille et al., 2006), families organize patterns around the crisis. They do this by withdrawing from potential support and becoming preoccupied with the crisis, leading to crisis being necessary for stability/predictability.

Family withdraws from potential social support. According to the FDM (Cornille & Boroto, 1992: Cornille et al., 1996; Cornille et al., 2006), some families believe that they need to resolve their crises without assistance. These families withdraw from potential social support (aid, association, affection), leading the family to become preoccupied with the crisis.

Family focuses intensely on (becomes preoccupied with) crisis. In the FDM (Cornille & Boroto, 1992: Cornille et al., 1996; Cornille et al., 2006), when families believe that they need to resolve their crises without assistance and withdraw from potential social support, the crisis overshadows issues that contribute to family well-being, and members' needs become secondary. The crisis becomes central to family functioning.

Family pattern becomes organized around crisis. Some families modify their patterns of family routines, rules, and roles into new patterns organized around the crisis. For example, rituals around holidays may be discontinued when a loved one dies, or routines surrounding a child's bedtime may be discontinued. These families experience temporary relief as long as they focus on the crisis, but this solution eventually increases distress and creates additional problems/stressors for family members with neglected needs. Having the family pattern organized around the crisis remains effective as long as the crisis exists.

Crisis becomes necessary for family stability. With the resolution of the crisis, the family experiences distress associated with the loss of focus on the crisis. Routines, roles, and rules adopted to deal with the crisis no longer work, and the family tries to maintain equilibrium by resisting resolution of the crisis or experiencing another crisis (returns to Phase III). This process may be unconscious. Often we observe this phenomenon when someone tries to recover from an addiction without involving the family in the process.

Phase V: Using Social Support to Cope With a Crisis

Families may enter Phase V from Phase II of problems, Phase III of crisis, or Phase IV of patterns being organized around crisis. In Phase V of the FDM (Cornille & Boroto, 1992; Cornille et al., 1996; Cornille et al., 2006), the family seeks potential social support, views the disruption in the context of its goals, resolves or manages the disruption, and develops a new pattern of stability.

Family Seeks Potential Social Support

When problems exceed a family's resources, members look outside the family for help. Families become aware that their strategies for coping have not worked and ask for external assistance, perhaps from a professional. Cornille and Boroto (1992), in discussing their model, refer to the sources of support put forth by Antonucci (cited in Cornille & Boroto, 1992) of aid, affiliation, and affection. Aid refers to concrete goods and services while affiliation refers to a sense of belonging or membership, and affection refers to emotional support.

Family Views Disruption (Crisis) in Context of Its Goals

According to Cornille and Boroto (1992), if the family receives useful outside resources, the family views the disruption/crisis in the context of its goals. Crisis managers need to remind families about their goals at this time without imposing their own values and goals (Cornille et al., 1996).

Disruption (Crisis) Resolved or Managed

Useful outside resources help the family to resolve the disruption/crisis. The resolution of the disruption/crisis allows a family to develop a stable new predictable pattern or to return to the previous pattern of Phase I.

Family Develops a New Pattern for Stability (Predictability)

Developing a new pattern involves second-order change and commonly occurs because of crises resulting from the stressors of transition. At this point, the family returns to Phase I of the FDM (Cornille & Boroto, 1992; Cornille et al., 1996; Cornille et al., 2006) until another disrupting event occurs.

Critique of the Family Distress Model

On the positive side, in their second version of the FDM, the authors changed the term *stage* (Cornille & Boroto, 1992) to *phase* (Cornille et al., 2006). This change helps to remove the idea that one must go from one stage to another in a linear fashion. In addition, *stable pattern* (Cornille & Boroto, 1992) changed to *predictable pattern* (Cornille et al., 2006), which is probably more readily understood by paraprofessionals who might perform crisis management. The FDM provides a model that considers family patterns like the Typology Model (McCubbin et al., 1988; McCubbin & McCubbin, 1987, 1989) and the Resiliency Model (McCubbin et al., 1995; McCubbin & McCubbin, 1991, 1993, 1996) but is somewhat simpler and easier to use as a guide for intervention with families.

On the negative side, in the discussions, Cornille and associates (Cornille & Boroto, 1992; Cornille et al., 1996; Cornille et al., 2006) use the word *problem* to refer to three different things: the disrupting event, the distress arising from the event, and the crisis. The use of the term *problem* for three separate concepts leads to confusion. Although paraprofessionals may understand the term *problem*, it would be helpful to use the term *problem* for the event, the distress, *or* the crisis. Better yet would be to not use *problem* at all and refer to the *event*, *distress*, and *crisis* instead. In Phase IV, the FDM purports that the *crisis* becomes necessary for family stability. It may be more appropriate to say that the *stressor* becomes necessary for family stability, as, by definition, a crisis is time-limited.

Summary of the Family Distress Model

The Family Distress Model (Cornille & Boroto, 1992; Cornille et al., 1996; Cornille et al., 2006), developed by a family therapist and a psychologist, provides a guide for research and for intervention. It considers family patterns yet provides a simpler model than earlier models that included family patterns. The model consists of five nonlinear phases with the disrupting event/stressor occurring between Phase I and Phase II: Phase I, the family's stable/predictable pattern; Phase II, problems; Phase III, family experiences crisis; Phase IV, patterns organized around the crisis; and Phase V, using social support to cope with the crisis. Like the Family Distress Model, the Contextual Model of Family Stress was developed by a family therapist.

The Contextual Model of Family Stress

The core of the Contextual Model (Boss, 2002) is Hill's (1949, 1958) ABCX Formula. Pauline Boss (2002), a marriage and family therapist, adds to the ABCX Formula in hopes of making it "more useful to a wider population of therapists, teachers, nurses, doctors, researchers, and policymakers who work with stressed families of different ethnic backgrounds and beliefs, young and old" (p. 35). She searched inductively for more general umbrella variables and with a new focus on meaning and perception aiming at multicultural application. Reviewing research of others as well as her own, Boss (2002) added the internal and external contexts to the ABCX Formula (Hill, 1949, 1958) to consider the unique experiences of individuals from diverse backgrounds, which affect their perceptions.

Conceptual Framework of the Contextual Model of Family Stress

Contexts

Some of the contexts of the Contextual Model (Boss, 2002) were included in earlier models using different terminology, but most were not. See Figure 9.2. Conflict between external and internal contexts creates more stress. Following appear discussions of each of the contexts.

External context. Boss (2002) defines the external context as elements the family cannot control that influence how families react to stressors, including the cultural, historical, economic, developmental, and hereditary contexts. The *cultural* context includes the rules of society as well as the rules of any subculture to which the family belongs. Sometimes the rules of the culture and of the subculture conflict, causing more stress on the family. The *historical* context includes both events going on at the time of the stressor and events experienced by ancestors as in trauma transmitted from generation to generation. The *economic* context includes the financial situation both in the community and in the larger society. Examples include an economic depression, recession, or boon on the societal level and

Figure 9.2 The Contextual Model of Family Stress

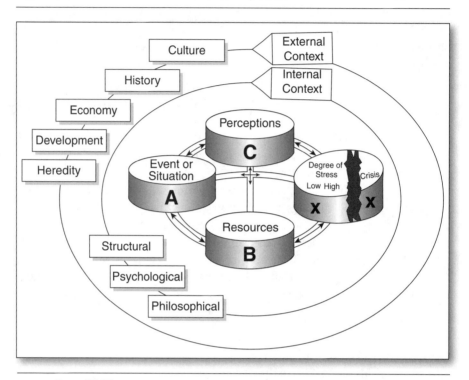

Source: Boss (2002).

changes in the economy because of natural disasters or plants opening or closing on the community level. The *developmental* context refers to the stages in the life cycle of both the family and each individual family member. The *hereditary* context refers to genetics, which influence such things as our health, stamina, and energy, which are resources.

Internal context. Boss (2002) defines the internal context as elements the family can change and control including the structural, psychological, and philosophical contexts. When performing crisis intervention, Boss focuses primarily on the internal instead of the external context because the internal context changes more easily than the external context. While it may not be possible to change the fact that the country is in a recession (economic context), it is possible to change role assignments within a family (internal context).

A family's internal context may change over time. In addition, at any particular time, family members may have different internal contexts from each other. The *structural* context means the form and function of boundaries, role assignments, and rules about who is in or out of boundaries of the family. Boss (2002) calls the situation of unclear rules about who is in or out of boundaries of the family *boundary ambiguity.* The *psychological* context refers to the family's perception of a stressor including both cognitive and affective (feeling) processes. The *philosophical* context, which is similar to the family schema in the Resiliency Model (McCubbin et al., 1995; McCubbin & McCubbin, 1991, 1993, 1996) discussed in Chapter 8, refers to the family's values and beliefs.

A, B, C, X, *and* X *in the* Contextual Model of Family Stress

In the Contextual Model of Family Stress, Boss (2002) includes and elaborates on the ABCX Formula (Hill, 1949, 1958). As in the original formula, *A* is the stressor event or situation, *B* is resources (strengths), and *C* is perceptions (individual and collective). In the Contextual Model of Family Stress, *C* (perceptions) receives primacy. In Boss's (2002) adaptation of the ABCX Formula to the Contextual Model of Family Stress, she adds an *X* to represent the degree of stress (*low* or *high*) while another *X* represents crisis.

Critique of the Contextual Model of Family Stress

The Contextual Model of Family Stress (Boss, 2002) was designed for use by practitioners as well as researchers and takes into account cultural differences. The inclusion of the external context in the Contextual Model of Family Stress (Boss, 2002) makes it helpful in understanding groups that experienced historical trauma such as American Indians. While adding the degree of stress to the model is a good idea, using *X* to represent both the degree of stress and the crisis is confusing. Generally, the linearity of the ABCX Formula (Hill, 1949, 1958) limits the formula and other models based on it such as the Contextual Model. Boss (2002), however, does attempt to alleviate this limitation of the ABCX Formula by including arrows between each of the elements, showing that the development of a crisis is not a linear process.

Summary of the Contextual Model of Family Stress

Boss (2002) added the external and internal contexts that influence how a family reacts to a stressor to Hill's (1949, 1958) ABCX Formula. The external context, the environment/ecosystem, tends to be elements the family cannot control. The external elements include cultural, historical, economic, developmental, and hereditary. The internal context falls into three categories, structural, psychological, and philosophical. Boss (2002) also added the degree of stress to the model but represented it with an X, causing confusion as she also uses X to represent crisis.

Chapter Summary

This chapter presented two of the latest family stress models, the Family Distress Model (FDM) and the Contextual Model of Family Stress, that can be used for guiding intervention as well as research. The FDM proposes five nonlinear phases. Although the Contextual Model, like many other family stress models, is based on the ABCX Formula, it shows the interactive nature of these components. In addition, the Contextual Model considers external and internal contexts, which had not been addressed in any previous model. A table comparing these two models to the other family stress models presented in this text appears in the appendix of this book. The variables appearing in the same rows are sometimes totally equivalent and at other times partially equivalent.

EXERCISES

9.1 Outline the crisis from Exercise 2.1 using Family Distress Model concepts. Following is an example of the assignment based on the case study presented in Chapter 2.

I. Phase I: Family's predictable pattern

A. Routines: had daily routines

B. Roles: had traditional roles at home

C. Rituals: had holiday rituals

D. Rules: husband and I made rules together

II. Disrupting event (external or internal): husband's death (internal)

III. Phase II: Problems

A. Pattern disrupted and family experiences distress (problem)

1. Routines: evening routines changed as my son and I started eating supper at my parents' home after my husband died

2. Roles: role as wife no longer existed

3. Rituals: rituals did not immediately change

4. Rules: metarules changed as I began to make rules alone

B. Resolve distress using preexisting strategies (or new strategies): did not resolve distress

IV. Phase III: Family experiences crisis

    A. Amount of consciousness and acceptance by each family member of his or her and others' family roles (better than average, average, below average): below average; my parents took care of my son for a period of time—a few days, I think—so I was not performing my role as parent

    B. Extent to which family members worked toward family and individual good (better than average, average, below average): below average; I was not taking care of my son, and self-care was based on what others told me to do

    C. How much family members found satisfaction with family unit (better than average, average, below average): below average; the family unit had been redefined, and ways to find satisfaction would need to be redefined as well

    D. Whether the family had a sense of direction and was moving in that direction (better than average, average, below average): below average; family goals would need to be redefined by me as a single parent

V. Phase IV: Patterns organized around the crisis: did not experience Phase IV

    A. Withdraws from potential social support

        1. Aid
        2. Affiliation
        3. Affection

    B. Family becomes preoccupied with crisis

    C. Family pattern becomes organized around crisis

        1. Routines
        2. Roles
        3. Rituals
        4. Rules

    D. Crisis becomes necessary for family stability

VI. Phase IV: Using social support to cope with a crisis

    A. Seeks potential social support

        1. Aid

            a. Used material aid from parents in the form of meals
            b. Used material aid from Veterans Administration (VA) in the form of tombstone
            c. Used material aid from Social Security Administration (SSA) in the form of dependent benefits

        2. Affiliation: Used association in the form of widows' group

        3. Affection: did not use affection

B. Family views crisis in context of its goals: used life insurance toward goal of buying home

C. Crisis resolved or managed: managed

D. Family developed a new pattern for predictability (or returns to old pattern): developed a new pattern for predictability

  1. Routines: evening routines of eating supper at my parents' home became new pattern

  2. Roles: role of single woman

  3. Rituals: rituals did not immediately change

  4. Rules: I made rules alone

Now complete the following outline based on your crisis.

  I. Phase I: Family's stable (predictable) pattern

   A. Routines

   B. Roles

   C. Rituals

   D. Rules

  II. Disrupting event (external or internal)

  III. Phase II: Problems

   A. Pattern disrupted and family experiences distress (problem)

    1. Routines

    2. Roles

    3. Rituals

    4. Rules

   B. Resolve distress using preexisting strategies (or new strategies)

    1. Preexisting

    2. New

  IV. Phase III: Family experiences crisis

  V. Phase IV: Patterns organized around the crisis

   A. Withdraws from potential social support

    1. Aid

    2. Affiliation

    3. Affection

   B. Family focuses intensely on (becomes preoccupied with) crisis (members' needs become secondary)

    C. Family pattern becomes organized around crisis

       1. Routines

       2. Roles

       3. Rituals

       4. Rules

    D. Crisis becomes necessary for family stability

VI. Phase V: Using social support to cope with a crisis

    A. Seeks potential social support

       1. Aid

       2. Affiliation

       3. Affection

    B. Family views disruption (crisis) in context of its goals

    C. Disruption (crisis) resolved or managed

    D. Family develops a new pattern for stability (predictability) (or returns to old pattern)

       1. Routines

       2. Roles

       3. Rituals

       4. Rules

9.2   Outline the crisis from Exercise 2.1 using Boss's (2002) Contextual Model of Family Stress. Following is an example of this assignment based on the case study presented in Chapter 2.

I. External context (environment/ecosystem): Elements the family cannot control that influence how family reacts to stressor

    A. Cultural

       1. Culture's rules: rules about men marrying younger women

       2. Subculture's rules: cannot think of any subculture rules impacting experience of stressor

    B. Historical

       1. Events going on at the time of stressor: cannot remember any historical events from that time

       2. Events experienced by ancestors (trauma may have been passed down): ancestors were exiled from Canada

    C. Economic

       1. Community's economy: recovering from oil bust

       2. Society's economy: interest rates were high

    D. Developmental: stage in the life cycle

       1. Family: child rearing

       2. Individuals: age 30 transition

    E. Hereditary: Genetic

       1. Health: poor eyesight

       2. Stamina: high stamina

       3. Energy: medium energy

II. Internal context: Elements the family can change and control

    A. Structural: Form and function of

       1. Boundaries: permeable

       2. Role assignments: traditional

       3. Rules about who is in or out of boundaries (boundary ambiguity when rules are unclear): unambiguous

    B. Psychological: Family's perception

       1. Cognitive: challenging; I believed that I would be successful in spite of my loss

       2. Affective

          a. Emotional shock

          b. Guilt

          c. Numbness

    C. Philosophical

       1. Values

          a. Family structure (extended vs. nuclear family): extended

          b. Self-/group orientation (we vs. I): we

          c. Spiritual beliefs (spiritual vs. religious): spiritual

          d. Land/nature (preserved vs. used): preserved

          e. Time orientation (present vs. future): future

       2. Beliefs

          a. Believed extended family was important part of family

          b. Believed needs of family were more important than needs of individual family members

          c. Believed that it was more important to be spiritual than to follow a particular organized religion

          d. Believed that it was important to plan and make decisions based on the future

III. The A, B, C, X, and X of Family Stress

    A. A = event or situation: husband's death

    B. B = resources

1. Integration (high, medium, low): medium
    a. Willingness to sacrifice personal interest to attain family objectives (high, medium, low): high; I sacrificed my personal interests to care for my husband and child
    b. Pride in the family tree and in the ancestral traditions (high, medium, low): medium; there was pride in the family tree from one side of the family but not the other
    c. Presence of strong patterns of emotional interdependence and unity (high, medium, low): low; we did not share our emotions very readily
    d. High participation as a family in joint activities (high, medium, low): low; other than going to doctors' visits, we did not share many activities
    e. Strong affectional ties between father and mother, father and children, mother and children, and children and children (high, medium, low): medium

        1) Father and mother (high, medium, low): medium; focused on illness and child

        2) Father and children (high, medium, low): low; father was not able to pick up and hold child because of illness; he seemed to disengage

        3) Mother and children (high, medium, low): medium; child was source of emotional satisfaction

        4) Children and children (high, medium, low): only one child

2. Adaptability (high, medium, low): medium
    a. Previous success in meeting family crises (high, medium, low): medium; had recovered from other crises as when the husband was diagnosed with cancer but not to prior level of functioning
    b. Predominance of nonmaterialistic goals (high, medium, low): high; goals were within financial means—for example, we lived in a mobile home at the time
    c. Flexibility and willingness to shift traditional roles of husband and wife or of father and mother, if necessary (high, medium, low): low; husband could barely perform his roles much less shift roles
    d. Acceptance of responsibility by all family members in performing family duties (high, medium, low): low; primary responsibility for all household duties and child care were mine due to husband's illness
    e. Presence of equalitarian patterns of family control and decision making (high, medium, low): high; decisions were made as a couple

3. Marital adjustment (poor, fair, or good): fair to good
    a. Wife (poor, fair, or good): good; there were no disagreements
    b. Husband (poor, fair, or good): fair; husband could not really participate as a marital partner in many ways
    C. *C* = perceptions

1. Individual: challenging; I believed that I would be successful in spite of my loss

2. Collective: same as individual as other family member was infant

D. X = degree of stress (low or high): high because of nature of stressor

E. X = crisis

  1. Amount of consciousness and acceptance by each family member of his or her and others' family roles (better than average, average, below average): below average; my parents took care of my son for a period of time—a few days, I think—so I was not performing my role as parent

  2. Extent to which family members worked toward family and individual good (better than average, average, below average): below average; I was not taking care of my son, and self-care was based on what others told me to do

  3. How much family members found satisfaction with family unit (better than average, average, below average): below average; the family unit had been redefined, and ways to find satisfaction would need to be redefined as well

  4. Whether the family had a sense of direction and was moving in that direction (better than average, average, below average): below average; family goals would need to be redefined by me as a single parent

Now complete the following outline using your crisis.

I. External context (environment/ecosystem): Elements the family cannot control that influence how family reacts to stressor

  A. Cultural

    1. Culture's rules

    2. Subculture's rules

  B. Historical

    1. Events going on at the time of stressor

    2. Events experienced by ancestors (trauma may have been passed down)

  C. Economic

    1. Community's economy

    2. Society's economy

  D. Developmental: stage in the life cycle

    1. Family

    2. Individuals

  E. Hereditary

    1. Health

    2. Stamina

    3. Energy

II. Internal context: Elements the family can change and control
   A. Structural: Form and function of
      1. Boundaries
      2. Role assignments
      3. Rules about who is in or out of boundaries (boundary ambiguity when rules are unclear)
   B. Psychological: Family's perception
      1. Cognitive
      2. Affective
   C. Philosophical
      1. Values
      2. Beliefs

III. The A, B, C, X, and X of Family Stress
   A. A = event or situation
   B. B = resources
   C. C = perceptions
      1. Individual
      2. Collective
   D. X = degree of stress (low or high)
   E. X = crisis

References and Suggested Readings

Boss, P. (1988). *Family stress management.* Newbury Park, CA: Sage.

Boss, P. (2002). *Family stress management: A contextual approach.* Thousand Oaks, CA: Sage.

Cornille, T. A., & Boroto, D. R. (1992). The Family Distress Model: A conceptual and clinical application of Reiss' strong bonds finding. *Contemporary Family Therapy, 14*(3), 181–198.

Cornille, T. A., Boroto, D. R., Barnes, M. F., & Hall, P. K. (1996). Dealing with family distress in schools. *Families in Society: The Journal of Contemporary Human Services, 77*(7), 435–445.

Cornille, T. A., Mullis, A. K., & Mullis, R. L. (2006, November). *How to use Internet coverage about disasters to teach about family resilience.* PowerPoint presented at the meeting of the National Council on Family Relations, Minneapolis, MN.

Hill, R. (1949). *Families under stress.* New York: Harper & Brothers.

Hill, R. (1958). Generic features of families under stress. *Social Casework, 49,* 139–150.

McCubbin, H. I., McCubbin, M. A., Thompson, A. I., & Thompson, E. A. (1995). *Resiliency in ethnic families: A conceptual model for predicting family adjustment and adaptation.* Madison: University of Wisconsin System.

McCubbin, H. I., Thompson, A., Pirner, P., & McCubbin, M. A. (1988). *Family types and family strengths: A life cycle and ecological perspective.* Edina, MN: Burgess International Group.

McCubbin, M. A., & McCubbin, H. I. (1987). Family stress theory and assessment: The T-Double ABCX Model of family adjustment and adaptation. In H. I. McCubbin & A. Thompson (Eds.), *Family assessment inventories for research and practice* (pp. 3–32). Madison: University of Wisconsin.

McCubbin, M. A., & McCubbin, H. I. (1989). Theoretical orientations to family stress and coping. In C. R. Figley (Ed.), *Treating stress in families* (pp. 3–43). New York: Brunner/Mazel.

McCubbin, M. A., & McCubbin, H. I. (1991). Family stress theory and assessment: The Resiliency Model of Family Stress Adjustment and Adaptation. In H. I. McCubbin & A. Thompson (Eds.), *Family assessment inventories for research and practice* (pp. 3–31). Madison: University of Wisconsin.

McCubbin, M. A., & McCubbin, H. I. (1993). Families coping with illness: The Resiliency Model of Family Stress, Adjustment, and Adaptation. In C. Danielson, B. Hamel-Bissell, & P. Winstead-Fry (Eds.), *Families, health & illness* (pp. 21–64). St. Louis, MO: Mosby.

McCubbin, M. A., & McCubbin, H. I. (1996). Resiliency in families: A conceptual model of family adjustment and adaptation in response to stress and crises. In H. I. McCubbin, A. I. Thompson, & M. A. McCubbin (Eds.), *Family assessment: Resiliency, coping and adaptation—Inventories for research and practice* (pp. 1–64). Madison: University of Wisconsin System.

CRISIS MANAGEMENT

Part II of this book made us fluent in various aspects of stress theory. This fluency prevents crisis managers from appearing mechanical when assisting people in crisis. Part III presents the history and practice of formal crisis management, which applies the models from Part II of this book.

CHAPTER 10

The History of Formal Crisis Management

I nformal crisis management assistance has probably existed since the beginning of humankind. People help other people all the time, providing resources and support in times of need. Formal crisis management assistance, however, is relatively new practice and has interdisciplinary roots. This chapter provides a chronology of the development of formal crisis management as well as the interdisciplinary contributions to the practice of crisis management. See Figure 10.1.

Chronology

1940s

Erich Lindemann, a sociologist, wrote the first major publication on crisis management in 1944 about the surviving family members of the 493 people who perished in the Cocoanut Grove Melody Lounge fire of 1942 in Boston. Based on his work with survivors and their grief, he believed that community volunteers (paraprofessionals) could help people work through grief. Before this time, only psychiatrists provided services for those with emotional symptoms of anxiety and depression, symptoms thought to stem only from personality disorders or biochemical illnesses (Kanel, 1998) rather than from loss.

After his study, Lindemann further operationalized his idea that community volunteers could help people and with Gerald Caplan established a community mental health program called the Wellesley project in Boston in 1948 with an emphasis on short-term preventive psychiatry and mental

Figure 10.1 Timeline of Formal Crisis Management

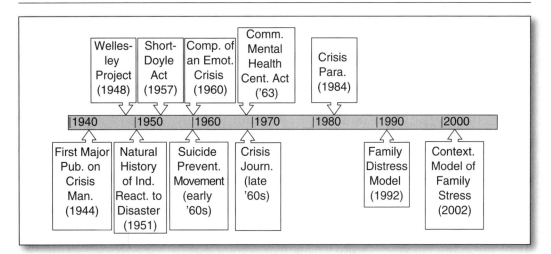

health consultation (Slaikeu, 1990). Out of the Wellesley project came some of the current-day individual stress theory (Kanel, 1998).

1950s and Early 1960s

In the 1950s and early 1960s crisis management saw the advent of the community mental health movement and the suicide prevention movement. The *community mental health movement* emerged in the United States beginning with the 1957 Short-Doyle Act, which authorized funding to provide mental health clinics for each county and resulted in the deinstitutionalization of mental patients. As a means of implementing the 1961 recommendations of the Joint Commission on Mental Illness and Health, Congress, with the support of the Kennedy administration, passed the Community Mental Health Centers Act of 1963 (Kanel, 1998; Slaikeu, 1990). Community mental health clinics, originally established to serve deinstitutionalized mentally ill patients, were directed by the U.S. government to provide short-term crisis management for clients who were not mentally ill (Slaikeu, 1990).

Parallel to the community mental health movement, the *suicide prevention movement* in the United States grew during the early 1960s, with community centers offering 24-hour hotlines manned by nonprofessional volunteers. Early centers in Los Angeles and Buffalo, New York, were aimed solely at preventing suicide (Slaikeu, 1990). Later, specialized, grassroots, nonprofit organizations met the needs of populations (e.g., abortion seekers, battered women, raped women) not being helped by government agencies (Kanel, 1998).

Late 1960s, 1970s, and 1980s

In the late 1960s and early 1970s, journals such as *Crisis Intervention* appeared (Kanel, 1998). The cognitive approaches of Ellis, Beck, Meichenbaum, and Lazarus blossomed in the 1970s and 1980s (Kanel, 1998). In the 1980s Hoff's Crisis Paradigm (1984, 1989, 1995, 2001) linked crisis management intervention techniques to crisis origins for individuals. Crisis management also became more valued because economics led to emphasis on diligence in the use of scarce resources (Slaikeu, 1990). Crisis management is economical in that it is short-term (lasting up to 6 weeks) and may prevent long-term mental health problems (negative crisis outcomes) that require treatment with more expensive long-term psychotherapy.

1990s and Early 2000s

In the 1990s and early 2000s, crisis management saw the development of new models aimed at guiding crisis management for families. The Family Distress Model (FDM) (Cornille & Boroto, 1992; Cornille, Mullis, & Mullis, 2006) and the Contextual Model of Family Stress (Boss, 2002) emerged at this time. Both models consider culture's influence on families' reactions to stressors.

Interdisciplinary Contributions

The evolution of formal crisis management was interdisciplinary. Psychiatry, psychoanalysis, and existential, humanistic, cognitive-behavioral, and family systems approaches influenced its development. Each is considered next, beginning with the psychiatry approach.

Psychiatry Approach

Preventive Psychiatry

Crisis management drew from both preventive psychiatry and military psychiatry. From *preventive psychiatry* we get the contributions of Lindemann (1944), Tyhurst (1957), Sifneos (1960), and Caplan (1964).

Caplan (1964) focused on preventing crises from occurring (primary prevention), using such techniques as public education programs. Caplan also developed a conceptual framework for understanding crises discussed in Part II of this book. In addition, he emphasized a community approach to crisis management and advocated consultation with the social network.

Lindemann (1944) focused on preventing negative crisis outcomes (secondary prevention). Although a sociologist, he contributed to the preventive psychiatry approach with his definition of the grieving process (grief work) to include processes that an individual needs to complete to have a positive outcome. Lindemann found that survivors who developed negative outcomes failed to go through the entire process. Grief work applies to any loss and therefore is one of the most important contributions to crisis management (Hoff, 1984, 1989, 1995, 2001). Grief work is discussed in detail in Chapter 11 of this book.

Also contributing to crisis management from the preventive psychiatry approach, Tyhurst (1957) helped us to understand individual responses to disasters and thus to help people when such disasters occur. Refer to Part II of this book for a more detailed discussion of Tyhurst's work as well as the work of Sifneos (1960) who reported on the components of an emotional crisis.

Military Psychiatry

Military psychiatry contributed to crisis management as well. From military psychiatry, crisis management draws the practice of giving immediate help (Hoff, 1984, 1989, 1995, 2001). Providing immediate help after a stressor can prevent a crisis from occurring. In addition to the psychiatry approach, the psychoanalytic approach contributed to crisis management.

Psychoanalytic Approach

Crisis management borrows an assumption, concepts, and techniques from Freud's psychoanalytic theory. Crisis management borrows from psychoanalysis the assumption that people are complex and capable of self-discovery and change (Hoff, 1984, 1989, 1995, 2001). From the theory crisis management also gets the concepts of psychic energy, ego strength, and equilibrium (balance). The concept of *psychic energy* refers to the idea that individuals have only a certain amount of psychological energy in order to deal with life stressors and helps explain the disequilibrium/unbalance that develops when an individual's coping skills fail to relieve distress and his or her psychic energy is depleted (Kanel, 1998). As previously pointed out, ego strength is a personal resource. Occasionally (e.g., when a person is psychotic or vegetatively depressed), crisis workers may be called upon to be the client's ego strength until the client can take over for him- or herself. Although at times this may be necessary, as a rule we perform crisis management *with* the individual or family rather than *for* the individual or family. In such a case, the client needs the worker to structure his or her behavior by setting goals and choosing strategies and/or to recommend medication so the person can take part in his or her crisis management (Kanel, 1998). This is a very important point. Performing crisis management with individuals or families empowers them at a time when everything seems beyond their control or agency. When we do things for clients in crisis, we make ourselves "the expert" and take away the power of the clients at a time when they are already disempowered and need to regain their sense of personal power. In addition, making decisions for the clients also affects the chances that crisis management will be successful. Clients are more likely to follow the intervention plan when they have made the plan themselves (Hoff, 1984, 1989, 1995, 2001) and thus are more likely to be successful in managing the crisis or to have a positive crisis outcome.

In addition to the concepts of psychic energy, ego strength, and equilibrium, the techniques of listening and catharsis (the expression of feelings) also stem from psychoanalytic roots. Techniques are discussed in greater detail in the next chapter of this book. Besides the psychiatric and psychoanalytic approaches, the existential approach contributed to crisis management.

Existential Approach

Existential theory addresses the meaning of our existence. From existential psychotherapy, crisis management acquired the idea that anxiety is a normal part of life and can actually help development. Anxiety acts as a motivator to grow to relieve the anxiety. Crisis helpers can use this idea to help clients redefine their situations as opportunities for growth (Kanel, 1998). The techniques of encouraging clients to accept responsibility and empowering them with choices also come from existentialism (Kanel, 1998). Crisis workers help clients realize their part in causing the crisis and then help them consider choices to recover. In addition to the psychiatric, psychoanalytic, and existential approaches, the humanistic approach influenced crisis management.

Humanistic Approach

From Carl Rogers (cited in Kanel, 1998), crisis management gets the belief that people can grow if they experience acceptance. When clients believe that they are accepted, they can better accept and trust themselves and make choices (Kanel, 1998). Crisis management also acquired reflective and empathic techniques from this approach (Kanel, 1998). The techniques help clients express emotions and contribute to positive crisis outcomes (Corsini & Wedding, 1989). In addition to the psychiatric, psychoanalytic, existential, and humanistic approaches, the cognitive-behavioral approach influenced crisis management.

Cognitive-Behavioral Approach

From the cognitive-behavioral approach crisis management borrowed the behavioral decision-making model on which crisis managers base all crisis management. The steps in the model include the following:

1. Defining the problem

2. Reviewing efforts to correct the problem

3. Deciding on desired outcomes

4. Brainstorming alternative interventions

5. Selecting alternatives and commitment to following through

6. Following up (Kanel, 1998)

From this approach, crisis management also acquired the idea of understanding the individual's or family's cognitive definition of the problem, and the technique of reframing (redefining) maladaptive definitions (Peake, Borduin, & Archer, 1988) to positive definitions. Besides the psychiatric, psychoanalytic, existential, humanistic, and cognitive-behavioral approaches, the family systems approach influenced crisis management.

Family Systems Approach

The family systems approach is particularly useful for distress and crises stemming from transitions. An assumption taken from the systems approach is that if a family member makes a major change, the rest of the family will also have to change to maintain balance. From the *structural* family systems approach we borrow the opposing terms *healthy* (balanced) and *unhealthy* (unbalanced) *family structures* (types) (Kanel, 1998). The *systems-based, family resilience approach,* the most recent to contribute to crisis management, focuses on strengths. Interventions build capabilities (resources and coping skills). Crisis managers consider *both* the individual and the family when using this approach (Walsh, 1998).

Summary of the History of Formal Crisis Management

Although informal crisis management has probably existed since the beginning of humankind, formal crisis management began in the 1940s with Lindemann's (1944) observations of grief work after the Boston Cocoanut Grove Melody Lounge fire in 1942. Based on his determination that community volunteers could help those in crisis, Lindemann, with Caplan, began the Wellesley project. The 1950s and early 1960s brought the suicide prevention movement, which led to other specialized organizations to meet the needs of particular populations. In the same time period, the U.S. government mandated that community mental health clinics appear in every county, first, to serve the deinstitutionalized mentally ill. The clinics evolved to serve the general population in times of crisis. The late 1960s, 1970s, and 1980s saw journals, new models, and crisis intervention becoming more valued due to economic constraints. In the 1990s and early 2000s, new family crisis models appeared to guide crisis management that considered culture. Approaches influencing crisis management throughout those years included the psychiatric, psychoanalytic, existential, humanistic, cognitive-behavioral, and family systems approaches, which contributed assumptions, concepts, and techniques.

References and Suggestions for Further Reading

Boss, P. (2002). *Family stress management: A contextual approach.* Thousand Oaks, CA: Sage.

Caplan, G. (1964). *Principles of preventive psychiatry.* New York: Basic Books.

Cornille, T. A., & Boroto, D. R. (1992). The Family Distress Model: A conceptual and clinical application of Reiss' strong bonds finding. *Contemporary Family Therapy, 14*(3), 181–198.

Cornille, T. A., Boroto, D. R., Barnes, M. F., & Hall, P. K. (1996). Dealing with family distress in schools. *Families in Society: The Journal of Contemporary Human Services, 77*(7), 435–445.

Cornille, T. A., Mullis, A. K., & Mullis, R. L. (2006, November). *How to use Internet coverage about disasters to teach about family resilience.* PowerPoint presented at the meeting of the National Council on Family Relations, Minneapolis, MN.

Corsini, R. J., & Wedding, D. (1989). *Current psychotherapies.* Itasca, IL: F. E. Peacock.

Hoff, L. A. (1984). *People in crisis: Understanding and helping* (2nd ed.). Menlo Park, CA: Addison Wesley.

Hoff, L. A. (1989). *People in crisis: Understanding and helping* (3rd ed.). Menlo Park, CA: Addison Wesley.

Hoff, L. A. (1995). *People in crisis: Understanding and helping* (4th ed.). San Francisco: Jossey-Bass.

Hoff, L. A. (2001). *People in crisis: Clinical and public health perspectives* (5th ed.). San Francisco: Jossey-Bass.

Kanel, K. (1998). *A guide to crisis intervention.* Pacific Grove, CA: Brooks/Cole.

Lindemann, E. (1944). Symptomology and management in acute grief. *American Journal of Psychiatry, 101*, 141–148.

Peake, T. H., Borduin, C. M., & Archer, R. P. (1988). *Brief psychotherapies: Changing frames of mind.* Newbury Park, CA: Sage.

Sifneos, P. E. (1960). A concept of "emotional crisis." *Mental Hygiene, 44*, 169–179.

Slaikeu, K. A. (1990). *Crisis intervention: A handbook for practice and research* (2nd ed.). Boston: Allyn & Bacon.

Tyhurst, J. S. (1957). The role of transition states—including disasters—in mental illness. In *Symposium on preventive and social psychiatry* (pp. 149–169). Washington, DC: Walter Reed Army Institute of Research and the National Research Council.

Walsh, F. (1998). *Strengthening family resilience.* New York: Guilford.

CHAPTER 11

The Practice of Formal Crisis Management

C risis management, although therapeutic (healing), is not therapy. Thus, trained paraprofessionals and family life educators as well as counselors and therapists can perform formal crisis management. When performed by trained individuals, crisis management is labeled as formal while, when performed by laypersons (family, friends, etc.), it is labeled as informal. Both formal and informal crisis managers can use all the techniques discussed in this chapter. Preferably, we prevent crises by intervening before an occurrence. Therefore, prevention is included in the discussion of crisis management.

Prevention

Borrowing terms from the preventive mental health movement (Caplan, 1964), there are two types of prevention called anticipatory and participatory. See Table 11.1. The purpose of anticipatory and participatory prevention is to prevent mental health problems, a possible negative outcome to a crisis. A discussion of the types of prevention follows.

Anticipatory Prevention

Anticipatory prevention occurs to reduce the likelihood of crises and to promote growth, development, and crisis resistance. Anticipatory prevention is a form of primary prevention. Primary prevention occurs either before or after a stressor. The forms of primary prevention are education and consultation and intervention when intervention occurs after a stressor (Hoff, 2001) but before a crisis. Education in the form of family life education or

Table 11.1 Comprehensive Crisis Management

Stressors	Approaches to Crisis Management			
	Anticipatory Prevention	*Participatory Prevention*		
	Primary Prevention	*Secondary Prevention*	*Tertiary Prevention*	
	Family Life Education/ Psychoeducation	*Crisis Intervention*	*Brief Psychotherapy*	*Psychoanalysis*
Suicide attempt	Education on where to get help for distress	Individual and family crisis counseling	Family counseling/ therapy	
Homelessness	Education on issues related to homelessness	Crisis counseling (personal, legal, residential focus)	Social change strategies	
School suspension	Education about personal responsibility, life goals, plans for achieving goals	Family and social network crisis counseling	Family counseling/ therapy	

Source: Adapted from Hoff (1989).

psychoeducation is a form of primary prevention found to be both effective and cost-effective (Coohey & Marsh, 1995).

Participatory Prevention

Participatory prevention can be further classified as secondary and tertiary prevention. The classifications are based on when the prevention occurs.

Secondary Prevention

Secondary prevention is crisis management, which takes place when an individual or a family is in crisis. The purpose is to shorten the time of the crisis (speed up recovery) and promote a positive outcome (Hoff, 2001; Walsh, 1998). Secondary prevention takes the form of crisis management services (Hoff, 2001).

Tertiary Prevention

Tertiary prevention is action taken when there are chronic stressors (e.g., mental illness, addictions) because of negative outcomes of previous crises. The purpose of tertiary prevention is to repair damage done (mental/ emotional disorders) by unresolved life crises. This chapter focuses on secondary prevention, also known as crisis management.

Crisis Management Skills

In order to assist someone in managing a crisis, one must possess certain skills in order to help and to "do no harm." We need basic attending skills to develop and maintain rapport (a state of understanding and comfort) needed for effective crisis management (Kanel, 1998). Rapport allows crisis managers to access sensitive information about the client. Crisis managers use the basic attending skills of listening, clarifying, reflecting, questioning, and summarizing throughout every session.

Listening Skills

The purpose of listening is to help gain an understanding of the crisis, as the client perceives it. Active listening, also called reflective listening, is the most basic skill of crisis helpers (Kanel, 1998). Active listening includes both verbal and nonverbal attending behaviors, which let the client know you are listening and convey warmth. Nonverbal attending behaviors include good, direct eye contact; body language that includes an interested face, relaxed posture, and leaning toward the client; and close physical proximity. Verbal attending behaviors include an expressive, soft, soothing voice and verbal following. In verbal following, the listener paraphrases the words (a clarifying skill) and the often unspoken feelings (a reflecting skill) so the speaker knows that the listener received the meaning. An elaboration of these skills follows.

Clarifying Skills

Crisis managers use clarifying to clear up confusion or ambiguity by paraphrasing or by asking a particular type of question called a verifying question (Kanel, 1998). Key to active listening, *paraphrasing* feeds back to the client the essence of what he or she said to encourage elaboration, let the client know the crisis manager is trying to understand, help focus on the specific problem, and highlight content (Slaikeu, 1990). An example of paraphrasing is "I hear you saying that since putting your cat to sleep, you've been depressed, and no one in your family seems to understand your feelings." Crisis helpers ask *verifying questions* to verify that what the crisis manager heard is what the client intended. An example of a verifying question is "Are you saying that you have felt very bad since your cat died and aren't receiving any support from your family?"

Reflecting Skills

Reflection, also used in active listening, is a statement rephrasing the affective/feeling/emotional part of a client's message (Kanel, 1998), such as "I can tell you are really upset." While clarifying skills convey an attempt to understand thoughts, reflecting skills convey an attempt to understand feelings. When we have reflecting skills, we convey empathy (understanding of feelings). In crisis management, not only do we want to reflect painful, ambivalent, and expressed feelings, but we also want to reflect positive and nonverbal feelings. Often, a person in crisis is "not in touch with" his or her feelings. The crisis manager can encourage such an individual to express those feelings by saying something like "If that happened to me, I would be very angry."

Questioning Skills

The purposes of questioning skills are to gain information and to encourage clients to express themselves. There are two types of questions— open-ended and closed. Closed questions have only one answer (e.g., yes or no). They are useful in gathering demographic information (e.g., age or marital status); otherwise we avoid closed questions in crisis management. Open-ended questions allow clients to express themselves (Kanel, 1998). We avoid open-ended questions that begin with the word *why* in crisis management because they tend to make people defensive (Ivey, Gluckstern, & Ivey, 1997). "What did you feel when that happened?" exemplifies a good open-ended question to use to elicit feelings (K. Elliot, personal communication, January 25, 2007).

Summarizing Skills

"Summarization is a statement that pulls together the various facts (stressor, definition of stressor, etc.) and feelings discussed" (Kanel, 1998, p. 62).

Crisis workers use summarization when they end a session, move from one phase of crisis management to the next, begin a session with a previously seen client, or simply do not know what to do next. The basic attending skills of listening, clarifying, reflecting, questioning, and summarizing are used throughout the crisis management process.

Crisis Management Phases and Techniques

Crisis management, a form of secondary prevention, seeks to prevent a negative outcome from a crisis, to shorten the length of a crisis, and to prevent future crises. Crisis management consists of the overlapping phases of assessment, planning, intervention, and follow-up (Hoff, 2001). These phases apply to all hazardous events, precipitating factors, and crisis origins as well as to crisis management with individuals, families, and communities. The chapter will refer to the client, which may be an individual, a family, or a community. The discussion begins with the crisis management phase of assessment.

Assessment

The crisis worker needs to perform two levels of assessment: Level I and Level II (Hoff, 2001). At Level I, the crisis worker assesses risk/threat to life of the individuals in crisis (suicide) and of others (assault or homicide) (Hoff, 2001). At Level II, crisis workers assess the ability to function in normal roles. See Table 11.2.

Level I Assessment

Suicide risk assessment attempts to answer the question "What is the likelihood of death by suicide?" In reality, many people have suicidal ideation (thoughts of suicide) at some time in their lives, and we are all on a continuum from wanting life more than death to wanting death more than life. Suicide may be an attempt to cope with a crisis when coping skills are lacking.

Presence of certain factors indicates a risk for suicide. These include

1. a specific suicide plan with an available, highly lethal method (see Table 11.3) that does not include rescue;
2. a history of highly lethal suicide attempts with accidental rescue;
3. very limited or nonexistent resources or perception of no resources; and
4. inability to communicate effectively (Hoff, 2001).

Table 11.2 Crisis Assessment Levels

	Focus of Assessment	*Assessment Done By*
Level I	Risk to life • Victimization • Suicide (self) • Assault/homicide (child, partner, parent, mental health or community worker, police officer)	Everyone (natural and formal crisis managers) • Family, friends, neighbors • Hotline workers • Frontline workers: clergy, police officers, nurses, physicians, teachers • Crisis and mental health professionals, family life educators
Level II	Comprehensive psychological and social aspects of the person's life pertaining to the hazardous event, including assessment of chronic self-destructiveness	Counselors or mental health professionals specially trained in crisis work, family life educators (formal crisis managers)

Source: Adapted from Hoff (2001).

In addition to the above, recent loss or threat of loss, physical illness, alcohol and other drug abuse, isolation, depression, social problems, and unexplained change in behavior increase risk (Hoff, 2001). These factors are often present in the general population, but when combined with the first four factors, they increase suicide risk.

Hoff (1989) lists areas to be addressed and questions to ask in suicide risk assessment.

1. *Suicidal ideas:* "Are you so upset that you're thinking of suicide?" or "Are you thinking about hurting yourself?" (p. 200)
2. *Lethality of method (see Table 11.3):* "What are you thinking of doing?" (p. 200)
3. *Availability of means:* "Do you have a gun? Do you know how to use it? Do you have ammunition? Why don't you put the gun away and . . . then let's talk about what's troubling you?" (p. 201)
4. *Specificity of plan:* "Do you have a plan worked out for killing yourself? How do you plan to get the gun? What time of day do you plan to do this? Is there anyone else around at that time?" (p. 201)

Table 11.3 Lethality of Suicide Methods

Highly lethal methods	Less lethal methods
Antidepressants (such as Elavil)	Nonprescription drugs (excluding aspirin and acetaminophen)
Acetaminophen (brand name Tylenol)	
Aspirin (high dose)	Tranquilizers (such as Valium)
Barbiturates	Wrist cutting
Car crash	
Carbon monoxide poisoning	
Drowning	
Exposure to extreme cold	
Gun	
Hanging	
Jumping	
Sleeping pills (prescribed)	

Source: Adapted from Hoff (2001).

The last two questions also assess the odds of rescue.

Assault or homicidal risk assessment attempts to answer the question "What is the likelihood of assault or homicide?" It includes assessment of the following: history of homicidal threats and/or assault, current homicidal threats and plan, possession of lethal weapons, use or abuse of alcohol or other drugs, and conflict in significant social relationships (such as infidelity or threat of divorce) (Hoff, 2001). The crisis worker may use similar questions to those used to assess risk of suicide for assessing risk of assault or homicide.

In Level I assessment, if a person is found to be at risk for suicide or homicide, the crisis worker intervenes immediately. Appropriate intervention for suicide or homicide risk appears later in this chapter under the intervention phase. If there is no risk of suicide, assault, or homicide, the crisis worker moves on to Level II assessment.

Level II Assessment

Level II assessment corresponds to the elements of the total crisis experience. An understanding of stress theory and the various stress models guides Level II assessment. One of the first things to determine is whether the client is in a vulnerable state or in crisis. If the client is in a vulnerable state and not yet in crisis, a crisis worker can intervene and prevent crisis (primary prevention). Interventions are similar in either case, but when the client is not yet in crisis, he or she is able to be more active in managing the distress.

Based on the stress models studied earlier in this book, Level II assessment identifies the following:

1. Hazardous event: "What happened?" (Hoff, 1989, p. 79) or "Tell me what happened. Can you tell me what happened?" (Hoff, 1989, p. 261)
2. Precipitating factor: "What brought you here today?" (Hoff, 1989, p. 80) or "What happened in this past week?"
3. Stressor origins (internal or external; situational, sociocultural, or transitional)
4. Definition of the stressor (threat, loss, challenge)
5. Vulnerability or crisis manifestations: "What do you feel about what happened?"
6. Resources (availability and use): "Is there anyone you can talk to?"
7. Coping strategies (negative and positive): "What have you done to try to take care of yourself?"
8. Contexts (internal and external)

While assessing the client, the crisis worker may begin to develop the crisis management plan.

Planning

According to Hoff (2001), a crisis management plan must be

1. developed with the client;
2. appropriate to the client's functional level and dependency needs;
3. problem oriented;
4. consistent with the client's culture and lifestyle;
5. inclusive of the client's social network;
6. realistic;
7. time limited;
8. concrete;
9. renegotiable; and
10. inclusive of plans for follow-up.

The plan is developed with the client rather than for the client. Helpers never do something for clients that clients can do for themselves. To do so would be disempowering at a time when clients need to be empowered. The level of clients' participation in developing the plan is related to their functional level and dependency needs. Dependency is on a continuum from independence to dependence with interdependence in the middle. Very dependent persons may want a helper to do everything for them. In such cases, helpers must be careful not to do things for clients that they can do themselves, such as making phone calls to family. In times of crisis, independent persons may need to accept help. Helpers may need to explain to independent clients that it is all right to accept help temporarily and that they can go back to being independent once the crisis is resolved.

Being problem oriented means that the plan is focused on the crisis and what led to it (hazardous event). Clients may have other problems in their lives, but those would be addressed in the plans for follow-up. If clients in crisis bring up marital problems during assessment, helpers can refer them to marital counseling once the crisis is resolved.

Plans must be consistent with clients' cultures and lifestyles to be successful. Clients will be more likely to follow plans that are consistent with their traditions. Plans that include clients' social networks are also more likely to be successful. Social networks are resources that clients can draw on in times of crisis. Social networks include intimate attachments, such as lovers/spouses, siblings, friends, parents, and children, as well as community affiliations, such as those at schools, at churches, in the medical community, in clubs, at work, and with neighbors (Hoff, 1989).

Successful plans are also realistic regarding needs and resources. A plan that includes clients who are having financial difficulties joining a health club to exercise for stress reduction is not likely to be successful.

Crisis management plans are time limited as crises are time limited. Plans are also concrete so that clients know specifically what to do. Plans are renegotiable in case circumstances change or plans do not work as expected. Lastly, crisis management plans include plans for follow-up. When follow-up will take place and what follow-up will include lets clients know that someone will check to see how they are doing once the plan is complete.

After planning, the crisis worker puts the plan in writing. Once it is in writing, the crisis management plan is referred to as a *crisis management contract* (Hoff, 2001). Intervention may begin during the assessing and planning stages, as attending to the client and planning with the client may begin the recovery process.

Intervention

Since it would be impossible to include interventions for every possible stressor in one book, general intervention strategies that apply in many situations follow. In addition, the discussion includes strategies specifically for suicide, homicide, and loss situations and for children.

Intervention for Suicide Risk

Some possible interventions for people at *low risk* for suicide include education, empowerment, connection to resources, and informal no-suicide contracts (Kanel, 1998). An interventionist might suggest reading books by people who have attempted suicide or might tell the client that thinking of suicide is common (educational interventions). Kanel (1998) suggests an empowering comment: "The part of you that sought help is obviously very strong, and you can take comfort in knowing you have this inner strength that helps you choose to cope with your problems actively" (p. 93). A no-suicide contract is an informal verbal or a formal written agreement from the suicidal person that he or she will not harm him- or herself without first speaking to the interventionist. With a low-risk person, a verbal agreement (informal contract) may be sufficient.

Intervention with people at *middle risk* for suicide includes formal, written no-suicide contracts (see the Suicide Contract Example at the end of this chapter), suicide watch, asking clients to bring in the planned means of suicide, addressing the client's ambivalence, and possibly hospitalization (Kanel, 1998). The contract is usually for 2 to 3 days until the next appointment with the interventionist. If the client will not contract for 2 days, ask if he or she will contract for 1 day. People at middle risk for suicide may need the crisis manager to see them every day. Kanel (1998) suggests shaking hands to seal the contract. If the person at risk will not contract with the interventionist, he or she will need to be on suicide watch 24 hours a day and, if this is not possible, hospitalized. Enlisting family members or friends to conduct the suicide watch is preferable to hospitalization, as hospitalization itself is a stressor (Hoff, 2001). A psychiatric hospital is preferable to a general hospital, as staff in the former generally receive training for such situations (Wyman cited in Kanel, 1998). Voluntary hospitalization is preferable to involuntary. If the client signs a no-suicide contract and/or will be on suicide watch, the interventionist can ask that the client bring the planned means of suicide to him or her. The interventionist can then destroy or lock it away. The interventionist can also address the client's ambivalence "and focus on the part that wants to live" (Kanel, 1998, p. 94). With someone at *high risk* for suicide, it may be necessary to call the police and an ambulance. When doubting what to do, consult with a supervisor or colleague if possible.

Intervention for Assault or Homicide Risk

For assault or homicide risk, crisis managers first need to remove themselves if they are in a dangerous situation. If the crisis manager is not in danger, crisis management for assault or homicide is similar to that for suicide. Helpers try to get people to postpone irreversible decisions. Usually in a matter of days, they will change their minds. Next, crisis managers need to make a report to the proper authorities. According to U.S. federal case law, crisis managers also have a legal obligation to notify the possible victims and their families. As in threatened suicide, the goal of saving human life supersedes allegiance to confidentiality (Slaikeu, 1990). If no risk to life is identified in the assessment process or when there is no longer a risk to life, the crisis manager may use general intervention strategies that apply to all crises.

General Intervention Strategies

Hoff (2001) identified general intervention strategies that apply to all crises.

1. Listen actively and with concern.
2. Encourage the open expression of feelings.
3. Help the client(s) gain an understanding of the crisis.
4. Help the client(s) gradually accept reality.
5. Help the client(s) explore new ways of coping with problems.
6. Link the client(s) to a social network.
7. Reinforce the newly learned coping strategies.
8. Follow up on resolution of the crisis.

In the case of a client experiencing loss, the above strategies may be supplemented with specific intervention for loss.

Intervention for Loss

No matter what the origin of a crisis, a crisis often includes the theme of loss (Hoff, 2001). The term *bereavement* refers to any loss (people, health, property, body integrity, etc.). Brabant (1996) defined *grief* as response to loss. Grief work refers to the intervention appropriate for grief. "*Grief work* is the work that must be done to move through the pain that we experience because of a loss" (Brabant, 1996, p. 5). Grief work includes the following tasks (Hoff, 2001), which can occur simultaneously and in no particular order.

1. Accept the pain of loss.
2. Express feelings.
3. Understand that the intense feelings are normal.
4. Resume normal activities and social relationships.

Crisis workers use general intervention strategies to assist their client(s) with grief work.

Boss (2006) addresses crisis intervention for *ambiguous loss.* See Chapter 2 for a discussion of ambiguous loss. According to Boss, the goals for intervention for ambiguous loss are to do the following:

1. Find meaning.
2. Temper mastery (moderate sense of control over one's life).
3. Reconstruct identity (know who one is and what roles one will play).
4. Normalize ambivalence (mixed feelings).
5. Revise attachment (to the lost person).
6. Discover hope.

According to Boss (2006), crisis workers can help clients do the following:

1. Name the problem (ambiguous loss).
2. Think dialectically. This refers to holding two opposing ideas at the same time. Clients can do this by talking about what is gone and talking about what is present (i.e., the lost person's ideas and/or work, symbols of the lost person's life, and/or physical features of the lost person seen in others).
3. Connect with the spiritual part of their lives (e.g., trust that things will work out). They may increase their faith in God or connect with nature.
4. Forgive. Forgiveness includes reconstructing thinking about revenge and evilness.
5. Do small good works/acts of kindness.
6. Use rituals. Canceling rituals is maladaptive. Clients may revise old rituals (e.g., the mother takes over roles of the father during rituals when he is deployed) and/or create new rituals.
7. Move forward to honor the loved one.

8. Recognize that the world is not always just and fair. Unfortunately, working hard and doing the right thing do not always guarantee a good outcome, and bad things happen to good people.
9. Increase self-care.
10. Strengthen connections (friends, relatives, and pets).
11. Rethink blame. Boss (2006) suggests that crisis workers help their clients decrease self-blame (shift view of fault for not having done a good enough job) and/or soften attribution of blame for loss (on God, bad luck, etc.) to a more accepting belief (destiny). Examples include beliefs such as "God has a plan."
12. Identify past competencies (resources). Boss (2006) suggests that if clients have difficulty identifying their past competencies, crisis workers assist them in reviewing their history. In doing so, they identify capabilities (resources and coping skills) used in the past. If that does not work, reviewing the history of others through literature or support groups may help.
13. Increase success experiences. Boss (2006) suggests that client(s) do activities in small steps to increase success experiences.
14. Accept what will not change.
15. Have a sense of invincibility.
16. Master one's internal self. Boss (2006) suggests that crisis workers assist clients with shifting mastery from control over environment and people to control of inner self. She suggests that we do this by helping clients reinterpret/redefine/reframe the situation (change the definition of the stressor) and/or change an assumption that they cannot cope without knowing the facts.
17. Define family boundaries. Boss (2006) suggests that to help clients establish who the family is (who is in, and who is out), crisis workers ask them to draw both the psychological and physical families. In the case of the psychological family, crisis workers can help the clients reassess and reconstruct the psychological family not necessarily based on what society says ("forget and move on") so they can include the missing member in the psychological family even when he or she is not in the physical family.
18. Reconstruct roles. To reconstruct roles, Boss (2006) suggests that crisis workers assist clients with both reassigning everyday roles and being flexible about gender and generational roles (e.g., an elderly mother acts like a mother one day and a child the next). In addition, she suggests that crisis workers assist clients with recognizing former identities and integrating who they were with

who they are, as well as with identifying whether "ex-people" (e.g., in-laws) are in or out of the family and what their roles are. Once the clients reconstruct their roles, crisis workers can help them use symbols to indicate reconstructed identities (e.g., how they dress to take a job).

19. Get to know people with different identities. Getting to know people with different identities is particularly important with a stressor of sociocultural origin as in the September 11, 2001, attacks on the World Trade Center. Boss (2006) indicates a way for clients to get to know people with different identities includes travel (sometimes just down the street). This discourages intergenerational transmission of hatred of other religious identities. Crisis workers can teach clients that it is not healthy for children to grow up in a vengeful atmosphere, since this leads to violence and killing. Reconnecting with clients' own past and ways of ancestors, such as language, also connects them with others. Other than American Indians, in the United States, we are all immigrants.

20. Uncover secrets about family identity. Boss (2006) suggests that this teaches clients that all families have both good and bad in them and that all people have both good and bad in them.

21. Broaden family rules for problem solving beyond blaming, shaming, and scapegoating. Boss (2006) suggests crisis workers assist clients with increasing self-responsibility for their part in things that happen to them and learning anger-management skills.

22. Identify positive family themes about resilience (sports, music, and religion vs. addiction, violence, abuse, and crime) through genograms (family maps). See *Genograms in Family Assessment* (McGoldrick & Gerson, 1985).

23. Tell story repeatedly.

24. Use the arts (film, dance, music, creative writing, literature, painting, theater). When the arts move people, change is less frightening, and relational revisions are more possible according to Boss (2006). The arts bring ambivalent (mixed) feelings to the surface. Through the arts, clients can see that ambivalence is common and not necessarily negative. Clients can also express themselves artistically.

25. See the community as family (support groups and/or therapy groups).

26. Talk about the dark side of feelings (negative feelings clients do not like to admit about the loss such as anger and vengefulness).

27. Manage ambivalence, once aware of it (tolerate it).

28. See conflict as positive (an opportunity for growth).

29. Know that closure (absolute absence or presence) does not lower ambivalence. Boss (2006) contends that the assumption that there is such a thing as closure makes people feel inept and guilty.
30. Listen to others' stories. Listening to others' stories offers opportunities to learn about other resources and coping strategies. Others' stories also help normalize clients' experiences.

These techniques for intervention for ambiguous loss can be used with all age groups. There are general techniques, however, that are particularly useful with children for distress from stressors from any origins based on their ages and development.

Intervention for Children

Children react to stressors differently based on their ages and stages of development. For that reason, this section presents specific intervention strategies for various age groups.

Intervention for preschool children (ages 1–5). *Preschool children (ages 1–5)* are particularly vulnerable and look to others for comfort because they lack verbal and conceptual skills to cope with crises by themselves (Greenstone & Leviton, 2002). They are also vulnerable to the reactions of important people in their lives. Since abandonment is a fear at this age, children who experience a loss need special reassurance that someone will be available to care for them. According to Greenstone and Leviton (2002), the goals of intervention with these children are "to help them integrate their experiences and reestablish a sense of security and mastery" (p. 69). To do this we can try the following:

- Encourage expression through play reenactment where appropriate.
- Provide verbal reassurance and physical comforting.
- Give the child frequent attention.
- Encourage the child's expression of feelings and concerns.
- Provide comforting bedtime routines.
- Allow the child to sleep in the same room with the parent. Make it clear to the child that this is only for a limited period. (Greenstone & Leviton, 2002, p. 69)

Intervention for early childhood (ages 5–11). In *early childhood (ages 5–11),* fear of loss is particularly difficult, and regressive behavior is the most common crisis manifestation. Recommendations made by Greenstone and Leviton (2002) include the following:

- Display patience and tolerance.
- Provide play sessions with adults and peers to provide an opportunity for open discussion of emotions.
- Conduct discussions with adults and peers about frightening, anxiety-producing aspects of events and about appropriate behavior (coping strategies) to manage the child's concerns and the stress.
- Relax expectations at school or at home, but make it clear to the child that this relaxation is temporary.
- Provide opportunities for structured, but not demanding, chores and responsibilities at home.
- Maintain a familiar routine as much as possible and as soon as possible.

Intervention for preadolescents (ages 11–14). Greenstone and Leviton (2002) suggest that, because peers are so significant for *preadolescents (ages 11–14),* they need to know that peers share their reactions. The suggested goals for this age group include lessening tensions, anxieties, and possible guilt feelings. The authors recommend the following:

- Provide group activities geared toward the resumption of routines.
- Involve clients with same-age group activities.
- Conduct group discussions geared toward examining feelings about the crisis and appropriate behavior to manage the concerns and the stress.
- Provide structured, but undemanding, responsibilities.
- Temporarily relax expectations of performance at school and at home.
- Give additional individual attention and consideration.

Intervention for adolescents (ages 14–18). Greenstone and Leviton (2002) recommend the following for *adolescents (ages 14–18)* in crisis, who get particularly distressed by disruption of peer activities and lack of full adult responsibilities:

- Encourage participation in the community and in individual responses, such as letter writing.
- Encourage discussion of feelings, concerns, and shared information with peers and extrafamily significant others.
- Temporarily reduce expectations for specific levels of both school and general performance, depending on individual reactions.
- Encourage, but do not insist upon, discussions of crisis-induced fears within the family setting. (pp. 71–72)

Follow-up

The main purpose of a follow-up is to check progress (Slaikeu, 1990). Follow-up plans may also include plans for long-term counseling or therapy for chronic situations identified during assessment (Hoff, 1989, 2001). Plans for follow-up are made when preparing the service plan. At that time, the crisis manager secures identifying information and explores possible follow-up procedures. Sometimes it is not appropriate to contact clients at their residences, as in the case of spouse abuse, since such contact could put clients in danger. In the case of rape, for instance, clients may not want other people to know that they used crisis services. In such cases, clients often initiate follow-up contact. During follow-up the crisis manager secures feedback regarding the crisis intervention. If the crisis plan did not work to resolve the crisis, crisis managers start the crisis management process again, beginning with assessment.

Summary of the Practice of Formal Crisis Management

Crisis management can be either informal or formal, with informal performed by laypeople and formal performed by paraprofessionals and professionals trained in crisis management. Since it is usually preferable to prevent crises before they occur, we discuss crisis management in terms of anticipatory and participatory prevention. Anticipatory prevention, also called primary prevention, occurs prior to a stressor or after a stressor but before a crisis, has the goal of reducing the likelihood of crises, and includes family life education or psychoeducation. Participatory prevention occurs once there is a crisis and includes secondary and tertiary prevention. Crisis intervention falls under secondary prevention. Trained paraprofessionals and professionals perform secondary prevention. Tertiary prevention, performed by counselors and psychotherapists, occurs after a negative crisis resolution.

Crisis managers use the basic attending skills of listening, clarifying, reflecting, questioning, and summarizing throughout every session. Crisis management consists of the overlapping phases of assessment, planning, intervention, and follow-up. The crisis worker performs two levels of assessment: Level I and Level II. Level I assesses risk to life while Level II assesses vulnerability and crisis. Planning begins with assessment, and when completed, plans are put into writing and called a service contract. If a risk to life is identified in assessment, intervention begins immediately. Once the risk to life is alleviated, general intervention strategies may be used for crises in all age groups along with specific techniques helpful with children of different ages and developmental stages. Loss occurs in almost every crisis and indicates a need for grief work. If the loss is ambiguous, special techniques help reduce the ambivalence experienced with the unique kind of loss. Follow-up occurs after the crisis resolution.

SUICIDE CONTRACT EXAMPLE

I, _____ agree that I will not kill myself or in any other way harm myself, either accidentally or on purpose, until I have seen and talked with, _____, my counselor, on _____ in his or her office.
I will not accidentally or on purpose take an overdose of my medication.
I will drive my car safely and pay attention any time I am behind the wheel.

Signed _____

Witnessed _____

Date _____

EXERCISES

11.1   Break up into groups of three or four. From the group, choose a client, crisis manager, and rater. A fourth person will be an observer. Take turns in each role, rating each other on crisis management skills.

References and Suggestions for Further Reading

Aguilera, D. C. (1990). *Crisis intervention: Theory and methodology.* St Louis, MO: C. V. Mosby.

Bernard, B. (1995). *Fostering resilience in children* (ERIC Document Reproduction Service No. EDO-PS-95). Champaign: University of Illinois.

Boss, P. (2006). *Loss, trauma, and resilience.* New York: Norton.

Brabant, S. (1996). *Mending the torn fabric: For those who grieve and those who want to help them.* Amityville, NY: Baywood.

Caplan, G. (1964). *Principles of preventive psychiatry.* New York: Basic Books.

Coohey, C., & Marsh, J. (1995). Promotion, prevention, and treatment: What are the differences? *Research on Social Work Practice, 5,* 524–538.

Corsini, R. J., & Wedding, D. (1989). *Current psychotherapies.* Itasca, IL: F. E. Peacock.

Greenberg, J. S. (1987). *Comprehensive stress management* (2nd ed.). Dubuque, IA: W. C. Brown.

Greenstone, J. L., & Leviton, S. C. (2002). *Elements of crisis intervention: Crises and how to respond to them* (2nd ed.). Pacific Grove, CA: Brooks/Cole.

Hoff, L. A. (1989). *People in crisis: Understanding and helping* (3rd ed.). Menlo Park, CA: Addison Wesley.

Hoff, L. A. (2001). *People in crisis: Clinical and public health perspectives* (5th ed.). San Francisco: Jossey-Bass.

Ivey, A. E., Gluckstern, N. B., & Ivey, M. B. (1997). *Basic attending skills* (3rd ed.). North Amherst, MA: Microtraining Associates.

Kanel, K. (1998). *A guide to crisis intervention.* Pacific Grove, CA: Brooks/Cole.

McGoldrick, M., & Gerson, R. (1985). *Genograms in family assessment.* New York: Norton.

National Council on Family Relations. (n.d.) *Families and disaster preparedness.* Minneapolis, MN: Author.

Rice, K. F., & Groves, B. M. (2005). *Hope and healing: A caregiver's guide to helping young children affected by trauma.* Washington, DC: Zero to Three Press.

Slaikeu, K. A. (1990). *Crisis intervention: A handbook for practice and research* (2nd ed.). Boston: Allyn & Bacon.

U.S. Department of Health and Human Services. (2003). *An activity book for African American families: Helping children cope with crisis* (NIH Publication No. 03-5362B). Washington, DC: National Institutes of Health.

Walsh, F. (1998). *Strengthening family resilience.* New York: Guilford.

Watzlawick, P., Weakland, J., & Fisch, R. (1974). *Change: Principles of problem formation and problem resolution.* New York: Norton.

Appendix

Comparison of Family Stress Models

Profile of Trouble	Truncated Roller Coaster Profile of Adjustment	ABCX Formula	Double ABCX Model	FAAR Model	Typology Model of Family Adjustment and Adaptation	Family Ecosystemic Model of Stress	Resiliency Model of Family Stress, Adjustment, and Adaptation	Family Distress Model	Contextual Model of Family Stress
a. Normal Interaction/ Organization	Precrisis Level of Family Organization				Adjustment Phase: T Factor—Family Type	First Process: Old/Normal Level	Adjustment Phase: Established Patterns of Functioning (T)	Phase I: Family's Predictable Pattern	Internal Context
		A. Crisis-Precipitating Event	Precrisis: a. Stressor	Adjustment Phase: a. Stressor	Adjustment Phase: A Factor	Second Process: Input(s) or Stressor(s)	Adjustment Phase: Stressor (A)	Phase II: Problems—Disrupting Event	A. Event or Stressor
				Adjustment Phase: Demands	Adjustment Phase: V Factor—Family System Vulnerability		Adjustment Phase: Vulnerability (V)	Phase II: Problems—Patterns Disrupted and Family Experiences Distress	Degree of Stress
		B. Family's Crisis-Meeting Resources	Precrisis: b. Existing Resources	Adjustment Phase: b. Existing Resources	Adjustment Phase: B Factor—Family Resources		Adjustment Phase: Family Resources (B)		B. Resources
		C. Definition Family Makes of Event	Precrisis: c. Perception of a	Adjustment Phase: Resistance (C). Definition and Appraisal of Demands	Adjustment Phase: C Factor—Family Appraisal		Adjustment Phase: Stressor Appraisal (C)		C. Perceptions
Anticipatory Stress Reactions				Adjustment Phase: Resistance Adjustment Coping Strategies	Adjustment Phase: PSC Factor—Family Management		Adjustment Phase: Problem Solving and Coping (PSC)	Phase II: Problems—Resolve Distress Using Preexisting or New Strategies	

X. Degree of Stress	X. Crisis				
		Phase III: Family Experiences Crisis	Phase IV: Patterns Organized Around Crisis		
	Adjustment Phase: Crisis (X) (Maladjustment)	Adaptation Phase: Inadequate and/or Deterioration of Family Patterns of Functioning (T)	Adjustment Phase: Bonadjustment or Maladjustment/Crisis Situation (X)	Adaptation Phase: Pileup of Demands (AA)	Adaptation Phase: Maladjustment/Crisis Situation (X)
			Third Process: Stress and Coping Levels I, II, and/or III		
	Adjustment; Adjustment Phase: X Factor	Exhaustion		Adaptation Phase: AA Factor—Pileup	Adaptation Phase: X Factor
Adjustment Phase: Bonadjustment or Maladjustment	Adjustment Phase: Crisis (x)	Exhaustion	Adaptation Phase: Accommodation Level 1—aA. Pileup		
	x. Crisis			Postcrisis: aA. Pileup	
X. Crisis					
Reaction to First Stressor					
b. Point Initiating Cause Takes Effect					
c. Point at Which Family Interaction Drops					

(Continued)

(Continued)

Profile of Trouble	Truncated Roller Coaster Profile of Adjustment	ABCX Formula	Double ABCX Model	FAAR Model	Typology Model of Family Adjustment and Adaptation	Family Ecosystemic Model of Stress	Resiliency Model of Family Stress, Adjustment, and Adaptation	Family Distress Model	Contextual Model of Family Stress
					Adaptation Phase: R Factor—Regenerativity				
					Adaptation Phase: T Factor—Family Type		Adaptation Phase: Patterns of Functioning [Retained (T), Restored (T), or New(TT)]	Phase V: Family Develops New or Returns to Old Pattern for Predictability	
			Postcrisis: bB. Existing and New Resources	Adaptation Phase: Accommodation Level 1—(bB), Resources and Support	Adaptation Phase: BB Factor—Family Resources and BBB Factor—Community Support		Adaptation Phase: BB Family Resources—Family, Social, Kin, and Community Support		
				Adaptation Phase: Accommodation Level 1—Restructuring Awareness					
			Postcrisis: cC. Perception of a (c) and Perception of $x + aA = bB$ (C)	Adaptation Phase: Accommodation Level 1—Restructuring (cC). Shared Definition of Situation	Adaptation Phase: Family Appraisal—CC Factor Situational Appraisal		Adaptation Phase: Situational Appraisal (CC)		

Adaptation Phase: Accommodation Level 1—Restructuring Search for Agreement on Solutions and Implementation			Adaptation Phase: Paradigms (CCC)		Internal Context: Philosophical	
			Adaptation Phase: Coherence (CCCC)			
Adaptation Phase: cC. Shared Family Life Orientation and Meaning		Adaptation Phase: Family Appraisal—CCC Factor Global Appraisal	Adaptation Phase: Schema (CCCCC)			
Adaptation Phase: Accommodation Level 1—Restructuring Search for and Agreement on Solutions and Implementation						

(Continued)

(Continued)

Profile of Trouble	Truncated Roller Coaster Profile of Adjustment	ABCX Formula	Double ABCX Model	FAAR Model	Typology Model of Family Adjustment and Adaptation	Family Ecosystemic Model of Stress	Resiliency Model of Family Stress, Adjustment, and Adaptation	Family Distress Model	Contextual Model of Family Stress
	Adjustment Process/Recovery		Postcrisis: Coping	Adaptation Phase: Accommodation Level 1—Restructuring Adaptive Coping/System Maintenance	Adaptation Phase: PSC Factor—Adaptive Coping	Third Process: Stress and Coping Levels, I, II, and III	Adaptation Phase: Problem Solving and Coping (PSC)		
				Adaptation Phase: Accommodation Level 2—Consolidation Agreement on Concomitant Changes and Implementation	Adaptation Phase: PSC Factor—Adaptive Coping	Third Process: Stress and Coping Levels I, II, and III	Adaptation Phase: Problem Solving and Coping (PSC)		
				Adaptation Phase: Accommodation Level 2—Consolidation Adaptive Coping	Adaptation Phase: PSC Factor—Adaptive Coping	Third Process: Stress and Coping Levels, I, II, and III	Adaptation Phase: Problem Solving and Coping (PSC)	Phase V: Using Social Support to Cope With a Crisis—Seeks Potential Support	
								Phase V: Family Views Crisis in Context of Its Goals	
d. Point of Recovery	Level of Organization After Adjustment/Recovery Is Complete		Postcrisis: Adaptation—Bon- or Mal- (xX)	Adaptation Phase: Bonadaptation or Maladaptation	XX Factor: Bonadaptation or Maladaptation	Fourth Process: New "Normal" Level	Adaptation Phase: Family Adaptation (XX)	Phase V: Crisis Resolved or Managed	

Index

About the Author

Janice Gauthier Weber, PhD, CFLE, CFCS, is an associate professor in the Child and Family Studies Program at the University of Louisiana at Lafayette. At the university, she developed and taught for over 20 years a course titled Families in Crisis. She has published in the area of family life education, including encyclopedia articles on stress and crisis in families ("Family Crises," *Human Ecology*, ABC-CLIO, 2003; "Stress Management Theory and Techniques in Families," *Encyclopedia of Family Health*, Sage, in press), as well as pedagogical materials (*Analyzing a Personal Crisis*, National Council on Family Relations, 1993). In addition, Dr. Weber has done numerous presentations on issues related to stress and crisis for both professional and lay audiences, such as *War Hits Home: How to Talk to Children; Living With Grief: Coping With Public Tragedy; Effects of Events of September 11, 2001, on College Students; Comparative Analysis of Bereavement Outcomes in Young Widowed and Divorced Women; Violence Against Teachers: High School Teachers' Fears of, Experiences With, and Perceptions of Prevention; Passages: Life, Loss, and Changes; Crisis Prevention and Management; Lens on Teaching Individual and Family Stress Theory and Crisis Intervention; Get Organized: Be CALM and RELAXED; Talking to Children About War and Disasters; Making Sense of Hurricanes Katrina and Rita: The Context of Disaster; De-stressing Your Family;* and *Ambiguous Loss in Staff, Children, and Ourselves: What Is It and What Can We Do About It?*